The
Campus
Cookbook

To Kathie

*Congratulations on
your graduation!*

*from Barb, Gary.
Kim & Heather*

6/78

The
CAMPUS
COOKBOOK

Moira Hodgson
with
Raeford Liles

The Bobbs-Merrill Company, Inc.
Indianapolis · *New York*

The Bobbs-Merrill Company, Inc.
Indianapolis · New York

CONTENTS

Introduction

In recent years there have been enormous changes in college life. Colleges that forever considered the admission of the opposite sex preposterous and nothing short of the downfall of the establishment have suddenly turned co-ed. Dorm rules have been relaxed, replacing the old policy of rooms where no member of the opposite sex was allowed after 7 o'clock; there are mixed dorms with kitchens and cooking equipment; and there are co-ed apartment buildings. No longer is the weekend the student's only salvation.

At the same time, students are still found living in rented rooms, with nothing to cook on but a hot plate, and more and more students are living in communes, where feeding a crowd is something that has to be done every day.

In the past, students were notorious for their bad eating habits. A snatched hot dog or spaghetti and meat balls in the college cafeteria, hamburgers in the crowded Saturday night place, a package of onion soup heated up over a cold chicken leg for dinner—this used to be the extent of the student's food consciousness.

This is rarely true today. Students, perhaps more than any other group, are tremendously aware of the importance of good food. Where are health foods consumed most but in colleges? Where is there more awareness of the harmful chemicals and sprays that saturate our food? Many students now have their own gardens. Many have turned vegetarian, in disgust with the loathsome commercial methods of raising meat and poultry.

At the same time, there may be readers of this book who will fling it aside after the first few recipes. Frozen, artificial, prepared foods and mixes won't be found here. With the exception of an occasional package of frozen peas or a can of chick peas, the recipes are made from real ingredients.

Whereas a sausage and a piece of bread are transformed into a delicious meal at the hands of a Frenchman or an Italian, when they fall into the hands of an American, they become the hot dog. This is changing. Just as most Americans are getting sick of pollution, so are they getting sick of that kind of food.

This book is intended for people who probably have neither a great deal of time nor a great deal of money. For this reason most of the recipes

1

are simple and quick. For someone new to cooking and to good food, it is hoped that this book will provide some groundwork and arouse an interest in the subject.

Just as you have to learn to appreciate music, painting, or books, so you have to learn to appreciate food. The first time you hear a symphony it may mean nothing to you. After hearing it three or four times, however, you begin to understand and enjoy the music.

Before you learn to cook, you have to learn to eat. Children love jam, cakes, sweets, sticky drinks—almost anything with sugar in it. Grownups like olives, oysters, caviar, and scotch. These are all acquired tastes.

If you don't like something, you have to keep on trying. Many people don't like liver, kidney, and brains, for example. Too bad, because they are cheap and very good for you. Others can't stand leeks, spinach, fish, or even eggs. But if you keep trying, unless you have a real block to a particular food, sooner or later you will start to enjoy it.

"Faites simple," said the great French epicure Escoffier. The best meals are the simplest ones, prepared without a great deal of fuss. If you are cooking for other people, cook something within your powers, don't try too hard, and don't overembellish the food. There is no point in having friends over if your evening will be spent toiling over the stove, a white sauce boiling over here, the meat burning over there, the vegetables overcooked because you put them on too soon and with one hand all the while trying to beat egg whites for a soufflé. A whole lot of things swimming in cream, flambé, or sautéed in red wine won't make you a great cook.

If you are trying something new, simplify the recipe, and when you've got the hang of it, build it up again. When you are entertaining, get as much as possible done in advance and, to begin with, don't serve more than one last-minute dish.

Cooking is a creative and relaxing art. Whether cooking for yourself, as a necessity, or cooking for others, cooking can be a positive pleasure.

Kitchen Hints

When you are setting up a kitchen in college, you don't want to spend a lot of money on things that you will not absolutely need during the time you spend there, or on supplies that you will never finish. This chapter deals with two kinds of kitchens, the communal kitchen and the one-person kitchen. A communal kitchen is much easier to set up because each person can contribute one or two items; the cost doesn't mount up in the alarming way that it can for the single person.

Utensils

By the time you have finished reading in some cookbooks the list of the utensils required for you to be able to cook anything at all, you may wonder whether you'd better forget the whole thing and eat in the cafeteria, however bad the food may be. A brioche cake tin, a marble slab for pastry making, an omelette pan: apparently no kitchen is complete without them, not to mention an ice cream freezer, a thing for piping whipped cream into fancy patterns, and a complete range of equipment for doing your own canning. The following list contains the basic essential utensils for both one-person and communal kitchens, and other important utensils that, if you are sharing, it would be a good idea to get.

When you are setting up a communal kitchen, buy utensils from a restaurant or hotel supplier. They are cheaper and you'll be able to get big ones.

1 big pot or casserole, heavy, with a tightly fitting lid. The best ones are those that can go both on top of the stove and inside the oven.
1 large heavy frying pan
1 good-sized saucepan for vegetables, etc.
1 small saucepan for sauces, eggs, etc.
1 large very sharp knife If it is not sharp, you cannot work properly.
1 medium-sized knife
1 paring knife
1 chopping block This is essential for chopping meat and vegetables. A cheap one costs less than a dollar.
1 large bowl for mixing; for desserts; for salads, if you don't have a salad bowl.

3

1 *colander* for draining vegetables
1 *sieve* (This can substitute for a colander, if necessary.)
1 *spatula* for getting up fried eggs, etc.
2 *wooden spoons*
1 *eggbeater*
1 *can opener*
1 *oven cloth*
1 *pepper grinder*

Other basic utensils:
1 *ladle* for soups and sauces
1 *vegetable peeler* (saves time and waste)
1 *garlic squeezer* (saves time and aggravation)
1 *Moka coffee pot* This excellent Italian coffee pot produces good strong
    coffee in no time at all. Comes in various sizes.
1 *knife sharpener*
1 *cheese grater* Get the kind with different-sized holes so that you can
    use it for bread, nutmeg, etc.
1 *rolling pin* A heavy glass works as well and functions as a cutter, too.

The Store Cupboard

If you are by yourself, buy small supplies of the goods that might go stale. Staples such as oil and vinegar should be bought in large amounts, because, as you will find, you use them a lot and you can save a tremendous amount of money by buying enormous quantities at once. A giant can of olive oil, for example, will cost you between $3 and $4. You can decant what you need into a small bottle. Gallon bottles of vinegar are very cheap and can be improved with the addition of chopped fresh herbs such as tarragon or basil.

Keep a bottle of cheap dry sherry (about a dollar) on hand for cooking, provided you can be trusted not to drink it. Cider is a good substitute for white wine. Opened bottles of red or white wine may turn into vinegar after a week. Use the wine you are drinking for cooking. Stale flat beer can sometimes be used instead of white wine or cider, and it is good with beef stews.

Save breadcrumbs or stale bread; the bought breadcrumbs are very odd indeed and come in an unlikely brilliant orange.

Below is a list of basic ingredients for your store cupboard. The herbs and spices are dealt with on page 6.

Mustard Use good Dijon or French mustard, not the bright yellow stuff.
Vinegar Use good cider or wine vinegar.

Oil Use olive, peanut, soy, sesame, or vegetable oil for cooking and for salads. Corn oil should be used only for frying.

Tomato purée or tomato paste

Garlic

Wholewheat flour

Sugar

Honey or molasses Use wherever possible instead of sugar.

Brown rice

Long-grain rice

Lemons

Onions

Grated cheese

Chicken and beef bouillon cubes

Soy sauce

Horseradish sauce

Tabasco sauce

Worcestershire sauce

Spices

Herbs

Coarse salt (Use kosher or sea salt. It has more flavor and texture than ordinary salt.)

Peppercorns

Also have on hand:

Aluminum foil This is especially useful for people with hot plates or electric skillets.

Plastic bags These can be washed, dried, and used again.

Glass jars Save and use for storing beans, etc.

Towel Use for drying salad vegetables.

If your kitchen consists of a hot plate balanced on the corner of a desk or table, you will need:

A bowl of water for dipping knives and forks

A wet rag for wiping up messes

A jug of water for cooking

A newspaper on the floor

An open window

Storing Food

When you buy meat or fish, always remove it from its wrapper, wipe or wash it, dry it, and either put it in a marinade, wrap it in fresh plastic, or put it in a covered bowl. Refrigerate. Don't ever leave it in the paper. The paper sticks to it and becomes almost impossible to remove, as well as imparting a flavor of its own.

Never leave food in open cans; it can become poisonous.

Never leave fish, garlic-flavored food, melon, or other equally smelly or absorbent things unwrapped in the refrigerator. Everything else will pick up the smell.

Keep bread wrapped in airtight plastic.

Keep milk out of the light. Light destroys its vitamins.

Herbs and Spices

If you are by yourself, you can make do with a jar of mixed herbs, using them in the recipes that call for specific herbs. Mixed sweet herbs usually consist of marjoram, savory, parsley, thyme, and celery. Blended herbs usually contain oregano, thyme, basil, sage, and bay leaf.

Always keep herbs in airtight containers, out of strong light, and in a cool place. They lose their flavor fast, so buy them in small quantities. Dry, stale herbs can ruin a recipe. Ground herbs and spices go stale very quickly. Nutmeg and pepper, for example, should always be ground or grated fresh.

If you are setting up a communal kitchen, each person can contribute a couple of jars of herbs or spices. This way you can get a complete spice and herb shelf.

Be careful with herbs; too much can ruin a dish. A chicken flavored with tarragon should taste more of the chicken than of the tarragon. You can use more fresh herbs than dried since they do not have such a strong flavor. Chop and add them to the dish.

Here is a basic list of herbs and spices, with explanations and uses for each one.

Basil   Used in stews, salad, with tomatoes, vegetables, and seafood, it has a wide flat leaf and a minty smell.

Bay leaf   A dried leaf used for flavoring stews, soups, marinades, stocks, and tomatoes.

Capers   Unopened flower buds, usually preserved in vinegar or salt. Delicious with eggplant, fish, tomatoes, and hot or cold sauces.

Caraway seeds   Tart little seeds that are good with cabbage, sauerkraut, pork, potatoes, and sausages.

Cardamom   A straw-colored round spice with little seeds inside. Use with curries, desserts, fruit salad, oranges, after-dinner espresso coffee, and mulled wine.

Cayenne A strong, fiery red pepper, good on meat, fish, and eggs, and in sauces.

Chili powder Ground Mexican peppers mixed with paprika, cumin, garlic, and oregano. Excellent for meat, stews, and sauces.

Chives Thin green stalks with an onion flavor, excellent when chopped and added to sauces, stews, etc. If not available fresh, can often be bought frozen.

Cinnamon The bark of the cinnamon tree. Excellent in spicy dishes, desserts, sauces, and mulled wine.

Cloves Excellent with apples, fruit, curries, ham, or pork.

Coriander Fresh coriander is used in avocado salads, stews, and soups. The dried seeds are good with curries, marinades, and soups.

Curry powder A blend of spices which varies a great deal but usually contains turmeric, cardamom, coriander, allspice, ginger, cinnamon, cloves, cumin, garlic, mustard, mace, nutmeg, paprika, and red pepper, among other things.

Dill A delicious feathery herb, excellent chopped fresh with lamb, fish, cream, and cucumbers. Dill seed is good with vegetables, soup, sauces, cheese, and salad dressings.

Ginger Ground ginger is good with curries, pot roasts, lamb, fish, and steaks, in moderation, and with desserts. Fresh ginger root is delicious sliced and cooked with vegetables or meat.

Juniper berries Not an essential part of your herb collection, but incredibly good with pork, sausages, or sauerkraut. A dark purple, dried berry, it is crushed and put into marinades or sauces.

Marjoram A strong aromatic herb from the mint family, it is good with lamb, beef, stews, soups, stuffings, pork, and sausages.

Nutmeg Best when bought whole and freshly ground. Excellent with vegetables, soup, cheese, desserts, mulled cider, or mulled wine.

Oregano Excellent for pasta, sauces, meat, fish, onions, and tomatoes.

Paprika The kind you normally find has little taste and is primarily useful for decorating food. Hungarian paprika has a strong flavor and should be used for stews and goulash.

Parsley Always makes dishes look attractive. Put it in stuffings, in large quantities in a white sauce (Sauce Béchamel, page 107) for fish, chicken, or ham. Chop it in a cup with scissors.

Rosemary Rosemary has long thin leaves and is delicious with chicken, lamb, pork, veal, and stuffings.

Sesame seeds   A nutty seed which is superb in salads, cakes, as oil, as a spread, or in homemade bread.

Tarragon   A delicately flavored herb with long tapery leaves. Excellent with chicken, veal, and eggs. Also great in salad dressing.

Thyme   Thyme is good with almost every savory dish, soups, stews, casseroles, meat, vegetable and fish dishes, and dishes flavored with wine.

Ways to Save Money

To save money, you have to spend time. Fast foods such as steaks and chops are much more expensive than slow ones such as stews or casseroles. Frozen and packaged food costs much more than fresh, homemade food.

If it is possible, try to think ahead and plan meals for a few days at a time. This way you will be able to stretch things like meat by using the leftovers. If you are having roast chicken one night, you might have creamed chicken the next day, and perhaps chicken curry the third night. If you are by yourself, you can eat for several days like this; by making different sauces, you won't get sick of having the same thing again.

Don't shop when you're hungry. The best time to go is after a meal, when the sight of food turns you off.

Shop with a list and stick to it. Remember that the whole point of the supermarket is to make you buy things you hadn't intended to buy. For that reason everything is displayed so that you need only help yourself to what you want. Try not to be tempted; if you're not hungry, you won't be.

Always check the weights against the prices. Note how much a box or jar contains and work out whether you really would save money by buying a big one. Some stores now display unit pricing. Ask the store manager where his list is if individual items are not marked.

Learn what fruits and vegetables are in season and avoid out-of-season hothouse vegetables.

Avoid delicatessen and late-night food shops. They charge wild prices. This means planning ahead a bit and not rushing out for barbecued chicken at 12:30 on Saturday night.

Get to know the shops and try to go to the ones outside the supermarket. Ethnic shops are usually cheaper and better because the shopkeepers know the clients personally and wouldn't dare sell them junk. You'll also discover intriguing ingredients you might not otherwise know about.

In the supermarket, the house brands of canned or frozen goods are usually cheaper than name brands.

Avoid such garbage food as soda pop, frozen TV dinners (some supermarkets even have the audacity to sell frozen omelettes), canned

9

meat, cookies, potato chips, ice cream, cakes, etc. They are more expensive than ordinary juice, fresh meat, vegetables, and homemade cakes, and they won't do a thing for you. Next time you're tempted, read the list of ingredients.

Instead of oil, use drippings. Save meat drippings in one jar, bacon in another, and keep both in the refrigerator. If you intend to eat a dish cold the next day, cook it in oil instead of fat.

Save leftovers to go in soups and stocks. But check your icebox every day or so and throw out the leftovers you had good intentions for but didn't use. An upset stomach costs you more in time and discomfort than the price of fresh food.

Save celery leaves for soup, stock, and marinades.

Save mushroom stems for sauces, soup, and stews.

Save water from canned vegetables for soup or stock. Also save any vegetable water from boiled vegetables.

Use bacon rind for soup or stew instead of bacon. Buy bacon in a hunk and cut it up yourself with a very sharp knife. Use less since your strips will be thicker than pre-sliced bacon.

Save all cast-off bits of meat trimmings from steaks, cubed meat, etc.; save chicken feet, gizzards, and bones for stock or soup. You can freeze meat bits in small containers, then use a container each time you need stock.

Substitute finely chopped scallion tops for chives.

Buy a thick soy sauce and water it down a little.

Buy a little more meat than you need and cook it the next day shredded and stir-fried the Chinese way (page 85) with vegetables.

For a quick meal, shred stewing beef and stir-fry it instead of buying steak.

Save ends of cheese and grate them. Keep in the refrigerator.

Use yoghurt or thin cream instead of thick cream for a sauce.

Use light beer instead of cider or white wine for cooking when you think it might be appropriate.

Save stale bread for breadcrumbs.

Meal Stretchers

To casseroles or stews, add hard-boiled eggs, chopped sausage, cooked beans, and chopped leftover meat or chicken.

Serve pasta or rice which can be cooked quickly at the last minute.

Serve creamed meat, fish, chicken, or vegetables in a pie shell.

Make a white sauce (Sauce Béchamel, page 107) and fold vegetables or chopped meat into it.

If you have steak, or chicken and vegetables, shred the meat and cook in the Chinese way with vegetables. Serve with rice. The meat goes further this way.

Miscellaneous Hints

Oil added to butter prevents it from burning.

Fat congeals on cold plates. Heat dishes either by putting them in the oven for a few minutes or by running them under hot water, then drying them.

Food keeps on cooking even after it has left the stove.

If fat splutters, throw a little flour or salt into the pan.

Use butter paper to grease pans.

Never add flour or cornstarch to hot liquid without blending it with a little water first.

Baby foods can be used in sauces if you don't have a blender.

Never put food you are frying into cold oil.

When food is added to the pan, it lowers the temperature. When frying food, add a few pieces at a time.

Don't let food get cold slowly. It spoils and can cause food poisoning. Refrigerate it at once.

Weights and Measures

Definite quantities for salt, pepper, and herbs are not usually given in the recipes. It is impossible to tell exactly how much you will need. Start by putting in about ¼ teaspoon, if you must measure, then taste and add more if necessary. Herbs and spices vary greatly in strength. Only you can be the judge.

When using oil for frying or sautéing, it is hard to give a specific amount. How large is your pan? As long as the surface is covered with the oil, there should be enough, but it will also depend upon what kind of dish you are making.

Dash = ⅛ to ¼ teaspoon	2 cups = 1 pint
1 teaspoon = ⅓ tablespoon	2 pints = 1 quart
2 tablespoons = 1 ounce	4 quarts = 1 gallon
4 tablespoons = ¼ cup	16 cups = 1 gallon
5⅓ tablespoons = ⅓ cup	1 pound = 16 ounces
8 tablespoons = ½ cup	1 fluid ounce = 2 tablespoons
1 cup = ½ pint	16 fluid ounces = 1 pint

Soup

An epicure dining at Crewe
Found a rather large mouse in his stew
Said the waiter "Don't shout and wave it about
Or the rest will be wanting one too."
—Edward Lear

A soup, or a stew? Some of the soups in this chapter are complete meals. Leftovers of all kinds can be used up in a soup of this kind: fish bones, meat and chicken bones, old lettuce, soft tomatoes, carrots, onions, wine, beans, stale bread can all be thrown in the cauldron. Served with hot French bread, garlic bread, a salad and cheese, you have a cheap, good, and nourishing meal which is particularly useful for after school or after theater.

Included in this chapter are good quick cold soups that make a summer meal go further, and light soups for lunch or dinner.

Leftover Soups

Bean dishes: Heat the beans in extra water or stock, add milk if you like, and diced sausage, bacon, herbs, celery, tomatoes, and other vegetables. Chopped egg, egg yolks to thicken, scallions and herbs also improve canned soups.

Rice: Heat some chicken broth or stock. Shape the cooked rice into little balls and roll them in lightly beaten egg and then in breadcrumbs. Fry in butter and add to the broth.

Potatoes: Heat some meat broth, dice and add the cooked potatoes. Serve sprinkled with chopped parsley and grated cheese.

Pasta: Heat some meat or chicken broth, add a couple of chopped tomatoes if you like, then the chopped, cooked pasta, and serve with plenty of grated cheese.

Canned Soups

These can be fixed up with grated cheese, chopped fresh watercress or parsley, cream, chives, chopped celery, grated cheese, small Italian noodles (vermicelli), or croûtons.

To make croûtons, trim the crusts off the bread, cube, and fry in oil or fat, then drain on paper towels. Or, toast the bread and then cut it up into cubes.

BLACK BEAN SOUP

This is a very economical soup and very filling. With cheese and salad you will have a complete meal. The beans should be soaked overnight in water.

1 pound black beans
  Water to cover, plus about four
    cups
1 large, peeled onion stuck with
    cloves
1 carrot, sliced
3 celery stalks, coarsely chopped
  Small herb bouquet (thyme,
    parsley, and bay leaf, tied in

    cheesecloth)
4 whole allspice
¼ teaspoon mace
¼ teaspoon cinnamon
2 cloves garlic, chopped
  Coarse salt and freshly ground
    black pepper
¼ cup rum (optional)
  Sour cream, to garnish

Soak the beans overnight. Put in a large saucepan with the water, vegetables, and herbs. Season, and simmer gently for about 4 hours, adding water if needed. Add the rum if desired. In each serving, place a spoonful of sour cream. Enough for 8 people.

LEEK AND POTATO SOUP

A simple and warming French soup. Serve this hot on a cold evening with black bread and unsalted butter, beer, and tomato salad. When put in the blender and served cold with cream it becomes the immortal vichyssoise.

1 pound potatoes
1 pound leeks
  Bay leaf
  Thyme
1 tablespoon chopped parsley

  Coarse salt and freshly ground
    black pepper
  Dash nutmeg
  Water or stock, to cover
  Cream (optional)

Peel and chop the potatoes. Cut the leeks in half and wash thoroughly in cold water. Chop and add to the pot with the potatoes. Add all remaining ingredients except the cream and simmer until the potatoes are cooked, about 40 minutes. To serve, put a little cream on the top of the soup in each bowl, if you like. Enough for 4–6.

MUSHROOM SOUP

Black bread, green salad, and white wine or beer are good here.

1 tablespoon butter	Dash nutmeg
1 tablespoon flour	Coarse salt and freshly ground
2 cups hot milk	black pepper
1 pound sliced mushrooms	Heavy cream (optional)

Melt the butter in a saucepan and gradually add the flour, stirring constantly over medium heat without browning for about 2 minutes. Add the hot milk all at once. Stir to prevent lumps and boil for a minute until mixture thickens. Add the mushrooms, nutmeg, and seasonings. Simmer gently for about 20 minutes. To serve, put a spoonful of heavy cream in each bowl if you like. Enough for 2 large or 4 small servings.

OKLAHOMA OKRA SOUP

Serve this soup over boiled rice and you will have enough to make a complete meal. Use leftover chicken if you have any. Or bone fresh chicken meat and add the bones separately, removing them before you serve the soup. They will give flavor to it.

2 tablespoons butter	1 pound okra, trimmed and sliced
1 large onion, chopped	4 tomatoes, peeled and chopped
4 strips bacon, chopped	Dash Worcestershire sauce
½ pound chicken, chopped	Coarse salt and freshly ground
2 pints chicken stock, or water and	black pepper
3–4 chicken bouillon cubes	½ cup heavy cream

Melt the butter in a heavy saucepan. Add the onion and cook over low heat until clear. Add the bacon and brown. Add the chicken and stock and simmer for 20 minutes. Add the okra and tomatoes. Cook until the okra is tender. Add the Worcestershire sauce to taste, stir in the cream, and heat through without boiling. Correct the seasoning. Serve with rice. Serves 6.

TULANE FRENCH ONION SOUP

This is an excellent party soup. Serve at midnight to sober those who've had too much to drink, and to fill those who missed their dinner.

6 onions, sliced
3 tablespoons butter
1 quart water
5 bouillon cubes (beef)
  Coarse salt and freshly ground

black pepper
1 loaf French or Italian bread
1 cup grated Parmesan or Cheddar
  cheese

In a large pot cook the onions in the butter until they are soft. Add the water and the bouillon cubes and bring to a boil. Then simmer gently for half an hour. Season.

Cut the bread into small slices and toast. Put some cheese on top of each slice and brown in broiler. Ladle out the soup into warmed soup bowls, putting some onion in each one, and float the toast on top. Serves 6.

CHICKEN SOUP

This is a very good way to use up the carcass of a roasted chicken. The soup is even better if the bones have some meat left on them.

1 onion, chopped
1 tablespoon butter
1 chicken carcass
  Water to cover
  Coarse salt and freshly ground

black pepper
2 tablespoons sherry (optional)
  About ½ cup cream
1 tablespoon chopped fresh parsley

Soften the onion in the butter over a low flame. Add the chicken and cover with water. Simmer gently for about 1 hour. Remove the bones and strip off any meat left on them. Chop it up and return it to the soup. Season and add the sherry, if you like. Simmer for a few minutes, then add cream, and remove from stove. Pour into soup bowls and scatter parsley over the top of each serving. Enough for 4–6 people.

FISH BONE SOUP

This is a delicious soup and not at all the cat's dinner that its title suggests. It is the best way to use up the remains and bones of cooked fish, and any suitable leftovers in the fridge can go in, too. Tomatoes are important, but apart from them you could add peppers, green vegetables, squash, potatoes, leftover rice, chicken, ham, etc.

Serve with hot wholewheat bread and red wine.

Fish Stock:

Fish bones and leftover pieces
1 onion, sliced
1 carrot, sliced
  Herbs, to taste

Place all ingredients in a large saucepan and cover with water. Bring to a boil, then simmer for 30–40 minutes. Strain, to remove bones. Vegetables may be returned to pot, if you like.

2 pints fish stock
1 cup noodles
1 6-ounce can of shrimp (with
  juice)
1 cup mushrooms, sliced
4 tomatoes, peeled
2 hot sausages, chopped

2 cups chopped beet greens,
  spinach, or kale
½ cup stoned black olives
  Dash curry powder
  Coarse salt and freshly ground
  pepper to taste

Garnish (optional)

2 hard-boiled eggs, peeled and
  chopped
2 tablespoons chopped fresh parsley
3 tablespoons grated Cheddar cheese

Bring the fish stock to a boil. Add all the ingredients except the garnish and cook for about 10 minutes, until the soup is thick and dark. Pour into heated soup plates and scatter chopped egg, parsley, and grated cheese over the top. Serves 4.

ICEBOX SOUP

"An extra meal at no extra cost." For this soup keep all discarded vegetable leaves, stalks, etc., and ferret around in your icebox for anything else that's likely.

This soup is the answer to the leftover problem, particularly for people living by themselves. Make lots of it, and use any leftover icebox soup as stock. Then add a can of asparagus, chicken, or tomato soup to it, to make it taste different the next time around.

Leftover or discarded leafy green
  vegetables such as lettuce,
  cabbage, broccoli, celery, etc.
Scallions, chopped

Overripe tomatoes
2 strips bacon, diced
4 cups chicken stock, or 4 cups water
  and 4 bouillon cubes

1 clove garlic, crushed
1 onion, chopped
1 carrot, chopped
   Fresh parsley and/or herbs, to taste
     (thyme, bay leaf, basil, etc.)
   Dash Tabasco

Coarse salt and freshly ground
   black pepper
Leftover meat or chicken, chopped
Parmesan cheese
Croûtons (optional)

Place all ingredients except the meat or chicken in a big pot. Bring to a boil, then simmer for 1 hour. Strain. Add the meat or chicken and heat through.

Sprinkle grated Parmesan cheese on each serving and toss in a few croûtons, if desired. Serve very hot to 4–6 people.

COLD SOUPS

CONSOMMÉ MADRILÈNE

To make this soup simply buy a can or more, depending on how many people you want to feed (allowing ½ can per serving), and chill until the soup jiggles like jelly. Then garnish with the ingredients below and you will have an excellent beginning to a summer meal.

Per Serving

½ can chilled consommé madrilène
1 tablespoon sour cream
   Chives, to garnish
   Freshly ground black pepper

Spoon out the consommé into individual bowls. Put a tablespoon of sour cream on top, sprinkle with chives, and season.

ICED BEEF CONSOMMÉ

If you want to make this soup a special one, open the can before you chill it and stir a tablespoon of dry sherry into the soup.

Per Serving

½ can chilled beef consommé
1 lemon wedge
   Freshly chopped parsley, to
     garnish
   Freshly ground black pepper

Spoon out the consommé into individual bowls. Place the lemon wedge on top and garnish with parsley. Season and serve.

Note: If it is a hot day, do not serve these soups until you are ready to eat; otherwise the soup will be almost melted by the time you sit down.

UNIVERSITY OF MIAMI
AVOCADO SOUP WITH CHIVES

This is superb as a last-minute soup if you have a blender. It requires no cooking and takes few minutes to make. If you don't have a blender, mix the ingredients together by hand. It's worth the trouble.

2 ripe avocados
1 cup yoghurt
1 tablespoon lemon juice
½ cup light cream
1 cup cold chicken broth

Dash curry powder
Coarse salt and freshly ground
    black pepper
2 tablespoons chopped chives

Peel and pit the avocados. Mash them and put them in a blender. Add the remaining ingredients, except for the chives. Purée. If you don't have a blender, mash the other ingredients into the avocado. Chill. When ready to serve, sprinkle chives on top. Serves 4.

COLD TOMATO SOUP

For people with little cooking equipment this soup is an excellent start to a summer meal. If you have a blender, all the better, but it works just as well mashed together in a large bowl.

3 cups tomato juice
2 tablespoons tomato paste
4 scallions, minced (including tops)
    Dash thyme
    Dash curry powder
    Dash Worcestershire sauce
    Dash Tabasco

Dash sugar
Juice 1 lemon
1 teaspoon grated lemon rind
1 cup sour cream or yoghurt
    Coarse salt and freshly ground
        black pepper
2 teaspoons chopped parsley

Mix ingredients together, reserving half the sour cream and all the parsley. Chill. Put in bowls and add a spoonful of sour cream to each serving. Sprinkle parsley on top. Enough for 4.

PIMIENTO AND SOUR CREAM SOUP

This soup is extremely inexpensive and very good for a summer meal. It's also very nourishing.

1 jar pimientos (preferably roasted)
6 cups tomato juice
  Coarse salt and freshly ground
      black pepper
1 tablespoon chopped fresh parsley
1 tablespoon sour cream per serving

Mash half the pimientos and simmer in the tomato juice for about 20 minutes. Cut the rest into strips and add to the mixture. Season, and then refrigerate for at least 4 hours, preferably overnight. When ready to serve, put a tablespoon of sour cream in each serving and scatter parsley over the top. Serves 6.

Fish

Buy from a good fishmonger and choose fish that have bright eyes, rosy gills, firm, slithery flesh and no smell. If it smells fishy and the eyes are dull, the flesh limp and listless, the fish is old; don't buy it.

Frozen fish is sometimes fresher than fresh fish. Unfortunately, freezing robs it of much of its flavor. If there is a deposit of frozen juices at the bottom of the package, it means that it has been thawed and frozen again.

A small package of frozen fish makes an excellent one-person meal. Let it thaw out at room temperature. If you run it under the hot tap, you will cook the outside and it will start to flake off, leaving a lump of ice in the middle.

As for canned fish, sardines and tuna are the most practical and the cheapest.

Shellfish

Clams, mussels, and oysters should feel heavy in the hand, and the shells should always be tightly closed. Throw away any open ones.

Scrub them well with steel wool if you will be eating the liquid in which they are cooked.

Lobster and crab should be bought alive (or frozen, if you're squeamish) and put into cold water. Bring it to the boil slowly so that they will faint before the water gets hot enough to give them any pain.

Grilled Fish

Grilling or broiling is one of the best and simplest ways of cooking small and medium-sized fish and fish steaks. Very small fish are good fried, and the big ones should be poached or baked.

Suitable for grilling are herring, mackerel, small striped or sea bass, bluefish, trout, small red snapper; salmon, halibut, or swordfish steaks; flounder, sole, small pompano, plaice.

Score the fish twice on each side diagonally, about one and a half inches apart, depending on the size of the fish, after you have cleaned, scaled, washed, and dried it thoroughly.

Season the fish with sea or kosher salt, freshly ground pepper, and oil and chopped parsley, dill, fennel, basil, or marjoram—whichever you like—and lemon juice. If you like, leave it to marinate in this mixture for a couple of hours.

If you don't wish to marinate it, score and season as above and use butter instead of oil, if you like.

You must have a very hot grill. Grease the pan or griddle on which you are going to cook the fish, so that the skin won't stick when you turn it.

Cook the fish in the broiler or grill under high heat until it becomes golden brown. Baste with marinade or oil if it looks dry. If the fish is a large one, remove it to a lower rung after you have seared it, so that it can get cooked through without getting dry or burned.

Turn the fish only once; otherwise, it will break. Cook it longer on the second side. About 7 minutes on the first, and 10–12 minutes on the second side should be enough for a fish under 1½ pounds. When it flakes it is done, but it shouldn't flake too much or it is overdone. Smaller fish may take less time.

Serve the fish with lemon quarters and butter, or Parsley Butter (page 50), Lemon Butter (page 87), or the following Green Sauce.

GREEN SAUCE

This is good for rather bland whole fish, but is not so good on fish steaks. It is a strong garlicky sauce, and you need lots of French or Italian bread to mop it up.

6 tablespoons olive oil	**1 clove garlic, chopped**
Juice of half a lemon	**Coarse salt and freshly ground**
¾ cup chopped fresh parsley	**black pepper**
1 tablespoon chopped capers	

In a small bowl, mix all the ingredients together. You should have a thick sauce. Leftover sauce can be used on salad or spaghetti.

BROILED SALMON WASHINGTON STATE

If you can't get fresh salmon, frozen salmon will have to do. Thaw it out and dry it thoroughly before you cook it.

Serve this with Broccoli au Gratin (page 94), Cucumbers Baked with Dill (page 105), Braised Fennel (page 110), or Braised Greens (page 113).

If you're drinking wine, cold white wine is the best. Make sure it's not a sweet one.

4 salmon steaks	3 tablespoons butter (or more, as
2 tablespoons lemon juice	needed)
Coarse salt and freshly ground	Sauce Hollandaise (page 87), or
pepper	Parsley Butter (page 50)
Dash thyme	

Dry the steaks thoroughly and marinate them in the lemon juice, seasonings, thyme, and melted butter for 1 hour. Put on a greased pan or griddle and cook under very high heat, turning once, for about 7 minutes on each side. Test by pressing your finger on one of the steaks. If it's cold in the middle, it's not cooked. Serve with sauce or butter. Serves 4.

Note: Halibut or swordfish steaks can also be prepared this way.

GRILLED MACKEREL

Mackerel are inexpensive fish; you can make a meal out of them for very little per person. They're at their best toward the end of the summer.

1 mackerel per person (in this case,	Coarse salt and freshly ground
the stuffing is for 4)	black pepper
1 onion, chopped	1 tablespoon olive oil
2 tablespoons butter	2 tablespoons chopped fresh parsley,
1 tablespoon prepared mustard	to garnish (optional)

Wash and dry the mackerel. Soften the onion in the butter over low heat and add the mustard and seasonings. Remove from heat. Mix well. Preheat grill or broiler. Stuff the fish cavities with the mustard mixture, sprinkle with oil and cook, turning once. The fish is done when the flesh pulls away from the bone. Scatter parsley over the fish. Serves 4.

Deep-Fried Fish

Small fish and flat fish fillets are good for frying. Fish steaks can also be fried, as can large fish cut into slices about an inch thick. Real fried fish (as opposed to the bright orange greasy fish fillets you get in roadside stands) is simply delicious, but surprisingly hard to do. The fish must be absolutely dry, you must use plenty of oil (not butter), and the oil must be smoking when you put the fish in.

If the fish is quite large, score the flesh before you fry it. This will help it to cook faster.

Don't salt the fish before you cook it because the salt will draw out the juices.

Dip the fish in milk, beer, or beaten egg and then in flour or bread-crumbs, corn meal, or a combination of these. Sometimes you can season the liquid with Worcestershire sauce, Tabasco, or curry powder if you like, or mix some dried herbs, chili, curry powder, cumin, or what you will into the flour. It makes it different.

Put plenty of oil in the skillet, enough to cover the fish. Butter burns at a lower temperature and for this reason it is not good used here. Turn the heat up, and don't put the fish in until the oil is smoking. Add the fish a few at a time, so that you don't reduce the temperature too dras-tically.

After about 7–8 minutes, the fish should be cooked. Allow about 5 minutes for fish slices. The fish is done when it rises to the surface.

Drain the fish on paper towels, then salt to taste.

Serve with lemon wedges and chopped fresh parsley.

Sauce Tartare (below) is also good with fried fish.

Other fish good for frying this way include fresh sardines, smelts, grunions, herring, sprats, whiting, and almost any small fish.

SAUCE TARTARE

2 hard-boiled egg yolks	1 tablespoon chopped capers
1 teaspoon dry mustard	1 tablespoon chopped chives
Coarse salt and freshly ground	1 tablespoon chopped parsley
black pepper	Tarragon, dried or fresh (optional)
2 teaspoons vinegar	1 tablespoon chopped pickle
1 cup olive oil	(optional)

Mix the egg yolks into a paste with the mustard, salt, and pepper. Add vinegar and mix well. Gradually work in 1 cup of olive oil. Stir in the capers, chives, and parsley. Tarragon and chopped pickle add extra flavor, if desired.

INSTANT SAUCE TARTARE

1 cup mayonnaise	1 tablespoon chopped pickle
1 egg yolk	1 tablespoon chopped parsley
1 pimiento, chopped	Coarse salt and freshly ground
1 tablespoon chopped capers	black pepper

Combine all ingredients.

Poached Fish

Although fish should never be boiled, unless for a soup, it is delicious when poached, or simmered gently in a seasoned liquid. Fish suitable for poaching, among others, are red snapper, skate, striped or sea bass, carp, and haddock.

Court Bouillon for Fish

2 quarts water	½ cup vinegar or 1 cup white wine
½ bay leaf	1 teaspoon salt
¼ cup chopped carrot	Parsley
¼ cup chopped celery	Bouquet garni
1 small onion stuck with 2 cloves	

Bring water to a boil and add all other ingredients. Boil for half an hour. Strain. Place fish in liquid and bring to simmer. Allow 5–8 minutes per pound of fish. Remove 1 fish from liquid with a spatula and test for doneness by flaking with a fork. If done, remove all fish and drain. It helps to place fish on warmed plates to retain heat if you are preparing a sauce to accompany it.

Save the liquid which, now that the fish have been cooked in it, is fish stock, for Fish Bone Soup (page 15).

SKATE WITH BLACK BUTTER

Skate is a very inexpensive fish and has an odd appearance, with great wings that make it look like a kite. It is simple to cook and, when served with black butter, makes an impressive meal. Rice to soak up the butter, a green vegetable, and white wine would make it into a really good dinner.

2 pounds skate
    Court Bouillon for Fish (See above)
¼ pound butter
 1 tablespoon vinegar
 1 tablespoon chopped capers

Cook the fish in a court bouillon for 20 minutes and drain. Meanwhile, melt the butter in a saucepan and heat until it starts to brown (not until *black*, even though that's its title). Add the vinegar and capers. When the fish is cooked, pour the sauce over it and serve. Enough for 4.

FISH PIE

Use leftover or cooked fish for this pie. Chopped tomatoes are excellent in it and any suitable leftovers can be added. Salad is all you need to serve with it. Brown under a hot grill for about 15 minutes until the potato crust has browned.

2 cups cooked fish, picked over and chopped	Dash nutmeg
1 tablespoon butter	Coarse salt and freshly ground black pepper
1 tablespoon flour	1½ cups mashed potatoes
¾ cup hot milk	Paprika
¼ cup grated Parmesan or Cheddar cheese	Extra butter

Put the fish in a baking dish. Heat the butter in a saucepan and add the flour. Cook together for 2 minutes over low heat, without browning. Add the milk all at once and boil until thick. Add some of the cheese, nutmeg, salt, and pepper. Pour over the fish. Put the potatoes on top, sprinkle with cheese and paprika, and dot with butter. Place in oven for 15 minutes, or until heated through. Then place in the broiler until the potato crust has browned. Serves 4.

CHUTNEY TUNA

Either serve this on rice or bake it in a pie shell. Use Wholewheat Pie Crust (page 197), or buy a frozen pie shell and partially cook it before adding the filling. Tomato salad or Cucumbers in Yoghurt (page 135) go well with it, as does cold beer.

2 7-ounce cans tuna fish	¾ cup mayonnaise
1 cup chopped chutney	Coarse salt and freshly ground black pepper
2 green peppers, chopped	
2 onions, chopped	1 egg, beaten
1 tablespoon oil	9-inch pie shell, partially cooked (optional)
3 stalks celery, chopped fine	

Preheat oven to 400°. Mash the tuna with the chutney in a mixing bowl. Soften the onions in the oil with the peppers and add to the tuna with the remaining ingredients, except the pie shell. Pour the mixture into the pie shell or into a greased baking dish and bake for 20 minutes in oven. Serve over rice if not using pie shell. Enough for 4–6.

FISH FILLETS IN CIDER

Any white fish fillets will do. Frozen ones, if fresh are not available, can be thawed and used here.

Peas and potatoes Gratin Dauphinois (page 176) are good with the fish. Cider is the best drink with it.

2 tablespoons butter	Coarse salt and freshly ground
8 white fish fillets	black pepper
1 cup cider	1 tablespoon butter mixed with 1
Juice of half a lemon	tablespoon flour

Butter a baking dish and put the fish fillets in. Cover with the cider and lemon juice, and season. If you have some, place a piece of grease-proof paper on top. Bake for 20–30 minutes in a preheated 350-degree oven.

Remove the cooking liquid and reduce it in a small saucepan over high heat. Gradually add the butter mixture and thicken the sauce. Correct seasoning and pour the sauce over the fish. Dot with butter and brown for a minute under the broiler. Serves 4.

Note: The potatoes can be put in the oven enough ahead of the fish to finish cooking at the same time.

See also
FISH WITH CAPERS, page 204
SAUTÉED FISH ROE, page 219

KEDGEREE

An English recipe has crept into this book. But since the English are old hands at cooking on a tight budget, it is inevitable that many of their dishes should appear here. This one is supposed to have originated in Victorian India. It makes a delicious light supper dish. It is also a good way to use up leftover cooked fish.

Beer is probably the best drink here, and a green vegetable such as broccoli or Brussels sprouts goes well.

2 cups poached white fish (above)	1 cup cooked rice
4 tablespoons butter	1 raw egg
2 hard-boiled eggs, chopped	½ cup cream (or more)
Coarse salt and freshly ground	Nutmeg
black pepper	

Flake the fish and put it in a saucepan with the butter. Heat through and add the hard-boiled eggs. Season, then add the rice and the raw egg. The cooked rice should be firm and the grains separate. (See page 171 for hints on cooking rice.) The worst kind of kedgeree is the sort that comes out mushy. Turn down the heat and cook slowly, stirring with a wooden spoon. Add the cream gradually, but don't let the mixture become runny. Sprinkle with nutmeg and serve. Enough for 4.

Note: Some people like a tablespoon of curry powder added to the butter at the beginning. Suit yourself.

BARNARD COLLEGE SALT COD

Obtainable in Italian and Puerto Rican markets, and often in fish or supermarkets, this salt cod makes a cheap, delicious dish and is easy to prepare. The cod is salted and dried after it has been caught and is sold in large white strips. Because it is salted, you must soak it overnight. Rinse as much salt off as you can and change the water you soak it in several times. If you don't rinse off the salt, it is inedible.

Once the cod has been soaked, it takes only a few minutes to cook it. Serve it with Brown Rice (page 172) and a green vegetable.

2 pounds salt cod, soaked overnight
  Milk
1 clove garlic, chopped
1 onion, chopped

1 tablespoon olive oil
3 tomatoes, chopped
Coarse salt and freshly ground
  black pepper

Test to see if there's still any salt on the cod by licking it. Chop it into large hunks and put it in a skillet. Cover with milk and bring to a boil. Simmer until done, when it will flake with a fork. Drain off milk and give it to the cat. Reserve fish. In another pan, sauté the garlic and onion in oil. Add tomatoes and simmer for a few minutes. Gently stir in fish and correct seasoning. When heated through, serve. Enough for 4.

BRANDEIS SARDINE PATTIES

Dirt cheap and quick to make, these are great with Watercress Salad (page 140) and fried or baked potatoes. Beer or cider to drink.

2 cans sardines
1 onion, chopped
1 tablespoon butter or oil
1 egg
1 tablespoon chopped fresh chives
  or parsley
Coarse salt and freshly ground

black pepper
Dash soy sauce
Dash Tabasco
½ cup dry breadcrumbs (more as
  needed)
Flour for dredging
Frying oil

Mash the sardines in a bowl. Soften the onion in the butter and add to the bowl with the egg, chives, and seasonings. Add the breadcrumbs and more if necessary to make firm patties. You should have about 4. Roll them in flour and fry over very high heat until brown. Serve immediately. Enough for 2.

See also
SARDINES WITH TOMATOES, page 218
SARDINES ON TOAST, page 218

EASY CLAMS WITH TOMATO SAUCE

There are three ways to make this dish. You can shortcut by buying a jar of marinara sauce and improve it with the ingredients below. Or you can make the Tomato Sauce on page 166 which is easy to make but takes an hour to cook. If you're feeling very lazy you could serve the ready-made sauce by itself, but it won't taste as good. This is great with spaghetti.

2 cups Tomato Sauce (page 166) or
   Improved Tomato Sauce
   (below)
2 dozen clams

Simmer sauce for 15 minutes. Scrub the clams free of sand and drain. Add clams to the sauce and simmer until shells open, about 5–10 minutes. Overcooking toughens clams. Serves 2.

Improved Commercial Tomato Sauce

1 onion, chopped	Pinch of thyme, parsley, and basil
1 tablespoon olive oil	¼ cup dry sherry or red wine
1 pint jar or can of marinara sauce	Coarse salt
Juice of half a lemon	Freshly ground black pepper

Sauté onion in the oil. Add the sauce, lemon juice, herbs, sherry or wine, and seasonings. Simmer for about 15 minutes.

SHRIMP WITH MAYONNAISE

This dish is incredibly simple and extremely good.

2 pounds fresh shrimp	1½ cups Mayonnaise (page 132) or
1 cup white wine	Improved Mayonnaise
Fresh herbs, to taste (parsley,	(below)
dill, etc.)	

Wash the shrimp and drain. Bring the wine and herbs to boil in a large skillet (an electric skillet may be used). Add the shrimp, cover, and cook for 3–5 minutes. *Do not overcook.* Drain the shrimp on paper towels or a newspaper. Place in the center of the table and let people help themselves, peeling the shrimp and dipping them into the mayonnaise. Serves 2–4.

Improved Commercial Mayonnaise

1½ cups commercial mayonnaise
  1 egg yolk
  1 teaspoon dry mustard
  Juice of half a lemon

Mix all ingredients together well and chill until flavors are mingled.

See also
BOSTON SHRIMP CHILI, page 203

LOUISIANA STATE UNIVERSITY GUMBO

When making gumbo, never put in the filé powder until just before serving. If it cooks, it gets bitter and makes the dish stringy. You can make this without the filé powder if you can't get it, but it is a very good natural thickening agent. If fresh shrimp and crab are unavailable, substitute frozen ones.

2 tablespoons olive oil	Herb bouquet (parsley, thyme,
1 pound okra, sliced	and bay leaf tied in a
1 onion, chopped	cheesecloth)
1 clove garlic, chopped or put	Water, to cover
through squeezer	1 pound headless raw shrimp,
2 sticks celery, chopped	shelled, washed and drained
3 tomatoes, or one medium-sized	½ pound crab meat
can tomatoes	1 teaspoon filé powder
2 rashers bacon, fried and chopped	Coarse salt and freshly ground
(optional)	black pepper

In a large casserole heat the oil. Add the okra, onion, and garlic, and sauté until golden. Add the celery and cook for one minute more. Add the tomatoes, bacon, herbs, and water. Simmer for 30–45 minutes, until the okra is almost done. Add the shrimp and crab meat, season, and cook for about 7 more minutes (do not overcook the shrimp). Stir in the filé powder quickly, remove from heat, and serve over rice in a soup bowl. Serves 6–8.

LOUISIANA EGGPLANT AND OYSTER CASSEROLE

For people living in many states a pint of oysters costs quite a bit; if they are too expensive, try using canned ones instead.

Serve this with French or Italian bread and Italian Pepper Salad (page 137).

1 eggplant	1 large tomato, chopped
1 pint oysters, with liquid	½ cup grated Parmesan cheese
2 onions, chopped	½ cup breadcrumbs
2 tablespoons butter	Coarse salt
1 tablespoon oil	Freshly ground black pepper
1 clove garlic, chopped	Cayenne pepper

Preheat oven to 350 degrees. Chop the eggplant into pieces the same size as the oysters. Salt and leave for half an hour. Meanwhile, sauté the onions in the butter and oil. Add the garlic and the tomato and cook together for a few minutes. In the baking dish arrange the eggplant, oysters (with their liquid), and onion-tomato mixture in layers, ending with eggplant. Top with breadcrumbs and cheese. Sprinkle with cayenne, dot with butter, and bake for an hour, or until the eggplant is cooked. Serves 4.

Poultry

Chicken used to be a luxury, something that you had once in a while for Sunday lunch or for someone's birthday. Nowadays this has all changed, for chicken has become one of the cheapest meats on the market. Unfortunately, as is often the case when things are mass-produced, it has lost the very thing which made it special in the first place. It no longer has any taste. Gone are the days when chicken roasted in a little butter and flavored with tarragon would be one of the most delicious meals you had ever tasted. Because the chickens are raised in "chicken factories," never allowed to see the light of day, fed on artificial feeds and injected with hormones, they emerge plump and tender, but that's it. Unless they are free-ranging chickens, there will always be a problem in getting the factory birds to taste of anything at all.

However, we have to make do with what we've got, and the recipes in this chapter are designed to give as much taste and flavor as possible to the poor old bird.

How to Buy Chicken

Choose chicken that is white, with a firm, soft skin. Never buy chicken that has a yellowed, wrinkled, or dry skin. If it is in a package (unfortunately most likely to be the case), check to see if there is a deposit of semi-frozen juices at the bottom and if the skin is moist and rather shiny. If so, the chicken has been frozen and thawed. Forget it. Frozen poultry is often tough because it has been frozen too soon after being killed. Often it has been thawed and frozen several times and has lost so much of its juices that it has become tasteless and rubbery. Also it can be a serious health hazard in that it supports the growth of salmonella bacteria. The best chicken comes from a butcher, preferably one that you know.

When you are buying chicken for frying and sautéing, buy a whole one and cut it up yourself. It is much cheaper.

What Kind of Chicken to Buy

A *squab* (about 2 months old, weighing about 1 pound) or a *broiler* (about 2–3 months old, about 1½–2½ pounds) is good for *broiling, grilling,* and *roasting.*

31

A *fryer* (about 3–5 months old, weighing 2–3 pounds) is good for *frying, sautéing, roasting,* and *casseroles.*

A *roaster* (about 5½–9 months old, weighing 3 pounds or more) or a *capon* (weighing over 4 pounds and 7 to 10 months old) is good for *roasting, poaching,* and *casseroles.*

Roast Chicken

Since chickens have little fat, they should always be roasted with butter or bacon; this keeps the bird at a lower temperature, makes the flesh more succulent, and produces a delicious gravy. While stuffing is unnecessary, it adds flavor and helps to make the dish go further. Recipes for stuffings, gravy, and sauce can be found below.

Good vegetables to serve with roast chicken are asparagus, green beans, broccoli, celery, spinach, mushrooms, okra, peas, and zucchini. Brown Rice (page 172), Roast Potatoes (page 176), Pommes Anna (page 177), or Gratin Dauphinois (page 176) make another good accompaniment.

1 chicken, cleaned, washed, and patted dry
Reserve wing tips, neck, and gizzard for stock (below) or

reserve liver, heart, and gizzard for Stuffing (pages 33–35)
Stuffing (optional)
Bacon (optional)

Preheat oven to 450 degrees. Place chicken on a rack, uncovered, in a large roasting pan. Place in oven and reduce heat to 350 degrees. Baste frequently with juices from pan for a browned bird. Chicken legs take 7–8 minutes longer to cook than the breast; to keep the breast from drying out you can cover it lightly with several slices of bacon. Remove for last 10 minutes so breast will brown. Roast about 20 minutes per pound for an unstuffed bird, 25 minutes per pound for a stuffed one. The chicken is done when the juices run clear when it is pricked with a fork, and when the leg moves easily in its socket. Remove to a warm platter.

If chicken is allowed to sit for a few minutes to allow its juices to settle from cooking, it will slice easily.

Serve with gravy or sauce if you like. The weight of the bird determines roughly the number of people it will feed amply: a 3-pound chicken will serve 2–3 people. If serving two, carve one side only, so that the remainder (if any) won't dry out.

CHICKEN STOCK

Wing tips and neck from a roasting chicken
Gizzard, chopped (optional)
1 onion, chopped

1 carrot, chopped
Herbs, to taste (parsley, thyme, bay leaf)
2 cups water

Cook together for 1 hour to produce a good stock for soup or gravy.

Sauces

Drain the fat off the pan or the casserole. If you want a thick gravy, add either a teaspoon of cornstarch mixed with a teaspoon of water, or a tablespoon of flour mixed with a tablespoon of water. Stir this in and scrape up the cooking juices with a wooden spoon. Add half a cup of chicken stock or bouillon. Bring to the boil. You can either season it and serve as it is, or improve it with a quarter to a half cup of red or white wine, dry sherry, dry vermouth, or port, depending on what kind of sauce you want to make. Remember that wine or spirits must be boiled so that the harsh alcohol taste is removed, leaving only the flavor.

You can, if you like, add a chopped scallion to the cooking juices at the beginning.

A tablespoon of butter stirred into the sauce at the end thickens and enriches it.

Half or a quarter of a cup of heavy cream, sour cream, or yoghurt stirred into the sauce at the end and heated through (but not boiled) is also good.

BREAD SAUCE

This is a delicious accompaniment to chicken which has been cooked with bacon and roast potatoes.

Heat a cup of milk with an onion studded with cloves for about ten minutes or until the milk is well flavored. Add two-thirds of a cup of breadcrumbs and leave to swell. Add two tablespoons butter, salt and pepper. Serve cold.

HERB AND GIBLET
STUFFING

Chicken gizzard, liver, and heart, chopped	1 tablespoon parsley, chopped fine
	Herbs, to taste (tarragon, thyme,
1 onion, chopped	or rosemary)
1 tablespoon butter or margarine	Coarse salt
1 cup soft breadcrumbs	Freshly ground pepper

Sauté the onion in butter. Add the meat and cook for 2 minutes. Remove from heat. Combine in a mixing bowl with breadcrumbs, parsley, and herbs. Season well and stuff loosely into the chicken (stuffing expands in cooking). Span the cavity with 2–3 trussing skewers and close it up by lacing string around the ends of the skewers.

WATERCRESS STUFFING

4 tablespoons butter	½ bunch fresh watercress, chopped
1 onion, chopped	¾ cup soft breadcrumbs
1 stalk celery, chopped	Pinch of thyme
Chicken heart and liver, chopped	Coarse salt
(optional)	Freshly ground pepper

Sauté onion in butter. Add celery and chopped meat, if desired, and cook for 2 minutes. Place in a mixing bowl and combine with remaining ingredients. Stuff loosely into chicken and close cavity with skewers and string.

MUSHROOM STUFFING

½ pound mushrooms, washed and sliced	¼ cup white wine or chicken stock
2 scallions, chopped	½ cup soft breadcrumbs
1 tablespoon butter	¼ cup cream cheese
1 tablespoon oil	Dash of tarragon
Chicken liver, gizzard, and heart, chopped	Dash of thyme
	Coarse salt
	Freshly ground pepper

Sauté mushrooms and scallions in butter and oil combined. Add the meat and cook for 2 minutes. Add wine or chicken stock to deglaze the pan. Scrape bottom of pan and put all in a mixing bowl. Combine well with remaining ingredients. Stuff cavity and close it up.

SAUSAGE STUFFING

1 onion, chopped	½ cup soft breadcrumbs
1 garlic clove, chopped	½ teaspoon sage
1 tablespoon butter	Dash of thyme
¼ pound sausage meat	Coarse salt
Chicken liver, heart, and gizzard, chopped (optional)	Freshly ground pepper

Sauté onion and garlic in butter. Add meat and cook for 4 minutes. Combine in mixing bowl with remaining ingredients. Stuff the chicken lightly and close cavity.

RICE STUFFING

1 onion, chopped	¼ cup raisins
1 garlic clove, chopped	Dash thyme
1 tablespoon butter or margarine	Dash tarragon
1 green pepper, chopped	Coarse salt
1 cup cooked rice	Freshly ground pepper
½ cup mushrooms, finely chopped	

Sauté the onion and garlic in butter. Add green pepper and cook for 2 minutes. Combine in a bowl with remaining ingredients. Stuff bird and close cavity.

ROAST CHICKEN
BASTED WITH CREAM

This is particularly good for stuffed chicken and produces a rich and creamy gravy. During the last 20 minutes of the chicken's cooking time baste it with heavy cream until you have used a cup. Remove the chicken from the pan and add about 3 tablespoons stock or bouillon. Add a little more cream, a tablespoon of chopped fresh parsley, salt and pepper, and serve.

CASSEROLE-ROASTED CHICKEN

Another way to roast chicken is in a casserole. The flavor is retained, and the vegetables you combine with it give it a delicious taste.

1 roasting chicken	Herbs, to taste (tarragon,
1 stick butter	rosemary, or thyme)
1 carrot, chopped	Coarse salt
1 onion, chopped	Freshly ground pepper
1 stalk celery, chopped	Lemon juice (optional)

Preheat oven to 450 degrees. Brown chicken thoroughly in butter in a heavy saucepan. Do not break the skin. Place vegetables and herbs in cavity of chicken. You do not need to truss it closed. Cover casserole and place in oven. Reduce heat to 350 degrees. If you squeeze a little lemon juice on the chicken before adding the cover, it will stay white. To brown, remove cover for last 15 minutes of roasting. Allow 20 minutes per pound for roasting.

LOUISIANA ROAST CHICKEN

In this delicious Southern recipe the chicken is stuffed with corn, peppers, and cream; roasted; and served with rice and fried bananas. It should be served in a large dish, with the rice and bananas arranged around it. No other vegetable is needed.

Canned creamed corn or frozen corn can be used for the stuffing, if fresh corn is not available.

1 roasting chicken	1 cup chicken stock (see page 32)
2 cups sweet corn	2 cups rice
2 green peppers, seeded and diced	1 tablespoon oil
½ cup heavy cream	2 tablespoons butter
Coarse salt	4 bananas or plantains, sliced
Freshly ground pepper	¼ cup heavy cream for sauce
2 strips bacon	1 tablespoon fresh chopped parsley

Set aside the wing tips, neck, heart, gizzard, etc., of the chicken for the stock. Salt the cavity and stuff with the corn mixed with the peppers, cream, and seasonings. Sew or skewer the cavity closed, cover the breast with the bacon, and roast the chicken in a moderate oven.

While it is cooking, make the stock and cook the rice.

When the chicken is done, take it out of the oven and let it sit for a while. Meanwhile, heat the butter and oil in a heavy skillet, and fry the bananas until they are golden. Keep warm.

Scrape up the chicken's cooking juices, drain off any fat, and add the stock. Boil until reduced. Stir in the cream, season, and serve separately. Arrange the chicken on a dish with the rice and bananas, garnish with parsley, and serve. Enough for 4–5.

HUNGARIAN STYLE CHICKEN

This is a simple and rewarding dish. It takes a little time to prepare, but needs no other accompaniment than, perhaps, a good red wine. You can make the sauce and prepare the rice while the chicken is roasting; don't forget to reserve the ingredients for chicken stock.

1 Casserole-Roasted Chicken (page 35)

Sauce

1 onion, chopped	Coarse salt
2 tablespoons butter	Freshly ground black pepper
1 tablespoon paprika (use good	2 tablespoons butter
Hungarian paprika)	1 tablespoon flour
1 cup dry white wine	2 cups hot chicken stock (page 32)
Pinch of thyme	Small amount of extra butter
Pinch of basil	(optional)

Sauté the onion in butter until transparent. Add the paprika and cook for 1 minute. Add the wine, herbs, and seasonings, and boil until liquid has reduced by two-thirds.

Meanwhile, melt 2 tablespoons butter in a saucepan, then gradually add the flour, making a smooth, thick paste. Do not let brown. Add the hot stock and boil for 1 minute, stirring constantly. Add the wine mixture and boil until thickened to the consistency of thick cream. Correct the seasoning. Dot with a little extra butter (to prevent a skin from forming on top) and reserve until ready to serve. It can be kept warm by placing in the top of a double boiler over hot (not boiling) water, or it can be reheated, very gently, at serving time.

Tomato-Rice Mixture

Cooked rice, enough for 4 people
    (page 171)
3 tomatoes
1 red pepper, seeded and chopped
    (optional)

Drain rice if necessary. Peel tomatoes and remove the seeds. (Tomatoes are easily peeled if allowed to sit in very hot water for a minute or two.) The seeds are discarded because their addition makes the rice too moist. Chop the tomatoes into small pieces and combine them with the rice. A chopped red pepper can also be included, if desired. Correct seasoning.

When you are ready to serve, arrange the roasted chicken on a large, warm serving platter. Pour the sauce over the chicken and mound the tomato-rice mixture around it. A little paprika may be sprinkled over the top. Serves 4.

Sautéed Chicken

Roasters or fryers are the chickens best suited to this method of cooking. They should be medium-sized, fleshy, and tender. They are cut into even-sized pieces and then cooked in butter, butter and oil, or oil.

1 chicken, washed, dried thoroughly, and cut into even-sized pieces	Clarified butter, butter and oil, or oil
Coarse salt	1 cup chicken stock or wine
Freshly ground pepper	Extra butter (optional)
Flour for dredging (optional)	1 tablespoon chopped parsley

The chicken will not brown unless it is completely dry, so pat with paper towels after washing until all excess water is absorbed. Dredging the chicken lightly in seasoned flour will also ensure its dryness. At any rate, season the chicken before sautéing it.

Butter burns quickly, and since the chicken must be browned at a high temperature, the addition of oil will prevent the butter from burning. Clarified butter doesn't burn, and if you will take a few minutes to prepare it, you can cook the chicken at a higher temperature. One method is to melt the butter over a low flame, and remove the scum as it forms on top. When no more forms, the butter is clarified. The danger here is in letting the butter burn before it is completely clear. Another method is to melt the butter, as above, then turn off the flame and allow the sediment to settle at the bottom of the pan. Then skim off the butter fat, or drawn clarified butter, into another container. Discard sediment.

Heat butter and add a few pieces of chicken at a time, allowing room around them. It helps to have the chicken at room temperature; cold chicken will lower the temperature of the butter. Brown on all sides until golden; reduce flame and cook 20–30 minutes, turning frequently. The dark meat will take a few minutes longer than the white meat.

When the chicken is done (the juices run clear), remove it to a hot dish. Remove the fat from the pan and deglaze the pan with boiling stock or wine, scraping up the good brown drippings. Boil liquid rapidly until it is reduced to about one-third of its volume. Correct seasoning, add a little extra butter (if you like), and the parsley. Pour over the chicken and serve.

CHICKEN SAUTÉED WITH EGGPLANT

All this dish needs with it is garlic bread and red wine. One skillet can be used for everything if the eggplant mixture is done first and reserved on the side.

1 medium-sized eggplant (skin on)	1 frying chicken, cut up
2 medium-sized onions	1 cup red wine
3 tomatoes	1 clove garlic, crushed
6 tablespoons olive oil	1 teaspoon tomato purée
	1 cup chicken stock or bouillon
	Coarse salt and freshly ground black pepper

Chop the eggplant into cubes and salt it; allow to stand for about half an hour. Salt removes the moisture from the eggplant. Chop the onions and the tomatoes. Dry the eggplant on paper towels. Heat 3 tablespoons oil in the skillet and sauté the onion until clear. Add the eggplant and brown lightly on all sides. When lightly browned, add the tomatoes. Cover and cook until the eggplant is done, about 30 minutes.

Dry the chicken pieces; heat remaining oil in a large skillet and brown the pieces on all sides. Reduce heat, put in dark meat, and cook, covered, for 7–8 minutes. Add the white meat and cook 15 minutes more. Remove to heated dish. Deglaze the pan with heated wine, scraping up cooking juices. Add remaining ingredients. Boil until reduced by about two-thirds. Correct seasoning. Add the chicken and eggplant mixture to the pan long enough to heat it through. Serves 4.

BERKELEY SAUTÉED CHICKEN WITH RICE

This is an excellent cheap dish for entertaining. Serve it with salad and white wine.

1 frying chicken, cut up
1 tablespoon butter
2 tablespoons oil
1 onion, chopped
¼ pound mushrooms, sliced

1 cup white wine
Dash rosemary
1 tablespoon chopped fresh
  parsley

Giblets, liver, and neck
¾ cups water
1½ cups rice
Coarse salt
Freshly ground black pepper

Dry the chicken thoroughly. Heat the butter and oil in the pan and brown the chicken. Remove. Drain off the excess fat. Add the onions and the mushrooms and cook for two minutes. Return the chicken to the pan and add the wine and herbs. Simmer gently for about 30 minutes, covered.

Meanwhile boil the giblets, liver, and neck in the water. Remove meat and reserve. Cook the rice in the same water. Test frequently to see if it's done. Chop the giblets and liver and add them to the cooked rice. Serve with the chicken, in a separate dish. Enough for 4–6.

See also
CHICKEN SAUTÉED WITH EGGPLANT, opposite
CHICKEN SAUTÉ WITH CUCUMBERS, page 205

BROILED CHICKEN LEGS WITH BACON

A simple and quick supper dish. Serve it with toast and bacon, and greens fried in the bacon fat (page 112). Beer is a good drink with it, as is cider.

4 chicken legs
  Peanut or vegetable oil
  Parsley Butter (page 50)
6 strips bacon

Coarse salt
Freshly ground black pepper
4 pieces toast

Brush the chicken legs with oil and broil for 9 minutes on each side, until golden brown and cooked. Meanwhile, make the Parsley Butter and cook the bacon. Drain the bacon and fry the greens, if you want to have them, in a small amount of the bacon fat. Put the toast on.

To serve, put the legs on a plate, crumble the bacon on the toast, and dot the chicken with the Parsley Butter. Serves 2–4.

MARYLAND UNIVERSITY CHICKEN

Serve this with buttermilk biscuits and salad. You can bake the biscuits while the chicken is frying.

1 frying chicken, cut up
1 beaten egg mixed with a dash of
  Worcestershire, a dash of soy
  sauce, and a dash of Tabasco

Flour seasoned with pepper and
  thyme
Vegetable or peanut oil

Dip the pieces of chicken into the egg mixture and then into the flour. Heat the oil until slightly smoking in the frying pan and fry the chicken for about 30 minutes, or until done. Serves 4.

UNIVERSITY OF TEXAS FRIED CHICKEN

Grated Parmesan cheese gives this chicken a slightly different flavor. Serve with corn and a salad.

1 frying chicken, cut up
1 egg
½ cup milk

1 cup flour
1 tablespoon grated Parmesan
  cheese
¼ cup yellow corn meal

Cayenne or paprika
Coarse salt
Freshly ground black pepper
Oil or fat for deep frying

Dry the chicken on paper towels. Beat the egg with the milk and dip the chicken into this mixture. Place the flour, cheese, corn meal, and seasonings in a plastic bag and shake to mix. Coat the chicken with the flour mixture by shaking a few pieces of the chicken at a time in the bag. In a deep pan, gradually heat the oil or fat. Do not allow it to smoke. If a cube of bread browns in 1 minute, the temperature is about right. Use a basket, and gradually lower chicken, a few pieces at a time, into the oil. Or pan-fry the chicken on all sides until golden. It is done when the juices run clear. Serves 4.

CHICKEN CASSEROLES

This is an ideal way to cook chicken and give it plenty of flavor. The chicken is first browned in butter, butter and oil, bacon fat, lard, or plain oil. It is then put into a casserole with vegetables, liquid, and seasonings.

If you fry the chicken in bacon or lard, vegetables such as turnips, carrots, potatoes, beans, and squash are good with it.

If you fry the chicken in butter, cook it with peas, string beans, celery, fennel, or mushrooms.

If you fry it in olive oil, cook it with eggplant, tomatoes, zucchini, okra, or peppers.

Hot chicken stock, tomato juice, apple cider, red wine, dry wine, and orange juice are all good liquids for cooking chicken.

The liquid that remains after cooking can be thickened with a *roux* or *beurre manié* to make a delicious sauce. To make a roux, cook together equal quantities of butter and flour over very low heat for 5 minutes or longer. *Beurre manié* consists of equal quantities of butter and flour rubbed together to make a paste, then formed into small balls and dropped into the hot liquid. Stir constantly at a simmer only, to thicken.

Sour cream, yoghurt, or cream can be added at the end.

JOHNS HOPKINS TOMATO CHICKEN CASSEROLE

Serve this with spaghetti or noodles and Green Salad (page 136). Red wine or beer goes well here.

1 frying chicken, cut up	2 cloves garlic, chopped
Flour for dredging (optional)	5 tomatoes, chopped (or 1 large
2 tablespoons butter	can tomatoes with juice)
2 tablespoons oil	2 tablespoons tomato purée
3 onions, chopped	½ cup chicken stock or bouillon

½ teaspoon cinnamon	Coarse salt
Bay leaf	Freshly ground black pepper
Dash thyme	Grated Parmesan cheese

Dry the chicken pieces thoroughly on paper towels. Dredge in flour if you like. Heat the butter and oil in a skillet or fireproof casserole. Fry the chicken until golden; remove and drain. In the same pan, sauté the onion and the garlic, then add the tomatoes. Add all remaining ingredients except the cheese. Return the chicken to the pan. Simmer for 30 minutes, or until the chicken is tender. Serve with pasta, and sprinkle with cheese. Serves 4–6.

CHICKEN MARENGO

Apparently named after the Battle of Marengo, for the dish Napoleon's cook created for him upon his return. Originally it contained shrimp and hard-boiled eggs.

New Potatoes (page 175), with butter and parsley, are the best accompaniment.

1 large fryer, cut up	or cider
2 tablespoons oil	2 tablespoons tomato purée
2 tablespoons butter	3 tomatoes, chopped
1 tablespoon flour	Dash thyme
1 clove garlic, chopped	Bay leaf
Coarse salt	½ pound mushrooms, sliced
Freshly ground black pepper	Cayenne pepper, to taste
½ cup dry white wine, dry sherry,	Fried croûtons (optional)

Wash and dry the chicken pieces thoroughly. Heat the butter and oil in a skillet or fireproof casserole and fry the chicken until golden. Sprinkle in the flour, cook for a minute, then add the remaining ingredients, except the croûtons. Cover and simmer for 30 minutes, or until the chicken is tender.

Serve the chicken garnished with croûtons (page 13), if you like. Enough for 4.

COQ AU VIN

For this dish you need either a large casserole that will go from the top of the stove to the table or a large stewing pot. You don't need any other vegetables with this dish, unless you feel like serving a salad after it. French bread is the best accompaniment.

It is cheaper to buy bacon in a hunk and cut off the amount you require, provided you have a sharp knife and can cut fairly thin slices. As far as the wine is concerned, a good strong red wine will do, such as Macon, Chianti, or California Mountain Red. Buy a gallon; use some for the chicken and drink the rest.

2 frying chickens (about 3–4 pounds)	12 mushrooms
1 tablespoon olive or peanut oil	Herb bouquet (thyme, parsley, bay leaf)
2–3 tablespoons butter	2 cloves garlic
4 ounces bacon (about 7–8 slices), chopped	Coarse salt
12 small white onions	Freshly ground black pepper
	4 cups red wine

Cut up the chickens and dry them well. In the casserole or stewing pan, heat the oil with the butter. Add the bacon and brown without burning. Remove the bacon and drain on paper towels.

To peel the white onions, drop them into boiling water for a couple of minutes. Drain them, remove their skins, and dry on paper towels.

Add the onions and mushrooms to the pan and brown. Remove and reserve for a few minutes. Now brown the chicken. Return the bacon, onions, and mushrooms to the casserole, together with the herb bouquet, the garlic (chopped or put through a squeezer), and seasonings. Pour in the wine and bring to a boil, then reduce heat and simmer gently for 30–45 minutes. Serves 8.

See also
CHICKEN BONNE FEMME, page 206

CHICKEN CURRY

Curry is the answer to feeding a lot of people cheaply and well. You can make it the night before and heat it up when you are ready to serve. This way the flavors develop overnight and the curry improves.

You can make an attractive table by setting out little bowls of condiments to go with the curry. All you need in addition is plenty of rice, French or Italian bread (unless you are lucky enough to have an Indian shop nearby), and a salad if you like.

Beer or cold rosé wine goes with curry.

Keep extra condiments in the refrigerator if you are cooking for a lot of people in case you run out. If you don't use them right away they will come in handy another day. Here is a list of condiments to go with curry:

chopped bananas with lemon squeezed on them
chopped apples with lemon squeezed on them
chutney
chopped peanuts
chopped or sliced tomatoes
sliced cucumbers (excellent in yoghurt with garlic)
grated coconut
chopped parsley
chopped chives
raisins
chopped hard-boiled eggs

These are, except for the chutney, cooling things which make a pleasant contrast to the hot curry. After curry, a cooling dessert such as ice cream or fruit salad is good.

2 chickens, cut up	½ teaspoon powdered ginger
1–2 tablespoons peanut or vegetable	2 teaspoons chopped fresh parsley
oil	Coarse salt
2 onions, chopped	Freshly ground black pepper
2 cloves garlic, chopped	Water to cover (or chicken
2–3 tablespoons curry powder,	broth or 1 cup red wine, as
according to taste	you like)
1 can stewed tomatoes	

Dry the chicken pieces thoroughly. In a heavy, fireproof casserole or a deep skillet, heat the oil. Add the chicken and, over high heat, brown on all sides. Remove to a side dish. Lower the heat, add the onions and garlic, and cook until the onions are limp and clear. Do not brown. Add the curry powder and cook, stirring, for about 3 minutes. Add the tomatoes and return the chicken to the pan. Add remaining ingredients and simmer for 30–45 minutes, or until chicken is done. The juice should run clear or yellow when chicken is pierced with a fork. Serves 8.

CHICKEN PIE

This is the basic pie; you can add or subtract from it as you wish. Chopped ham or tongue, hard-boiled eggs, nuts, vegetables—put in any leftovers you think will go with it.

Green Salad (page 136) and beer or cider are good with it.

2 tablespoons butter	chopped
2 cloves garlic, chopped	1 chicken, cooked and cut up
1 onion, chopped	3 tomatoes, chopped
2 green peppers, seeded and	Coarse salt

Freshly ground black pepper   ¼ cup milk
Dash chili powder or curry   2 cups mashed potatoes
   powder   ¼ cup grated Parmesan cheese
Dash thyme

Preheat oven to 375 degrees. In a fireproof casserole or skillet, melt the butter and cook the onion, garlic, and peppers until softened. If using a skillet, transfer the mixture to a baking dish. Add the chicken and remaining ingredients and top with the mashed potatoes. Sprinkle with cheese and bake for about 20 minutes, until browned and sizzling. Serves 4–6.

See also
DEVILED CHICKEN, page 219

For chicken livers, see
CHICKEN LIVERS WITH MUSHROOMS, page 221
PINEAPPLE AND CHICKEN LIVERS, page 221
CREAMED CHICKEN LIVERS, page 206
CHICKEN LIVERS AND TOMATOES WITH RICE, page 239

Meat

The best way to shop for meat is to go to a butcher. He is usually reliable, especially if you are a regular customer and show an interest, and he will give you good advice. You can learn what good meat looks like by looking in the windows of the best butcher in town.

Although the butcher may be a little more expensive than the super-market, you will probably be saving yourself money in the long run. Rather than confront those rows of trimmed, cut, tenderized, and plastic-wrapped parcels at the supermarket and wonder which "roast" will be best for your Stroganoff and what size package will feed six, consult your butcher. He will tell you which cut is suitable for stew, pot roast, grilling, etc., and, if he knows and likes you, may even suggest cheaper alternatives.

The toughest parts of the animal are the ones that have worked the hardest, such as the neck, the legs, and so on. Long, slow cooking suits these cuts of meat. The tender parts, such as sirloin and fillet, have less flavor than the tough ones, but are good cooked fast.

To store meat, remove the paper, and wrap it loosely in plastic. Place in the coldest part of your fridge. Freezing robs the meat of flavor, and you can keep most cuts in the fridge for 2–3 days. Chops and steaks can be held for 2–4 days, cubed meat for 4 days, and large roasts for 3–5 days. Ground meat should be used within 24 hours. If you haven't got a fridge, buy meat as you go.

A marinade can be useful if you are living on a budget. It will tenderize a tough cut of meat as well as give flavor to a rather tasteless variety. It has an acid base—usually wine, vinegar, or lemon juice—which works to break down the fibers of the meat. Herbs and spices are added for flavoring. There are cooked and raw marinades, cooked ones used for the longer periods. You can figure about ½ cup marinade per pound. Any food being marinated for longer than 1 hour should be re-frigerated.

A rule of thumb in judging the quantity of meat to buy is to allow 4–6 ounces of boneless meat per person, 6–8 ounces if bone is in.

Take meat out of the refrigerator an hour before you are going to cook it. If it is cold when started, the juices are lost rapidly.

Meat tastes better when served on heated plates. If you don't have a very low oven available to warm them in for a few minutes, run them under the hot tap and wipe them dry.

BEEF

The best beef is red, marbled with fat, and surrounded by a creamy white layer of fat. The interior of the bones is rosy and the texture of the meat firm, moist, and silky. If the meat looks dark and dry and the fat is yellow, it is old and stale. If packaged meat has a very damp look, it may have been frozen and thawed.

Some states and cities have their own inspection laws, but most meat in the United States is graded by federal meat inspectors. The best grade is *Prime*. It is expensive and not always available locally. *Choice* is of high eating quality and should be chosen for roasts, steaks, and most other purposes, although *Good* is still relatively tender and can be used for roasting and broiling. *Standard* and *Commercial* are low-quality grades and should be avoided for most purposes, although the *Commercial* grade is excellent for soups and stock.

The tougher cuts of meat are just as nourishing as the tender ones, and much can be done to make them more tender. They are tough primarily because they have more connective tissue than fat, so you can lard them to add fat, and marinate them or cook them slowly in liquid to break down the tissue.

Roast Beef

Trouble, time, and disaster can be saved by the small investment of about one dollar in a meat thermometer. It is almost impossible to go wrong if you use one, provided you don't stick it in right next to the bone.

Meat is best cooked at a fairly low temperature, so that it shrinks less and loses less of its juices. It should not be salted until after it has been cooked, since salt will draw the moisture out. If you have a sprawling piece of meat, tie it up like a parcel to prevent the juices from evaporating. If you are serving something rather more pedestrian than a fillet or rib roast, larding can make a tough cut juicier. Fat, cut into quarter-inch strips, can be inserted through the roast at intervals of about 2 inches with a larding needle.

Wipe the roast carefully to remove moisture. If it is dry when placed in a preheated oven, the heat will seal the moisture in. You may brown it first, if you wish, in as little fat as possible, or lightly brush it with oil.

Place the roast on a rack in a roasting pan, fat side up, so that the hot air can circulate around it; the fat will baste the roast as it cooks.

If your meat is a good cut, of *Prime* quality, roast it at 350 degrees according to the following table:

Rare   18–20 minutes per pound
Medium-rare   20–25 minutes per pound
Medium   22–25 minutes per pound
Well-done   27–30 minutes per pound

If your meat is *Choice,* roast it at 300 degrees according to the following table:

Rare   40–45 minutes per pound
Medium-rare   45–50 minutes per pound
Medium   55–60 minutes per pound
Well-done   60–65 minutes per pound

Your meat thermometer will register 140° at *rare,* 150° at *medium-rare,* 160° at *medium,* and 170° at *well-done.* When the roast is done (to your taste), remove it to a warm platter and allow to stand for 15 minutes before carving.

BASIC GRAVY
FOR ROAST BEEF

To the cooking juices add a minced scallion if you like. If you want a thick gravy add either a teaspoon of cornstarch mixed with a teaspoon of water, or a tablespoon of flour. Stir into the cooking juices and cook for two minutes.

Then add half a cup of beef stock or bouillon and bring to the boil. If you wish, add a quarter to a half cup of dry red wine and bring to boil. Season with salt and pepper and stir in some freshly chopped parsley at the end.

If you don't want to thicken the sauce, add a quarter to a half cup of stock or wine, depending on how much liquid you have. Boil down to reduce the sauce, season, stir in the parsley and serve.

A tablespoon of chopped butter added at the end will thicken the sauce.

A quarter of a cup of cream or sour cream can be added to the sauce. Heat through without boiling.

Accompaniments for Roast Beef

Plain roast beef is good with broad beans, green beans, broccoli, Brussels sprouts, Braised Celery (page 103), greens, okra, Buttered Peas (page 120), Creamed Onions (page 118), Braised Turnips (page 128), or zucchini.

Roast potatoes, baked potatoes, or Pommes Anna (page 177) also go well.

Horseradish and mustard are excellent on rare roast beef.

To Reheat Roast Beef

Slice the beef very thin and place on warmed plates. Bring the gravy to a boil, then pour over the meat. It takes a long time to heat through a large piece of meat, and the roast will get dry in the process.

Steak

Use only *Prime* or *Choice* grade. T-Bone, Porterhouse, rib, and sirloin are the best steaks. Tenderloin or fillet steaks are the tenderest of all, but out of our budget. Rump steak, cubed steak, and Swiss steak are better cooked with moisture and are not usually served as steak, as their names imply.

Steaks, in order to be juicy, should be not less than an inch thick; they should have a good layer of fat around them. The fat helps to seal in the steak's juices while it is cooking.

While cubed steak is cheap, it never produces a satisfactory steak. A cheap cut of meat is punctured and lacerated to make it tender (which it does), but most of the juices escape while it is cooking and it comes out stringy. Better to have hamburger.

Your steak should be at room temperature when you cook it. You may marinate it in oil, if you wish, and add pepper and garlic to the marinade for flavor. Of course, use a decent oil. Do not salt it until after cooking, or the juices will be lost.

If you broil it, first sear it on each side to seal in the juice, about 4 inches from the flame. Then cook until it is done as you like it.

To pan-broil it, you may use a skillet on top of the stove, but you must pour off the fat as it accumulates, to keep from frying the steak. If it is not *Prime* meat, you should rub the skillet with a little fat before searing. Sear each side, then cook until done.

You can serve steak with its cooking juices scraped up into a sauce —see Basic Gravy for Roast Beef (opposite), with Hollandaise Sauce (page 87); or with a savory butter. Sauces are served separately, so that the meat will stay crisp. The special butter is prepared earlier and refrigerated; at serving time, a slice is placed on each person's steak. You might try one of the following recipes.

GARLIC BUTTER

For ½ stick of soft butter (2 ounces), finely chop or put through a garlic squeezer 1 clove of garlic. Mix thoroughly and season. If you like, add some chopped fresh herbs (not dried ones) or parsley. Season, roll into a cylinder shape and refrigerate until ready to use. Enough for 4 small pats of butter.

PARSLEY BUTTER
Make as above without the garlic.

HERB AND MUSTARD BUTTER

Add a tablespoon of good dark mustard to ½ stick (2 ounces) softened butter. Add a tablespoon of chopped fresh parsley and a tablespoon of chopped fresh basil, tarragon, thyme, or oregano. If you can't get fresh herbs, add a tablespoon of chopped chives or an additional tablespoon of parsley. Season, roll into a cylinder shape, and refrigerate. Enough for 4 small pats of butter.

Accompaniments for Steak

Baked potatoes, Pommes Anna (page 177), or Gratin Dauphinois (page 176) are excellent potato dishes to serve with steak, and you might add a vegetable such as broad beans, green beans, Broccoli au Gratin (page 94), Braised Celery (page 103), greens, mushrooms, grilled tomatoes, Buttered Peas (page 120), or zucchini; and a salad such as Green Salad (page 136), Tomato Salad (page 139), Endive and Watercress Salad (page 136), or Italian Pepper Salad (page 137). Also delicious with steak is garlic bread.

See also
STEAK AU POIVRE, page 207

Hamburger

The hamburger is an American food that gives you a sinking feeling every time it is mentioned. Unfortunately, a good original idea has degenerated and left us with a tasteless, greasy, overcooked piece of meat stuck between two halves of cottonwool buns which would have been better used as sponges. It is absolutely unnecessary for hamburgers to taste this way, and with a little care and imagination they can be transformed into a very good and extremely inexpensive meal.

First of all, the meat has to be good. For the best, get it ground in front of you at the butcher's. The supermarket meat is never as good as freshly ground meat that has not been lying around in a package all day. If you must use packaged meat, try to avoid buying ground meat that looks too fatty.

Don't keep hamburger meat in the refrigerator for more than two days and don't freeze it. It must be fresh; freezing removes much of its flavor and makes it damp.

Allow at least one-quarter pound per serving. Put the meat into a bowl and to it add mustard, spices (such as thyme, basil, a dash of curry powder, a dash of cayenne pepper), Tabasco, Worcestershire sauce, seasonings using freshly ground pepper and coarse salt, and perhaps some chopped onion, garlic, or freshly chopped parsley. When you have flavored the meat the way you like it, heat the oil in the pan (a sliced garlic clove or some fresh ginger slices added to the oil will add more flavor). Turn the meat, made into patties, in wholewheat flour and immediately put the patties into the oil. Don't leave them sitting around in the flour or they will get soggy.

When you serve them, try to avoid putting them on those buns. If you want to use bread, why not try English muffins, fresh black bread, or even French bread? Hamburgers make an excellent dinner when served with a sauce or garnished with vegetables, potatoes, or cheese. Here are some different ways of serving hamburgers and producing a full meal.

HAMBURGERS WITH BLUE CHEESE

These are good for a snack, a party, or outdoor cooking. For a crowd, increase the proportions.

Let the cheese stand at room temperature for several hours before you use it, so that its flavor will develop. If the onion is very strong and you think it might overpower the taste of the cheese, soak the slices for about half an hour in cold water. Drain thoroughly before using. Mustard goes well with this combination.

4 hamburger patties (see master
    recipe above)
4 slices blue cheese
  Onion rings
  Fresh black bread, sliced

Cook the hamburgers to taste. Arrange them on the bread with the cheese and onion rings. Serve at once. Serves 4.

HAMBURGERS WITH ANCHOVIES

Serve these hamburgers with rice (preferably, brown rice) and a green vegetable.

4 hamburger patties (see master
  recipe, page 51)
8 strips of anchovy
1 tablespoon chopped fresh parsley

Heat the grill until very hot. Place the hamburgers on the tray and cook on one side. Turn them over, place two anchovy strips across each one, and grill until done according to taste. Sprinkle parsley over each hamburger and serve immediately. Serves 4.

HAMBURGERS WITH HAM

Baked sweet potatoes and Parsley Butter (page 50) are good companions for these hamburgers. Shape the butter into four small patties and place one over each burger just before serving.

4 hamburger patties (see master   1 tablespoon butter
  recipe, page 51)   1 tablespoon oil
1 tablespoon dark mustard   Parsley Butter (page 50),
4 slices ham   optional

Spread the surface of the hamburgers with mustard and place 1 ham slice on each. In a skillet, heat the butter and oil and cook the hamburgers on both sides. Put a slice of Parsley Butter on each hamburger just before serving, if desired. Serves 4.

HAMBURGER VIENNOISE

Prepare the garnishing ingredients *before* you cook the hamburger. Rice and grilled tomatoes go well here.

1 tablespoon oil   4 anchovies
4 hamburger patties (see master   1 tablespoon capers
  recipe, page 51)   4 slices of lemon
2 hard-boiled eggs   Chopped fresh parsley, to garnish

Chop the eggs, then the anchovies. Heat the oil, cook the hamburgers, and remove them to a heated dish. Scatter chopped egg, chopped anchovy, and capers on each, then top with a lemon slice. Garnish with parsley and serve at once. Serves 4.

HAMBURGER CATALANE

You can cook the eggplant with the tomatoes, if you like, but the sauce is really better cooked separately and poured over the hamburger at the end. Since this is a filling dish, you need serve only French bread and perhaps a salad with it.

1 medium-sized eggplant, cubed
2 tablespoons olive oil

Sauce

1 tablespoon olive oil   **Large pinch of basil**
1 onion, chopped   **Large pinch of thyme**
3 tomatoes, chopped   **Freshly ground black pepper**
1 tablespoon tomato purée   **Coarse salt**

6 hamburger patties (see master
  recipe, page 51)
2 tablespoons grated Parmesan
  cheese

Place the eggplant in a bowl and salt it, stirring well. Let it stand for about an hour until excess moisture is removed. Dry with paper towels.

Heat 2 tablespoons olive oil in a large skillet and brown the eggplant lightly on all sides. Reduce heat and simmer gently for about 30 minutes.

Meanwhile, in another pan, start the sauce. Sauté the onions in olive oil until they are clear. Add the tomatoes, tomato purée, spices, and seasonings. Simmer for 20–30 minutes.

Remove the eggplant when it is tender and drain on paper towels. Add the hamburgers (and extra oil, if necessary), brown on both sides, then cook until done.

Place the hamburger on heated plates, surround with eggplant, pour sauce on top, and garnish with Parmesan cheese. Serves 6.

SPANISH-STYLE HAMBURGER

Prepare the hamburgers according to the master recipe and be liberal with the paprika or curry powder. Rice, potatoes, or beans are fine with this dish, and red wine or beer goes well with it.

4 hamburger patties (see master   ¼–½ cup dry sherry
   recipe, page 51)   1 tablespoon chopped fresh
2 tablespoons olive oil   parsley
1 clove garlic, crushed   Coarse salt
2 large tomatoes, green ones if   Freshly ground black pepper
   available, sliced   8 black olives, pitted and halved
1 tablespoon flour

Heat the oil in a large skillet, and add the garlic and tomatoes. Cook for about three minutes and remove. Place in an ovenproof casserole. Brown the hamburgers in the skillet and cook until done. Remove them to the casserole dish containing the tomato mixture, and keep warm by holding in a very low oven while you make the sauce. Add 1 tablespoon flour to the skillet and stir into the scraped-up cooking juices. Add the sherry and boil until liquid is reduced to a thick sauce. Correct seasoning. Pour sauce over the hamburgers, scatter parsley on top, and garnish with black olives. Serves 4.

See also
STEAK TARTARE, page 222

Stews, Casseroles, and Pot Roasts

Stewing is one of the simplest and most economical ways to cook beef. Long, slow cooking with vegetables, herbs, and stock brings out the best in the cheaper cuts of meat. A stew should never boil; it should simmer gently for a long time. Little fuel is required because you need very little heat. You can cook it all afternoon on a very low flame and forget it until evening.

Try to buy a whole piece of meat for stew and cut it up yourself. You will save money, since cheap stewing meat is often fatty and tough and has been frozen. Bones added to the stew or casserole give flavor.

To get the best results, you need a deep, heavy pan with a tight-fitting lid. At least 1–2 inches of liquid should always be present during cooking. When adding liquid, always use hot stock or bouillon; a cold addition reduces the temperature.

Casseroles can be done in advance, the ingredients can usually be combined in one pot, they smell good, and they rarely burn.

BOEUF BOURGUIGNON

This dish is perfect with new potatoes and a green salad. It goes without saying that if you're having wine, it should be red. The meat is better, too, if marinated overnight in wine. The brandy is optional, but you can buy a miniature bottle for under a dollar.

2 pounds stewing beef, cut in cubes	Herb bouquet (thyme, parsley, and bay leaf tied in cheesecloth)
½ bottle dry red wine	
4–6 slices bacon, cut up	12 white onions, peeled
1 tablespoon flour and 1 tablespoon soft butter, mixed into a paste	12–15 mushrooms cooked in butter
	Coarse salt
1 shot glass brandy (optional)	Freshly ground black pepper

Marinate the beef overnight in the wine. Dry it on paper towels, and reserve the marinade. Fry the bacon, remove, and drain. Brown the beef cubes in the bacon grease over high heat; remove. Pour out most of the fat, add the butter-flour mixture, and cook, stirring constantly, for about 3 minutes. Return the beef to the pan and add the marinade, the brandy, and the herb bouquet. Bring to a boil, then cover and simmer for about 2 hours, either on top of the stove or in the oven. Peel the onions by immersing in hot water for a few minutes. Add the onions to the pot and cook 30 more minutes. Add the mushrooms; cook another 30 minutes. (Total cooking time is about 3 hours.) Make sure there's enough wine in the pot and add more if you have to, but be sure to boil it first. Correct seasoning. Serves 8.

BEEF STROGANOFF

The real thing doesn't contain either mushrooms or tomatoes, but both can be used in this dish, so add them if you like.

Serve with boiled potatoes sprinkled with chopped fresh dill (if available) and noodles or rice.

2 pounds chuck, cut in 1½-inch cubes	2 cups beef bouillon or stock
	1 cup sour cream or yoghurt
2 tablespoons flour	Parsley, to garnish
1 tablespoon paprika	Coarse salt
1 stick butter (4 ounces)	Freshly ground black pepper
2 onions, chopped	

Roll the meat in the mixed flour and paprika and, if possible, leave it overnight. Heat the butter in a skillet and brown the meat on all sides. Add the onions and cook until softened. Place the meat and onions in a large pot and add hot stock. Simmer for about 1½ hours, or until the meat is tender. Stir in the sour cream until heated, but do not let it boil. Add the parsley, and season. Serves 6.

HUNGARIAN GOULASH

Try to use good paprika in this dish if you can find it. In any case always look for the most expensive Hungarian paprika. You save money in the long run because you need less and the taste is better and much more pronounced.

Serve the goulash with noodles and parsley bread. This makes a good party dish.

2 pounds chuck steak, cubed
Flour for dredging
1 slice bacon, chopped
2 tablespoons oil or cooking fat
3 onions, chopped
2 cloves garlic, chopped
1 tablespoon of paprika (more or
less, to taste)
1 tablespoon tomato purée
3 tomatoes, peeled and chopped
2 cups beef stock or bouillon
Coarse salt
Freshly ground black pepper
3–4 tablespoons sour cream

Wipe the steak dry with paper towels and dredge in flour. Heat the bacon and oil in a skillet, add the meat, and brown on all sides. Remove and drain. Add the onions and garlic and cook until clear. Add the paprika, tomato purée, tomatoes, and stock, and return the meat to the pan. Season and bring to a boil. Reduce heat and simmer on top of stove or in a slow oven for about 2½ hours, or until the meat is tender. Add the sour cream and heat through without boiling. Serves 6.

CARBONNADE DE BOEUF
(Beef Braised in Beer)

This is an excellent way to use up flat beer. With it serve potatoes or a green vegetable (or both). Naturally beer is the best accompaniment.

1½ pounds stewing beef, cubed
1 tablespoon oil
2 onions, chopped
1 tablespoon flour
1¾ cups stale beer (or more, to cover)
Herb bouquet (thyme, bay leaf,
and parsley, tied in a cheesecloth)
1 tablespoon mustard
1 tablespoon tomato paste
Coarse salt
Freshly ground black pepper

Dry the cubed stewing beef with paper towels. In a skillet or heavy casserole heat the oil and brown the meat over high heat. Remove meat, lower heat, and sauté the onions until clear. Sprinkle the flour over them, and cook and stir for 2–3 minutes. Return the meat to the pan, add the beer to cover, and all remaining ingredients. Bring to a boil, then reduce heat, cover and simmer gently for about 2½ hours. Serves 4–6.

See also
BEEF AND BEAN CASSEROLE, page 181
POTATO, BEEF, AND WALNUT PIE, page 178
CHILI CON CARNE, page 182

BRAISED BEEF WITH ANCHOVIES

This is a very good way of cooking inexpensive cuts of meat. Buy a chuck roast that has been tied and larded. Simmer in a casserole with a tight-fitting lid very slowly on top of the stove.

If you can, use fresh nutmeg and grate it yourself.

2 slices bacon	Freshly grated nutmeg
1 tablespoon olive oil	1 teaspoon thyme
1 onion, chopped	½ cup white wine
2½ pounds chuck roast, rolled and larded	1 cup beef bouillon
	4 anchovies

Brown the bacon in a heavy casserole. Add the oil and heat. Reduce heat and sauté the onion until clear. Add the roast and brown it thoroughly on all sides. Stand it upright and grate nutmeg over it. Add the thyme, wine, and bouillon and lay the anchovies over the roast. Bring to a boil, then reduce heat and cover casserole. Simmer very slowly on top of the stove for 3½ hours. Enough for 6–8 people.

PRINCETON POT POT ROAST

Serve this with hard-boiled eggs and fried potatoes. If you're serving wine, have red wine.

3 pounds chuck roast	2 garlic cloves, crushed
2 tablespoons olive oil	½ teaspoon ground cloves
2 cups red wine	Dash of paprika
1 onion, coarsely chopped	1 tablespoon flour mixed with a
1 carrot, chopped	little cooking juice
Juice of half a lemon	Coarse salt
Pinch of thyme	Freshly ground black pepper
Bay leaf	

Wipe the meat, tie it together if it is a sprawling piece, and brown it in the olive oil. Place in a heavy casserole or baking dish and add the wine, vegetables, and herbs. Bring to a boil, then cover and reduce to a simmer. Cook very slowly for 3 hours on top of the stove or in a low oven, basting occasionally. When tender, remove to a heated platter. Stir the flour into the cooking juices, season, and boil until reduced to one-third in volume. Serve separately with the roast. Enough for 6.

For
BEEF KIDNEY, HEART, LIVER, see pages 239–240.

For
SWEETBREADS AND BRAINS, see page 245

LAMB

Genuine spring lamb, or *baby lamb* (3–5 months old), is available in April, and a leg of lamb at that time weighs 3–4 pounds. As the year progresses, the cuts get heavier and in the late winter can often weigh as much as 7 pounds.

From 5 months to 18 months, it is sold as *lamb*. After that, it is sold as *mutton*. Good spring lamb has pale red flesh, white fat, and slightly translucent bones.

If lamb has not been sufficiently aged after it has been killed, it will be tough. It is a good idea to keep a leg for two or three days in the refrigerator before you cook it. It should be dried, the blue stamps taken off, and covered with a marinade. This makes it very tender.

Lamb absorbs flavors very well. Recipes from the Middle East, North Africa, and the Mediterranean include marvelous lamb dishes using aromatic spices such as cumin, coriander, and sesame seeds. In Europe and America, garlic and rosemary are often used with lamb.

Roast Lamb

The best cuts for roast lamb are the leg and the shoulder. The leg has a small amount of bone and is the most economical; the shoulder often has a more delicate flavor.

Trim off the blue stamps and leave a thin layer of fat.

If possible, marinate the lamb in one of the following marinades, preferably for two or three days but at least overnight. Turn the lamb occasionally in the mixture.

YOGHURT MARINADE

This is one of the best marinades. It makes the lamb very tender, soft, and juicy.

1 cup yoghurt
1 tablespoon dark mustard
  Dash soy sauce

1 teaspoon rosemary
1 clove garlic, chopped
  Freshly ground black pepper

Mix all the ingredients together and cover the lamb with the mixture. Cover, and leave to marinate overnight.

SOY SAUCE MARINADE

½ cup soy sauce
2 cloves garlic, chopped
1 tablespoon dark mustard
½ cup dry sherry

Freshly ground black pepper
Pinch of thyme or rosemary
  (optional)

Combine all ingredients and cover lamb with the mixture. Cover and refrigerate for several hours, turning occasionally.

SPICY MARINADE

This is not strictly a marinade, and most of the mixture should be scraped off before roasting. If coated meat is refrigerated overnight, however, it will serve the same purpose.

1 onion, chopped fine
1 clove garlic, chopped
½ teaspoon curry powder
  Dash cayenne
  Dash turmeric
  Dash coriander

Dash nutmeg
Dash ginger
1 tablespoon lemon juice
1 tablespoon brown sugar
  Freshly ground black pepper

Mix together and spread on the lamb. Cover and place in fridge overnight. Scrape off most of mixture before roasting and coat meat with a little oil.

Coatings for Roast Lamb

If you have not had time to marinate the lamb, one of these coatings will make all the difference. Apply before roasting.

An interesting way of roasting lamb is to mash a can of anchovies with a tablespoon of brown sugar, a chopped clove of garlic and some pepper, and spread it on the lamb. At first it will smell strange, but after some time in the oven it will produce a delicious aroma.

You can also coat it with mustard and make little slits in the lamb and insert tiny pieces of garlic. Rub plenty of oil into the flesh with the mustard.

Breadcrumbs, mashed to a paste with garlic, parsley, softened butter and lemon juice, also makes a good coating.

Cook the lamb for about 15–20 minutes per pound for medium-rare, 20–35 for well done, in a low oven, about 300 to 325 degrees. If lamb is overcooked it turns out dry and loses much of its flavor. If it is too rare, its flavor will not have developed properly. Lamb should be pink on the inside with a good dark crust. If it's bright red, put it back in the oven; if it's gray-brown and dry, call a restaurant and make a reservation for dinner.

When the lamb is cooked remove it to a heated dish and let it sit on the back of the stove while its juices come back. Meanwhile scrape up the cooking juices with a little stock, wine, or dry sherry. See Basic Gravy for Roast Beef, page 48, for instructions on how to make the sauce.

Some people believe that lamb should be put in a hot oven and browned, then cooked at a moderately high temperature for a very short time. This shrinks the meat and makes it tougher than when it is cooked slowly.

Sauces to Go with Lamb

These sauces can be served instead of or with the gravy.

MINT SAUCE

This is great if you're drinking a lousy wine; the vinegar somehow softens the harshness. However, if you're drinking a really good wine, you'll probably ruin it.

Use fresh mint, not some dry old stuff that's been lying around in the back of the cupboard for five years.

Bring four tablespoons of water to the boil with two tablespoons wine vinegar. Add two tablespoons brown sugar, dissolve, and add two tablespoons of chopped fresh mint.

ONION SAUCE

Chop an onion and simmer in 1½ cups of milk with salt, pepper and half a teaspoon of mace. Mix together in a separate saucepan a tablespoon of flour and a tablespoon of butter. Cook for two minutes and add the onion mixture. Bring to a boil and cook until thick.

CURRANT JELLY is also good with lamb.

Accompaniments for Roast Lamb

Green beans, broad beans, broccoli, Brussels sprouts, cabbage, Braised Celery, page 103, Cucumbers Baked with Dill, page 105, Stewed Eggplant, page 108, Creamed Greens, page 113, Braised Fennel, page 110, okra, tomatoes and zucchini.

Rice, Brown Rice, page 172, roast potatoes, Potatoes Provençales, page 179, Gratin Dauphinois, page 176, Pommes Anna, page 177, and baked sweet potatoes, are all good with lamb.

STUFFED SHOULDER OF LAMB

This is a good, inexpensive way to feed 6 to 8 people. The stuffing helps to stretch the servings, and there is little clean-up afterwards, because the potatoes are cooked with the lamb.

2 pounds boned shoulder of lamb

Stuffing

½ pound sausage meat	1 egg
1 clove garlic, crushed	Coarse salt
1 tablespoon parsley	Freshly ground black pepper
Lemon juice	8 potatoes, sliced
1 onion, chopped and sautéed in 1	3 onions, sliced
tablespoon butter until clear	2 strips bacon, chopped
½ cup soft breadcrumbs	

Trim the lamb. In a bowl, mix the stuffing and put it inside the lamb. Tie it up with string.

Put the chopped bacon, potatoes, and onions in a large roasting pan. Place the lamb, fat side up, on a rack, and place it on top of the vegetables in the roasting pan. Roast in a moderate oven for 1½–2 hours, or until the lamb is done. Serves 6–8.

See also
LAMB CHOPS WITH WATERCRESS, page 223

Lamb Patties

These "lamburgers" make a delicious change from hamburgers and are just as economical. Get the butcher to grind lean meat in front of you.

Proceed just as you would for hamburgers (see following recipes for variations in ingredients), and shape the mixture into patties. You may roll them lightly in flour if you wish and fry them in oil or broil them. They should be cooked a little longer than beef, about 3–5 minutes on each side, so that they are browned on the outside and pinkish in the middle.

When the patties are cooked, set them aside on a heated dish while you prepare the sauce.

LAMB PATTIES WITH GARLIC AND HERBS

This is the basic recipe for lamb patties. A garlic clove, halved and put in the cooking oil, adds flavor.

Grilled tomatoes; fried, baked, or mashed potatoes; and a green vegetable such as broccoli, peas, or spinach make excellent accompaniments.

1 pound freshly ground lean lamb	Coarse salt
1 clove garlic, mashed	Freshly ground black pepper
1 tablespoon chopped fresh parsley	1 tablespoon olive oil (or more as
1 tablespoon minced scallions	needed, to cover bottom of
Dash thyme	pan)
Dash ginger	Flour (preferably wholewheat)
Dash allspice	for dredging

Sauce for Lamb Patties

½ cup red or white wine, canned bouillon, or stock	1 tablespoon chopped fresh parsley
1 teaspoon dark mustard	Coarse salt
	Freshly ground black pepper

Put the ground meat in a large bowl and mix in the remaining ingredients. Shape the mixture lightly into four patties. In a skillet, heat the oil. Toss the patties lightly in flour and place in the hot oil. Cook on each side for about five minutes. Remove to a heated dish. Pour off excess fat, add hot wine, stock, or bouillon, and scrape up the juices over high heat. Swirl in the mustard, parsley, and seasonings. Serve separately, with the patties. Makes 4.

LAMB PATTIES WITH ONION AND HERBS

This is a variation of the preceding recipe. They are almost interchangeable.

1 pound freshly ground lean lamb	1 egg, beaten
1 onion, chopped	Coarse salt
1 tablespoon butter	Freshly ground black pepper
1 tablespoon fresh breadcrumbs	Flour (preferably wholewheat)
1 clove garlic, mashed	for dredging
½ teaspoon rosemary	1 tablespoon olive oil (enough to
1 tablespoon chopped fresh parsley	cover bottom of pan)

Sauce

See Sauce for Lamb Patties, above. Sauté onions in butter over low heat until clear. Mix the meat with remaining ingredients and shape into four patties. Heat the oil in a skillet. Toss the patties in the flour and cook on each side for about 5 minutes. Remove to heated side dish. Make Sauce for Lamb Patties and serve separately. Makes 4.

LAMB PATTIES WITH BLACK OLIVES

Proceed as for Lamb Patties with Onion and Herbs (above) or Lamb Patties with Garlic and Herbs (page 62). Add 2 tablespoons pitted, chopped black olives to the mixture, and serve with tomato sauce.

For a vegetable, have green peppers, stewed okra, eggplant, or zucchini. Rice also goes well with this dish.

Tomato Sauce

1 onion, chopped	1 tablespoon fresh basil or oregano
1 tablespoon olive oil	(or ½ tablespoon dried)
3 tomatoes, chopped	Coarse salt
	Freshly ground black pepper

Soften the onion in the oil over low heat. Add the tomatoes, herbs, and seasonings and cook for about 3 minutes. Serve separately with the lamb patties. Enough for 4 patties.

LAMB PATTIES WITH MUSHROOMS AND HAM

Use leftover or cooked ham for this recipe. Leftover tongue or chicken could also be used.

Sweet potatoes, spinach, or braised celery goes particularly well here.

1 pound freshly ground lean lamb	Salt
1 onion, chopped	Freshly ground black pepper
1 tablespoon butter	1 tablespoon olive oil (or enough to
2 tablespoons diced mushrooms	cover bottom of pan)
2 tablespoons diced ham	Flour (preferably wholewheat)
Dash thyme	for dredging

Sauce

½ cup red or white wine, stock, or	1 tablespoon chopped fresh parsley
bouillon	Coarse salt
¼ cup heavy cream	Freshly ground black pepper

Place the lamb in a large mixing bowl. Add thyme, salt, and pepper. Soften the onions in the butter over low heat, add the mushrooms and ham, and cook for 3 minutes. Add to the lamb mixture. Blend well and shape into 4 patties. Heat the oil in a skillet. Toss the patties lightly in flour and cook in the oil for about 5 minutes on each side. Remove to a heated side dish. Pour the fat out of the skillet and scrape up the cooking juices over high heat with the wine, stock, or bouillon. Reduce heat, add the cream and parsley, and heat through without boiling. Season and serve separately with the lamb patties. Makes 4.

LAMB PATTIES, MIDDLE EASTERN STYLE

In the Middle East, lamb is traditionally served with pine nuts, onions, raisins, and spices. Roast lamb is often stuffed with this mixture, and lamb patties can also be prepared this way.

Serve with zucchini, eggplant, or okra and rice. If you have a local Arabic store, buy some flat bread and garnish the patties with stuffed vine leaves.

1 pound freshly ground lean lamb	Freshly ground black pepper
1 onion, chopped	1 tablespoon olive oil (to cover
1 tablespoon olive oil	bottom of pan)
Dash cumin	Flour (preferably wholewheat)
Dash allspice	for dredging
1 tablespoon chopped raisins	Coarse salt
2 tablespoons pine nuts, chopped	Freshly chopped parsley

Put the lamb in a large mixing bowl. Soften the onion over low heat in the olive oil. Add to the lamb and mix, together with the spices, pine nuts, raisins, and pepper. Heat the oil in the skillet, dredge the patties with flour and cook about five minutes on each side. Remove, drain, and place on a heated side dish. Salt, and sprinkle parsley over the top. Makes 4.

See also
LAMB PATTIES WITH WHEATGERM, page 238

Lamb Stews and Casseroles

The inexpensive cuts of lamb, such as breast, neck, and shoulder, are very good for stews and casseroles. They are quite fatty and are excellent cooked with potatoes or beans which absorb the fat.

Always ask the butcher to throw in a few bones when you buy stewing lamb. Not only do they add flavor, but they also contain calcium, which is very good for you. Ask him to saw the bones, not to chop them; otherwise little pieces of bone flake off into the stew. Cut the meat into even-sized pieces.

When you are making stew for a large number of people, increase the amount of cheap vegetables. Dried beans are extremely good with fresh spring vegetables such as green beans, peas, small onions, carrots, and new potatoes. The stew is also delicious with zucchini and eggplant.

SPRING NAVARIN OF LAMB

Navarin is a French word meaning stew. Somehow a navarin for dinner seems much more exotic than plain old stew. This is the basic recipe for the dish served in France. Traditionally it is served *printanier,* with spring vegetables in season. If you serve it at that time, it is quite economical.

Leftover ham, bacon, or bacon rinds could be used in this recipe, and partially cooked navy beans or lentils could be substituted for the potatoes.

2½ pounds lamb (breast or
    shoulder), cut into cubes
  Lamb bones
 2 tablespoons oil
 1 tablespoon butter
 1 tablespoon brown sugar
 2 tablespoons flour
  Coarse salt
  Freshly ground black pepper
  Water or stock, to cover
 1 pound tomatoes, peeled and
    chopped

Dash thyme
Bay leaf
1 clove garlic (optional)
  Dash nutmeg
4 small turnips, peeled and
    quartered
6 carrots, peeled
12 small onions, peeled
12 small potatoes (skins on, if new;
    peeled and quartered, if old)
½ pound green beans

Dry the lamb cubes and bones well and brown lightly in the oil and butter in a heavy fireproof casserole or saucepan. Add the sugar and cook for 2 more minutes, stirring constantly to prevent burning. Add the flour, salt, and pepper and cook for 2 minutes. Skim off extra fat. Cover with water or stock. Stir well, add the tomatoes and seasonings, and bring to a boil. Reduce heat, cover, and simmer for 1 hour. Meanwhile, prepare the vegetables. Remove meat after 1 hour and cool slightly, so that you can skim off the excess fat that rises to the top before adding turnips, carrots, onions and potatoes. Simmer until they are three-quarters cooked, about 30 minutes. Add the beans and cook for 20 minutes. (Total cooking time is about 2 hours.) Serves 6–8.

LAMB AND ZUCCHINI CASSEROLE

This is another economical dish. You need only serve the meat and vegetables in the casserole; however, if you want a starchy vegetable, too, try mashed potatoes or rice.

This dish is very good reheated, for the flavors develop overnight.

2–2½ pounds boned lamb (shoulder or neck)	2 tablespoons chopped fresh parsley
4 tablespoons olive oil	Coarse salt
1 onion, chopped	Freshly ground black pepper
1 clove garlic, chopped	4 medium-sized zucchini, sliced
4 large tomatoes, chopped	2 tablespoons butter
Basil or oregano	1 tablespoon olive oil

Cut the meat into 2-inch cubes. In a heavy casserole, heat the oil, and brown the meat lightly on all sides. Add the onion and garlic and cook for several minutes over low heat. Add the tomatoes, herbs, and seasonings and simmer, covered, over low heat for 1–1½ hours. Meanwhile, sauté the zucchini lightly in butter and oil. Add them to the casserole for the last 15 minutes of cooking time. Serves 4–6.

LAMB AND EGGPLANT CASSEROLE

To economize, use less meat than called for and more eggplant. Cut lamb and eggplant into 1–1½-inch cubes.

This dish can be made successfully in an electric skillet. It tastes even better heated up the next day. Serve plain rice with it.

1 medium-sized eggplant, cubed
   (do not peel)
½ cup olive oil
1 onion, chopped
1 clove garlic, chopped
¾ pound lamb, cubed

1 can tomatoes, with the juice
2 cups beef stock or bouillon
Dash turmeric
Dash oregano
Coarse salt
Freshly ground black pepper

Salt the eggplant and let it stand in a bowl for 30–40 minutes to remove excess moisture. Drain and dry thoroughly on paper towels.

Heat the oil in a heavy skillet or fireproof casserole. Add the onion and garlic and brown lightly. Add the eggplant and brown on all sides. Remove eggplant and drain on paper towels. Add the lamb and brown over low heat. Pour out excess fat. Return the eggplant to the casserole and add hot stock, spices, and seasonings. Bring to a boil, then cover and simmer gently for 1½ hours, or until lamb is tender. Serves 4.

See also
PERSIAN PILAF, page 174

For
LAMB KIDNEYS, LIVER, AND HEART, see pages 239–40

For
SWEETBREADS AND BRAINS, see page 245

PORK

Not only is pork one of the cheapest meats available, it is also one of the most nourishing. It is a fat and rather rich dish and is especially good during the winter since it has the effect of "heating you up."

Good pork has pale pink, firm and fine-grained flesh. It should have no smell. The fat should be white. Pork has more flavor when it is cooked on the bone. It may also be boned and marinated, preferably overnight, and tastes especially good cold when prepared this way.

Pork should never be underdone. It can transmit trichinosis, a parasitic disease, if it is not cooked properly. In order to kill the trichinae the internal cooking temperature must reach 185°. Never serve pork rare. However, this does not mean you should cook the meat to death. Dry tasteless pork is not fit to eat.

Roast Pork

The best cuts for roasts are the loin, which is best boned and rolled, and the loin end, a good combination of fat and meat. You may also roast a pork shoulder. Pork has so much fat that it is really self-basting.

The meat should be at room temperature before roasting. Take it out of the refrigerator at least two hours before roasting.

You may marinate before roasting, if you wish. See Marinades for Pork, below. Allow ½ cup marinade per pound of meat, and cover, refrigerated, overnight. Remember to use a pyrex, china, or enameled container, since a marinade has an acid base.

Pork can be roasted in an open pan, with or without its crackling (the skin which turns to a crisp brown), or it may be cooked in a casserole, covered, with vegetables.

Pan Roasting

Trim off all but a thin layer of fat. Score it across the top in a lattice pattern and rub it with brown sugar, honey, or soy sauce. If you prefer the skin on, score and prepare in the same manner. Place on a greased rack in a large roasting pan.

CASSEROLE ROASTED PORK

Dry meat thoroughly with paper towels and sear on all sides in about 4 tablespoons of oil. If your casserole cannot be used for this on top of the stove, sear in a skillet and then transfer to a heavy, ovenproof casserole. Pour off the fat. Add a chopped carrot, a chopped onion, a couple of crushed garlic cloves, and a pinch of thyme or parsley (or both) to the casserole, along with the meat. Roast the pork as is, or add vegetables if you wish (red cabbage, potatoes, or turnips) before covering and placing in a moderate oven.

Allow about 30–45 minutes per pound if the bone is in and cook in a 350-degree oven. If the roast is boned, rolled, or stuffed, add 10–15 minutes more cooking time per pound. A meat thermometer should register 185°. It must reach this temperature internally to kill the trichinae. When done, the juices should run clear and yellow when the meat is pricked, and the meat should be white. Never serve pink pork.

When the pork is cooked, remove it to a warm plate and let stand for a few minutes before carving. For details on making a sauce, see

Basic Gravy for Roast Beef (page 48). Red, white, or rosé wine goes with pork.

Accompaniments for Pork

Winter vegetables are particularly good with pork. Try Brussels sprouts, cabbage, Red Cabbage with Sour Cream (page 97), carrots, cauliflower, greens, Braised Leeks (page 114), squash, turnips, sauerkraut, or onions.

Roast potatoes, baked potatoes, or sweet potatoes are also good.

Applesauce and cranberry sauce are delicious with roast pork.

Marinades for Pork

These marinades are especially good for roasts and chops. In addition, Yoghurt Marinade (page 58) and Soy Sauce Marinade (page 59) are also good with pork.

RED WINE MARINADE

1 cup red wine
2 tablespoons oil
Bay leaf
Dash thyme

A few peppercorns
A few juniper berries, crushed (if available)

Mix well and pour over meat. Turn meat frequently. Cover and refrigerate.

LEMON JUICE MARINADE

2 tablespoons olive oil
Juice of a lemon
½ teaspoon allspice, sage, or thyme
1 clove garlic, chopped
Freshly ground black pepper

Rub mixture onto the pork and turn meat often.

HERB MARINADE

1 clove garlic, chopped
Pinch of allspice
½ teaspoon thyme or sage

Bay leaf, crushed
Salt
Freshly ground black pepper

Work mixture into the meat, turning meat often. Cover and refrigerate.

ORANGE JUICE AND HONEY MARINADE

Juice of an orange
3 tablespoons honey or molasses
Dash of soy sauce

Pinch of thyme
2 tablespoons olive oil
Freshly ground black pepper

Mix together and pour over the pork. Turn meat frequently. Cover when refrigerating.

WHITE WINE MARINADE

1 cup white wine
1 garlic clove, chopped
Pinch of thyme

4 whole cloves
½ teaspoon coriander (if available)
Freshly ground black pepper

Pour over the pork and turn meat often while marinating.

ROAST PORK WITH WHITE BEANS

This is an inexpensive way to serve a small gathering.

3-pound pork shoulder or pork loin
    Lemon Juice Marinade (page 69),
        Herb Marinade (page 69),
        Yoghurt Marinade (page 58),
        or Soy Sauce Marinade (page 59)
    Garlic, chopped
    Thyme

White or navy beans (see Basic
    Beans, page 180)
2 strips bacon
                    OR
2 cans white beans
2 strips bacon
1 onion, chopped

After marinating, follow instructions for Roast Pork (page 68), seasoning well with garlic and thyme.

Either cook Basic Beans (page 180), adding 2 strips of bacon to the pot; or cook 2 strips bacon in a skillet, sauté the onion in the bacon grease, and add to 2 cans of store-bought beans.

When the roast is three-quarters done, add the beans.

Serve pork in a casserole or on a heated platter surrounded by the beans. Serves 6–8.

ROAST PORK WITH PRUNES

This is a Swedish dish and very inexpensive. When you carve it, it has an attractive design. It is also very good cold. Serve it with applesauce and sweet potatoes.

1 4–5-pound pork loin	Coarse salt
About 15 medium-sized pitted prunes	Freshly ground black pepper
Juice of half a lemon	Oil for browning

Preheat oven to 350 degrees. Take the bone out of the meat (or have the butcher do it) and wipe it inside. Boil the prunes for about 30 minutes, so that they swell up. Drain the prunes, but reserve the boiling liquid. Squeeze the lemon juice over the inside of the pork, season it, and insert the prunes. Tie the meat together with string. Brown the meat either on top of the stove or under the grill, and place on a rack in a roasting pan or in a casserole. Roast for about 2 hours, basting with the prune juice, until the juices run clear and the meat is tender. Serves 8.

Pork Chops

Pork chops are very cheap and, when properly cooked, can compete with a steak at half the cost. Choose thick-cut chops if possible. If you are cooking chops for a group of people, it is often cheaper to buy a loin roast and cut the chops yourself.

Center loin and rib loin are the best and meatiest cuts. Shoulder chops are cheapest, but they are often greasy.

You can achieve great variations in flavor by using one of the Marinades for Pork (page 69). The chops should be marinated for at least two hours, longer if possible.

Casserole Chops

If you are cooking for several people, this is one of the best ways to cook chops, particularly if you have a casserole that can go either on top of or inside the stove. Dry the chops well and brown them in hot fat. Place them in the casserole with herbs (thyme, rosemary, oregano, or marjoram) and a crushed clove of garlic, if you like. Cook them in a moderate oven for 45 minutes to 1 hour. They will come out tender and juicy and evenly cooked.

Pour off the fat. Scrape up the juices with white wine, stock, or bouillon, and add the marinade for your sauce. See Basic Gravy for Roast Beef (page 48) for complete instructions.

Grilled Chops

Tomatoes or mushrooms can be grilled at the same time. Check to make sure they don't get too brown. Cook the chops under a moderate grill for about fifteen minutes on each side, until they are browned and cooked through. Don't use a fork to turn them or their juices will run out. Prick them at the end to be sure they are done. The juices should run clear and yellow.

Fried Chops

Brown the dried chops in oil on both sides. Cover and cook over low heat for 30–40 minutes. The pan juices can be used in a sauce.

PORK CHOPS WITH APPLES

If you like, marinate the chops overnight in Lemon Juice or Herb Marinade (page 69). Sautéed potatoes and string beans would go well here, with cider or beer to drink.

4 pork chops	Dash cinnamon
2 tablespoons butter	Coarse salt
3 apples, peeled and sliced	Freshly ground pepper
Extra butter	

Preheat oven to 350 degrees. Wipe the pork chops dry with paper towels. Brown them on both sides in the butter. Put the apples in a baking dish, dot with butter, and sprinkle with cinnamon. Put the pork chops on top, cover, and bake for 45 minutes to 1 hour. Serves 4.

CHOPS WITH BARBECUE SAUCE

If you like, marinate the chops in the sauce overnight. You can vary the ingredients to include chopped or canned tomatoes, cloves, coriander, or thyme, if you wish.

Serve the chops with sweet potatoes, baked potatoes, Pommes Anna (page 177), or cauliflower.

4 pork chops
  Oil for browning

Barbecue Sauce

1 teaspoon dry mustard	Dash Worcestershire Sauce
4 tablespoons red currant jelly	Dash Tabasco
2 tablespoons vinegar	1 clove garlic, chopped (optional)
2 tablespoons brown sugar, honey, or	Coarse salt
molasses	Freshly ground black pepper
1 teaspoon tomato purée	1 teaspoon cornstarch

Grill or fry the chops in a little oil (see Fried Chops, page 72). When done, remove to a warm platter. Combine sauce ingredients and simmer for a few minutes. Pour off excess fat, then add hot sauce to pork chop skillet. Scrape up cooking juices with the sauce and add the cornstarch mixed to a paste with a little water. Correct seasoning. When barbecue sauce has thickened, pour it over the chops. Serves 4.

COLUMBIA UNIVERSITY CHOPS IN RED WINE

This is delicious with potatoes Gratin Dauphinois (page 178), mashed potatoes, or baked potatoes. Broad beans, broccoli, Brussels sprouts, and Braised Celery (page 103) are also good with it.

You may marinate the chops overnight in Herb Marinade (page 69), if you like.

4 pork chops	1 tablespoon oil
1 tablespoon flour	1 scallion, chopped
Dash thyme	1 cup red wine
Freshly ground black pepper	Coarse salt, to taste
1 tablespoon butter	1 tablespoon chopped fresh parsley

Season the flour with thyme and pepper. Sprinkle on the chops. Heat the butter and oil and brown the chops on both sides. Add the scallion and the wine, bring to a boil, then simmer gently for 30–45 minutes. Or put into a baking dish and bake, covered, for 30–45 minutes in a preheated 350-degree oven. Remove the chops to a heated platter, boil down the sauce as necessary, and correct seasoning. Pour the sauce over the chops and garnish with parsley. Serves 4.

OHIO PORK CHOPS WITH TOMATOES

Delicious with mashed, new, or baked potatoes, or Potato Casserole with Cheese (page 178), minus the ham. A green salad and beer or cider go well with this.

If you like, marinate the chops for a few hours or overnight in Yoghurt Marinade (page 58).

4 pork chops
1 tablespoon butter
1 tablespoon oil
2 onions, chopped
1 clove garlic, chopped
1 tablespoon flour
4 tomatoes, chopped

1 tablespoon tomato paste
1 cup beef or chicken stock or
    bouillon
Dash thyme or basil
Coarse salt
Freshly ground black pepper

Dry the pork chops and brown them in the butter and oil. Remove and drain. Add the onions and garlic and brown. Add the flour and cook for 2 minutes. Return the chops to the pan and add the remaining ingredients. Bring to a boil, then simmer gently for 30–45 minutes. Add more stock, *hot,* if it gets too dry. Serves 4.

EXTRA EASY PORK CHOPS
WITH MUSHROOM SOUP

No claims will be made for this dish, but suffice it to say that if you haven't got the time to cook, this is an easy way out.

For four people dry 4 pork chops and brown them in a tablespoon each of oil and butter. Add 1 can cream of mushroom soup, some herbs if you like, then cover and simmer or bake for 30–45 minutes. That's all. Serves 4.

PORK CHOPS WITH ORANGES

These are excellent with spinach and sweet potatoes. Marinate the chops overnight in Orange Juice and Honey Marinade (page 70), if you like.

4 pork chops
1 tablespoon butter
1 tablespoon oil
1 onion, chopped
1 clove garlic, chopped

Dash marjoram
1 orange, peeled and sliced
Stock or red wine, as needed
Coarse salt
Freshly ground black pepper

Preheat oven to 375 degrees. Dry the pork chops and brown them in the butter and oil. Remove chops, add the onion and garlic and sauté. Put the chops, onion, and garlic in a baking dish. Add the marjoram and place an orange slice on top of each chop. Squeeze the rest of the orange juice over the pork chops. Bake for 30–45 minutes. Add stock or wine if it gets too dry. Season. Serves 4.

BARBECUED SPARERIBS

When they say spareribs, they mean it. There's usually not much meat on them, so buy plenty. At least they are cheap.

These are good with a potato casserole or a rice dish. Corn, tomatoes, okra, squash, and zucchini also go well with them.

2 pounds spareribs

Barbecue Sauce

1 teaspoon dry mustard	Juice of an orange
2 tablespoons vinegar	1 tablespoon soy sauce
Dash Worcestershire sauce	Juice of half a lemon
Dash Tabasco	Dash paprika or cayenne
1 tablespoon brown sugar and	1 tablespoon cornstarch
1 tablespoon molasses or honey	Coarse salt
or 2 tablespoons brown sugar	Freshly ground black pepper

Preheat oven to 375 degrees. Combine ingredients for sauce. Separate the spareribs and marinate them in the sauce, overnight if possible. Wrap the ribs in aluminum foil, allowing enough foil to seal the package completely, and place in a roasting pan. If you have not marinated the ribs, pour the sauce over them before sealing in foil. Bake in oven for 1 hour, uncovering them for the last 15 minutes. Turn the oven down if sauce is evaporating too quickly. Remove ribs to a heated platter.

Empty sauce and cooking juices into a pan. Mix the cornstarch in a cup with a tablespoon of the juice. Add to the sauce and bring to a simmer. When the sauce has thickened, correct seasoning, and pour it over the ribs. Serves 4.

Note: Spareribs often have a lot of fat on them. Skim off excess fat before thickening sauce. You could also increase slightly the amount of cornstarch to help absorb grease.

PORK AND CABBAGE STEW

This cheap, delicious dish goes well with buttered boiled potatoes and cider, white wine, or beer. If you like, marinate the chops overnight in Herb Marinade or Lemon Juice Marinade (page 69).

You need a large pot for this, since the cabbage takes up a lot of room when it is first put in.

1½ pounds pork, in 1½-inch cubes	1 glass cider, stock, or white wine
½ pound sausage meat	1 tablespoon caraway seeds
3 strips bacon, diced	(optional)
1 tablespoon butter	Coarse salt
1 onion, chopped	Freshly ground black pepper
1 carrot, chopped	Water to cover
1 tablespoon flour	1 white cabbage, chopped coarsely
Bay leaf	

Mash the sausage meat and toss lightly with the pork. Cook the bacon in the butter, add the onion and carrot and brown lightly. Add pork and sausage and brown. And flour and cook for 2 minutes, stirring constantly. Add bay leaf, cider, caraway seeds, and seasonings. Add water to cover, bring to a boil, then reduce heat and simmer slowly for 1 hour. Add cabbage and cook for another 30 minutes, or until tender.

If the stew gets too dry, add *hot* stock or water. Serves 6.

See also
PORK WITH SAUERKRAUT, page 224
CHINESE PORK WITH WATERCRESS, page 224
HUNGARIAN POTATOES AND PORK, page 208
SWEET AND SOUR PORK WITH CABBAGE, page 208
BREADCRUMBED PIG'S FEET, page 246

SAUSAGES WITH SAUERKRAUT

Serve this with buttered black bread and beer or cider.

1 pound link sausages	3 tablespoons chopped pickles
1 onion, chopped	Coarse salt
1 can sauerkraut, drained	Freshly ground black pepper

Fry the sausages and sauté the onion in the sausage fat. When almost cooked, add the drained sauerkraut and the pickles. Season. Heat through and serve very hot. Enough for 3–4.

TOAD IN THE HOLE

This is a simple and very filling English dish, a relic of another day when a little had to go a long way. (It still does.)

Green salad and plenty of mustard are good with this. The English some-times make a gravy out of brown gravy mix. Suit yourself.

2 eggs	Freshly ground black pepper
1 cup flour	8 sausages, skinned
1 cup milk (or half milk, half water)	1 tablespoon drippings, melted
Coarse salt	

Preheat oven to 400 degrees. If you have a blender, put in the eggs, milk, and flour and blend for 1 minute. Otherwise, beat the eggs, add the flour slowly, and beat thoroughly so as not to get any lumps. Add the milk and season. Let mixture rest for 30 minutes (or overnight, if pos-sible) before you use it.

Chop the sausages into pieces about 1½ inches long. Put the drip-pings in a baking tin, add the batter, and bake for 5 minutes. Remove pan from oven and carefully add the sausages. Return to oven and cook for 35–40 minutes, until both the sausages and the batter are browned. Serves 4.

BANGERS AND MASH

"Bangers" is a British slang word for sausages. Sausages served this way with mashed potatoes have long been a favorite economy dish in British households, particularly on winter nights.

8 pork sausages	Freshly ground black pepper
Dash thyme	2 cups cooked potatoes
Dash sage	1 beaten egg
½ teaspoon crushed juniper berries	¼ cup milk
(if available)	Extra butter
Coarse salt	Paprika

In a heavy skillet, cook the sausages. Place them in a buttered bak-ing dish, add the herbs and spices, and season. Mash the potatoes with the egg and milk. Season and spread over the sausages. Dot with butter, sprinkle on a little paprika, and brown quickly in the broiler. Serves 4.

See also
SAUSAGE AND CHICK PEAS, page 228
SAUSAGES WITH CORN AND TOMATOES, page 211

CHICKEN LIVER AND SAUSAGE PÂTÉ

Pâtés are easy to make and are delicious served as an hors d'oeuvre or with salad as a main course.

After cooking, they should be weighted. This compresses them and brings out the excess moisture. A good way to weight them down (without actual weights) is to put the pâté into the refrigerator with a strong plate on top, just small enough to cover the actual pâté without touching the side of the dish holding it. Place it on a lower shelf of the refrigerator. Now pile on more plates, a bowl, etc., and make a pyramid until it reaches the next shelf. Stack on enough to wedge it tightly against the shelf above. Now your pâté is weighted and should stay there overnight. If anyone tries to steal some, they'll probably bring down the whole upper shelf, which serves them right.

This particular pâté is very inexpensive and takes no time at all to make. If you can afford it, buy a miniature bottle of brandy and throw it in. It will make all the difference.

½ pound chicken livers, chopped	Freshly ground black pepper
2 tablespoons butter	Dash thyme
½ pound pork sausage, skinned	1 teaspoon crushed juniper berries
1 glass sherry or brandy (optional)	4 strips bacon
Coarse salt	Split pig's foot, cooked (optional)

In a skillet, sauté the chicken livers in butter. Remove chicken livers. Add the sausage and cook for about 10 minutes, stirring constantly. Return the chicken livers to the pan and add the sherry or brandy and seasonings. Mix well and turn into a small oven casserole. Place in a larger pan containing about an inch of water. Put the bacon on top and cook for about 1 hour, or until the pâté has shrunk from the sides of the casserole. Weight and refrigerate overnight. Serves 4.

Note: A cooked split pig's foot placed over the pâté gives it a delicious flavor. Remove and eat separately when the pâté has cooked.

VEAL

Good veal should be very pale pink with firm, pale, satiny fat. The bones should be tender and translucent. Don't buy veal that is yellowish, flabby, or dark pink.

Veal is very expensive meat and milk-fed veal is quite hard to come by. Real veal is supposed to come from milk-fed calves 5–12 weeks old. In America the calves are often put out to graze or are fed artificial feeds in addition to the milk; this toughens the flesh and makes it reddish. It is neither one thing nor the other, lacking the tenderness and delicacy of milk-fed veal and the flavor and nourishment of beef.

Veal is versatile, however, and for people on a college budget lends itself to a variety of inexpensive dishes.

Roast stuffed shoulder of veal, veal stew, and other excellent dishes made with very little veal can be had from the cheaper, darker cuts. Rather than buy fiendishly expensive veal escalopes from your butcher, cut them yourself from the leg or loin and pound them flat. Use the roast another day. Good substitutes can be made from escalopes cut from a large pork leg or loin and beaten flat. They should be cooked longer than veal, of course. See Ten-Minute Meals for escalope recipes.

Veal must be cooked very carefully. If it is cooked too long it dries out and becomes tough. It is usually better to cook it in a covered casserole with vegetables rather than in an open pan. You should always lard veal with bacon or fat so that it is kept moist while cooking.

ROAST VEAL

The most expensive cut is the loin. Rump and sirloin are medium-priced; and the cheapest of all is the shoulder. All these cuts are best boned and rolled, preferably stuffed with a good moist stuffing.

Never overcook the meat. Twenty to 25 minutes at a moderate to low temperature (about 300 degrees) should be sufficient per pound. It is done when the juices run yellow when pricked with a fork.

Always lard the meat with bacon or fat so that it is kept moist when it cooks.

Breast, loin, or shoulder of veal, larded	**Bacon**
	1 onion, chopped
Herb and Breadcrumb Stuffing	**1 carrot, sliced**
(page 80)	**1 celery stalk, chopped**

Preheat oven to 300 degrees. Wipe the roast dry, then rub with a cut clove of garlic. If you are using a breast or shoulder, make a pocket and fill it with the stuffing. If using a rolled roast, first unroll it, spread with stuffing, then reroll and tie together with string. Cover the roast with strips of bacon. Place in a greased casserole or roasting pan and distribute vegetables around it. The juices should run clear when it is done. Test by pricking with a fork. Remove to a heated plate and allow to rest for a few minutes before carving.

Pour off any excess fat before making pan gravy (see Basic Gravy for Roast Beef, page 48). Remember to substitute chicken bouillon for beef in that recipe, or use red or white wine, dry sherry, or dry vermouth. Tarragon, sour cream, and cream also are good additions to veal.

Roasting Times

Allow 20–25 minutes per pound, and 30–35 minutes per pound for a rolled, stuffed roast.

Meat thermometer should register 175 degrees.

HERB AND BREADCRUMB STUFFING

1 onion, chopped	¼ teaspoon thyme
1 tablespoon butter	1 egg, lightly beaten
1 cup soft breadcrumbs	Coarse salt
1 tablespoon grated lemon peel	Freshly ground black pepper
1 tablespoon parsley, chopped	

Sauté onion in butter until clear. Then place in a mixing bowl with all other ingredients. Mix together well.

Accompaniments for Roast Veal

The vegetables that go with veal are endless. Delicately flavored ones are the best. Asparagus, Jerusalem artichokes, green beans, broccoli, Braised Celery (page 103), cucumbers, greens, Braised Fennel (page 110), leeks, mushrooms, peas, tomatoes, and zucchini are very good.

Pasta (particularly noodles) has a great affinity for veal. New, mashed, or roast potatoes; Pommes Anna (page 177), Gratin Dauphinois (page 178), and Potato Casserole with Cheese (page 178) are also delicious with roast veal.

SAUSAGE-STUFFED BREAST OF VEAL

Ask the butcher to bone the meat; keep the bones for stock. Before roasting the meat, consult the instructions on page 79.

This can be cooked in a roasting pan with strips of bacon on top, or in a covered casserole with vegetables.

It is good with noodles, or Pommes Anna (page 177) cooked in the oven at the same time, and Greens (page 111).

2 pounds breast of veal

Stuffing

¼ pound sausage meat
1 cup breadcrumbs
1 egg, slightly beaten
1 onion, chopped
1 teaspoon sage
1 tablespoon chopped parsley

Coarse salt
Freshly ground black pepper
Bacon
2 carrots, chopped
1 onion, chopped

Preheat oven to 325 degrees. Dry the veal. Mix the stuffing ingredients together and season. Stuff into the veal and tie together with string. Place in a roasting pan and cover roast with strips of bacon, or put in a heavy casserole with vegetables and cover. Roast for 1 hour, or until done. Juices should run clear when meat is pricked with a fork. Serves 4.

BRAISED SHOULDER OF VEAL MICHIGAN STATE

This is good hot or cold. Coat the leftovers with the sauce and it will turn to jelly when refrigerated. You can serve it the next day with lemon wedges and chopped fresh parsley.

Boiled buttered potatoes, brown rice, or noodles are good with this casserole.

2 pounds shoulder of veal, boned
1 clove garlic, chopped
  Dash thyme
  Dash rosemary
1 tablespoon oil
  Juice of half a lemon
1 carrot, sliced

1 onion, sliced
2 stalks celery and leaves, chopped
2 cups chicken stock
  Coarse salt
  Freshly ground black pepper
  The bone

Wipe the veal dry and sprinkle the garlic, thyme and rosemary into the cavity. Brown the meat in the oil in a fireproof casserole. Add the remaining ingredients, bring to a boil, then reduce heat, cover, and simmer for 2 hours. Correct seasoning. Remove bone. Serves 4.

BLANQUETTE DE VEAU

This veal stew is good with noodles, rice, boiled potatoes, or mashed potatoes. Because veal tends to make a scum when it is boiled, you should boil it first and skim off as much as possible. Then simmer it with the vegetables in the usual way.

2 pounds stewing veal
  Water or white wine, to cover
1 lemon, quartered
1 onion, chopped
1 carrot, sliced
2 stalks celery with leaves, chopped

Thyme
Parsley
Rosemary
1 clove garlic, crushed
Bay leaf
Chicken stock, to cover

Sauce

2 tablespoons butter
2 tablespoons flour
½ cup light cream
1 egg yolk
2 tablespoons cream

1 tablespoon lemon juice
1 tablespoon butter
1 tablespoon chopped fresh parsley
Coarse salt
White pepper

Chop the veal into 1½-inch cubes. Bring to a boil in water or wine, with the lemon, and skim off the scum. Drain. Add the vegetables, seasonings, and stock. Bring to a boil, cover, and simmer for about 1 hour. Drain and reserve stock.

Melt the butter in a saucepan and add the flour. Stir together for two minutes, without browning. Add 2 cups of the veal stock, hot, and bring to a boil. When thickened, reduce heat and add the cream. Heat through without boiling. Remove from heat. Mix egg yolk and 2 table-spoons cream together and stir into sauce (off heat) until sauce is slightly thickened. Stir in lemon juice, butter, and seasonings. Add veal and turn in sauce. Serves 4–6, depending on quantity of noodles.

PAPRIKA VEAL CHOPS

These are good with spinach and noodles.

4 veal chops
3 tablespoons butter
1 onion, chopped
1 clove garlic, chopped
1 tablespoon paprika

Dash thyme
Coarse salt
Freshly ground black pepper
½ cup chicken stock
¾ cup sour cream

Preheat oven to 350 degrees. Dry the chops and brown them in the butter. Remove chops and sauté the onion and garlic in the butter. Place chops, onion, and garlic in a baking dish and sprinkle with the paprika. Add thyme, seasonings, and stock. Cover and bake for 20–30 minutes.

Remove and stir in the sour cream. Heat through without boiling. Serves 4.

Note: This can also be cooked on top of the stove. Simmer on low heat.

For
VEAL ESCALOPES see
ESCALOPES WITH CREAM AND MUSHROOMS, page 224
ESCALOPES WITH TOMATOES, page 225
WIENER SCHNITZEL, page 225
VEAL ESCALOPES WITH ASPARAGUS, page 212

HUNTER COLLEGE VEAL STEW

Serve this with new potatoes in parsley butter or with noodles. White wine would be the best drink with it.

1½ pounds stewing veal	1 small jar pimientos, chopped
1 tablespoon butter	1 package frozen peas (or fresh)
2 tablespoons pork drippings or oil	Coarse salt
1 onion, chopped	Freshly ground black pepper
1 cup white wine or chicken stock	Dash marjoram
2 tomatoes, chopped	

Cut the veal into 1½-inch cubes. Heat the butter and fat in a frying pan and brown the veal. Remove veal and drain. Add the onion and brown. Transfer veal, onions, and drippings to a stew pot, add the remaining ingredients, and bring to a boil. Reduce heat, cover, and simmer gently for 1½ hours. Serves 4–6.

Vegetables
and Vegetarian Dishes

In this chapter each vegetable is dealt with separately. You will find vegetable dishes suitable as a main course for a vegetarian meal, as well as side vegetable dishes. If you are a vegetarian you may omit the ham, tongue, or bacon called for in some recipes and substitute cheese instead. Vegetarians should eat plenty of eggs and cheese in order to get enough protein.

The nutritional value of raw or partially cooked vegetables was first discovered by the Chinese. Many were Buddhists and necessarily vegetarian and they perfected the method of cooking vegetables which to me is the best of all. (See Chinese Method of Cooking Vegetables, page 85.) This method preserves most of the vitamins and minerals, and the vegetables are bright in color, crisp, and fresh.

In contrast, most vegetables in the Western world are sprayed regularly with harmful insecticides before they are picked, sprayed again with preservatives or coloring agents or stuff to make them shiny; packed, dispatched, received, displayed, and bought, and finally any remaining vestige of taste or vitamins is boiled out, the water is thrown down the drain, and a gray mush is forced down the throat of the unhappy eater.

If you are a vegetarian it is particularly important that the water in which vegetables are cooked not be thrown away—if you must cook them in water. Use the water to make a soup or sauce, and use as little as possible so that the vegetables are steamed rather than boiled. As often as possible, cook your vegetables the Chinese way.

When buying vegetables avoid large, overgrown ones. They may win prizes but they have little taste. Store vegetables, wrapped, in the bottom of the refrigerator or in a cool, dry place until you are ready to use them. Never soak vegetables to "freshen" them.

CHINESE METHOD OF COOKING VEGETABLES

Stir-frying vegetables is the Chinese way and consists of just that—stirring and frying in a small amount of oil. Some vegetables require the addition of a small amount of liquid to complete cooking after they have been stir-fried. An electric skillet is ideal for this method of cooking.

First, prepare the vegetables. Wash, dry thoroughly, and dice or cut into strips. Most hard vegetables can be done this way. Leafy vegetables such as cabbages or lettuce should be shredded.

Heat 2–3 tablespoons peanut, vegetable, soy, or sesame oil in a large frying pan. You may add a chopped scallion, a tablespoon of chopped fresh ginger, or a chopped garlic clove if you like before adding the vegetables. Fry, stirring constantly, for several minutes, until bright and crisp.

If necessary, add additional liquid and continue to stir-fry for 2–5 minutes. Use about ½ cup liquid, stock or bouillon. You can also season with a small amount of soy sauce, sherry, or vinegar. If some sugar is added with the vinegar, you'll have a sweet-sour taste. Salt should be added only at the end of cooking.

These vegetables need only be stir-fried; they do not need extra liquid: canned or frozen vegetables, cabbage, lettuce, spinach, chard, mushrooms, snow peas, peas, and tomatoes.

The following vegetables need to be cooked in a little liquid *after* they have been stir-fried: asparagus, broccoli, Brussels sprouts, carrots, cauliflower, potatoes, cucumber, turnips, squash, string beans, eggplant, peppers, and onions.

Artichokes

Artichokes are the undeveloped flower heads of members of the thistle family. There are a great many varieties, but only one, the green artichoke, is usually found on the American market. Artichokes are relatively inexpensive in season and lend themselves to a variety of preparations. Unfortunately, some people are put off by their odd appearance and never try them because they don't know how to cook or eat them.

Artichokes should be heavy and have a fresh green color, with their leaves clinging tightly around the globe. They should not be rubbery or darkened, with badly split leaves.

How to Prepare Artichokes for Cooking

Cut off the stem so that the artichoke can stand upright. Discard old and tough outer leaves. Cut off the tips of the spikes with scissors. Wash them under running water. The artichokes are now ready for boiling.

How to Eat Artichokes

Pull off each leaf as you go and dip it into the sauce. Scrape the fleshy part off the bottom of the leaf with your teeth. As you finish the leaves, pile them up on one side of your plate. Eventually you will come across a furry choke which covers the heart. Pull it off or cut it off with a knife and discard it. You will be left with the heart—the best part. The heart is eaten with a knife and fork.

PLAIN ARTICHOKES

Method One

Artichokes, prepared for cooking
Boiling salted water, to cover
Juice of 1 lemon

Add lemon juice to water to avoid discoloration of artichokes. Place artichokes, bottoms down, in rapidly boiling water and cook for 40 minutes with the lid off. They are cooked when the leaves come off easily. Test by pulling a leaf quite near the middle. Remove and place upside down to drain. Squeeze each artichoke gently just before serving to rid it of any excess water.

You may lose vitamins using this method, so reserve liquid for use in soup.

Method Two

Artichokes, prepared for cooking
1 cup boiling water, unsalted
Juice of 1 lemon

Boil lemon juice with water. Place artichokes, bottoms down, in a heavy saucepan with a tight-fitting lid. Add water and steam for 40 minutes. Continue as in Method One, above.

Serve artichokes hot with Lemon Butter Sauce or Sauce Hollandaise (below); serve cold with Sauce Vinaigrette (page 131) or Mayonnaise (page 132).

LEMON BUTTER SAUCE

This is simple to do and goes well with most vegetables, especially asparagus, broccoli, and leeks.

1 stick butter
Lemon juice, to taste
Coarse salt
Freshly ground pepper

In a small saucepan, melt the butter over low heat without burning it. Squeeze in some lemon and season. Serve hot.

SAUCE HOLLANDAISE

A tricky sauce since you have to be very careful not to cook it over too strong a heat. If you do, it will curdle and be ruined. Keep the heat low rather than too high. It takes only about five minutes to make and should not be kept hot. If you have a double boiler, use it for this recipe. Do not add the butter too fast or the sauce will curdle.

Once you have learned how to make this sauce (and with patience it should come out right the first time) you will find it useful for all kinds of dishes. It is a delicious creamy yellow sauce with a delicate lemon flavor. It goes well on most vegetables and with steak, veal and chicken. It should look like mayonnaise when it is cooked.

2 egg yolks   Coarse salt
1 tablespoon lemon juice (or   1 stick butter (4 ounces), chopped
   vinegar)   up
1 tablespoon cold water

Separate the whites from the yolks and beat the yolks with a wire whip or fork until they are sticky. This will help them to absorb the butter. Add the lemon juice and water and beat some more. Season. Add a little of the butter and put over very low heat, stirring all the time. The sauce will start to thicken, like thick cream. Remove from heat every time you think it is cooking too fast. (A pan of cold water kept nearby into which you can dip the bottom of the saucepan will help you.) Keep adding the butter bit by bit until it is all used up. You should have a thick, creamy sauce. Correct seasoning, add more lemon juice if necessary, and serve. *Don't* try to keep it hot. In an emergency you can keep it at the back of a warm stove or over warm water.

How to Prepare Artichokes for Stuffing

Prepare as for boiling and boil for 30 minutes. Drain. Open up the middle leaves and remove the pale yellow leaves inside. Take out the prickly choke and squeeze some lemon juice on the heart to keep it from going brown. Get all the prickly stuff out because it is very unpleasant if you get any in your throat.

When stuffing, place your mixture in the center of the artichokes and between the leaves, too. Pull them back and push filling down between the leaves. Follow specific recipe for cooking time.

Jerusalem Artichokes

No one knows where these small brown tuber-like vegetables got their name. They are not from Jerusalem at all, but they do have a slight taste of artichoke. This vegetable is popular in France, where it goes by the even more unlikely name of *topinambours*.

Jerusalem artichokes are in season during the winter months. They are very much like potatoes and can be cooked the same way. The only problem is that they are knobby and a drag to peel. Probably the simplest way is to slip off the skin after they are cooked. They can also be served raw in salads, since they taste very much like water chestnuts.

A simple way to serve them is to boil them in a little water for 15–20 minutes, peel them, and pour melted butter on them. Season, and sprinkle chopped fresh parsley on top. Test for doneness after they have cooked for 15 minutes, for cooking too long toughens them again.

JERUSALEM ARTICHOKES WITH CHEESE
(main dish)

Serve this casserole as a main course with green vegetables and a salad. Cut ingredients in half if using as a side dish.

Leftover meat or nuts can be added to it.

2 pounds Jerusalem artichokes, cooked, peeled, and sliced	Freshly ground black pepper
2 tablespoons butter	¼ cup wheatgerm or fresh, soft breadcrumbs
4 scallions, chopped	½ cup grated cheese
Coarse salt	Paprika

Preheat oven to 350 degrees. Slice the artichokes. In a skillet heat the butter and sauté the scallions over low heat for about 5 minutes until softened. In a fireproof casserole, layer the artichokes with the scallions and butter, and season. Cover with breadcrumbs or wheatgerm. Put the cheese on top, sprinkle with paprika, and bake for 15–20 minutes, to brown the cheese. Serves 4.

Asparagus

When asparagus is in season, its price is not outrageous. Choose bright green, crisp stalks with closed tips. Try to select those of a uniform size. The fat ones are a little tougher and thus take longer to cook, but they are just as nutritious as the skinny ones.

To prepare the asparagus for cooking, wash the stalks well and scrub off any sand. Cut off the tough bottoms, 1–2 inches. These trimmed-off ends can be used in soups. Sort the asparagus into sizes, putting the fat ones in one bunch, the skinny ones in another. Tie up the bunches with white string. You don't have to do this, but they are easier to cook this way and can also be done in serving-size bundles. Allow ½ pound per person.

To cook, use a deep stew pot with a tight-fitting lid or a double boiler with its top inverted. Stand up the bundles in about 1 cup of boiling water. The water will cook the tough feet and the tops will steam without overcooking. Cover and cook for 12–20 minutes, depending on thickness of your stalks. Drain.

To cook in an electric skillet, leave the tops sticking out over the side. Push them down into the water for the last 5 minutes of cooking time.

Serve asparagus hot with Lemon Butter Sauce or Sauce Hollandaise (page 87); serve cold with Mayonnaise (page 132) or Sauce Vinaigrette (page 131). If you use this oil and vinegar dressing, pour it over the asparagus stalks while they are still hot, so they can marinate in the dressing while chilling.

ASPARAGUS CASSEROLE
WITH SWISS CHEESE AND SOUR CREAM
(main dish)

Serve this for lunch or at dinner with mashed potatoes and tomatoes.

2 pounds asparagus, cooked and
   drained
1 cup sour cream
Coarse salt
Freshly ground black pepper
8 slices Swiss cheese

Lemon juice
½ cup fresh breadcrumbs or
   wheatgerm
¼ cup butter
Paprika

Gently mix the asparagus with the sour cream and season. In a greased fireproof casserole, alternate layers of the asparagus-sour cream mixture with Swiss cheese. Squeeze lemon juice over all, top with breadcrumbs or wheatgerm, and dot with butter. Sprinkle with paprika and brown in the oven. Serves 4.

CREAMED ASPARAGUS WITH HAM
(main dish)

You need only a salad with this filling dish. Tongue would also do in place of the ham. Thin ham slices (not the chemically preserved packaged kind) are best here. If you can find a packaged kind free of chemicals, it will do. Otherwise get it freshly sliced.

2 pounds asparagus, cooked and
   drained
3 tablespoons butter
2 tablespoons flour (wholewheat
   if possible)
1½ cups of asparagus water or
   boiling milk
Nutmeg
Coarse salt

Freshly ground black pepper
8 thin ham slices, cut in half (or
   tongue)
4 hard-boiled eggs, sliced
½ cup grated cheese
Paprika
Extra butter
Chopped fresh parsley

Preheat oven to 350 degrees. Melt the butter in a saucepan. Add the flour and cook for 3 minutes, stirring constantly, without browning. Add the hot asparagus water or milk all at once and stir over medium heat until the sauce thickens like heavy cream. Add the nutmeg and season. Remove from heat. In a fireproof casserole put a layer of asparagus, a layer of ham, a layer of sliced hard-boiled eggs, and a layer of sauce. Repeat, ending with a layer of sauce. Scatter the cheese over the sauce, sprinkle with paprika, and dot with bits of butter. Bake for 20–30 minutes, until the casserole is brown and bubbling. Scatter parsley over the top. Serves 4.

Broad Beans

Broad beans (also called fava beans), lima beans and butter beans can be used interchangeably. They are sold fresh in their pods when they are in season during the summer, and dried throughout the rest of the year. In this section we will deal with the fresh kind. For dried beans, see under Beans (page 180).

Choose beans with firm, bright green pods; do not use limp, dry, or blackened ones. Choose the youngest beans possible and buy them when they are cheapest. You need about three-quarters of a pound per person because once podded the amount of beans you are left with is pitiful in comparison with the great pile of pods.

Cook them 20–30 minutes in boiling water, and drain. Serve with melted butter and a little chopped parsley.

Broad beans are very good cooked with bacon, ham, and pork. They are also nice with Sauce Béchamel (page 107).

BROAD BEANS WITH BACON
(main dish)

This is a good little supper dish and helps to stretch the beans. A tomato salad would go well with it.

3 pounds broad beans, podded and cooked	½ cup heavy cream
	Coarse salt
8 strips bacon	Freshly ground black pepper
1 tablespoon chopped fresh chives or parsley	4–6 slices wholewheat bread

Cook the bacon in a skillet. Mix the chives and parsley with the cream and combine with the beans. Drain the bacon, chop, and add to the beans. Season. Fry the bread on both sides in bacon fat and drain. Serve the beans on the fried bread. Serves 4–6.

Green Beans

Runner beans, snap beans, string beans, French beans—they come under a variety of names. There are many different kinds, but the ones in the market are all the same: longish, bright green beans, at their best when they are small. They should be clean and crisp and snap, not soft, malleable, or dry. Small ones don't need to be stringed, the bigger ones must be, and the very big ones should be stringed and sliced diagonally.

To prepare the beans, wash, then snap off one end and pull off the string. Do the same at the other end. This may be done with a vegetable peeler run down the sides.

Although the beans take time to prepare, the actual cooking time is short. They are so good when they are fresh that it is worth the trouble.

If you use frozen ones, cook them with a little butter, covered, over very low heat. Use *no water*.

To cook fresh green beans, put them in a little boiling water and cook, covered, for 10–20 minutes, until barely tender. They should always be a little firm. Drain them (saving the water for sauces, soups, or stocks) and put a lump of butter in the saucepan. Toss the beans until they are well coated with the butter.

These beans, particularly the older ones, are sometimes good cooked with pork fat or bacon. They can also be cooked with a peeled onion for flavor, sautéed Chinese style (an excellent method for these beans), or served with almonds, sour cream, cream, cheese sauce, Sauce Mornay (page 115), lemon, parsley, or sautéed mushrooms.

SWEET AND SOUR GREEN BEANS

Serve lots of this, with noodles or rice, for a good, quick dinner. Leftover diced meat can be added to the noodles or rice unless you are a vegetarian.

2 pounds green beans, prepared for
    cooking (above)
1 cup water or stock

Sweet and Sour Sauce

¾ cup water or bean water	1 teaspoon water
¼ cup brown sugar	1 tablespoon soy sauce
¼ cup red wine vinegar	Freshly ground black pepper
1 teaspoon cornstarch mixed with	

Cook the beans until barely tender in water or stock. Drain. Boil the bean water in a small saucepan and add the sugar and vinegar. Cook, stirring, for 5 minutes, or until the sugar is dissolved. Add the cornstarch mixture and soy sauce and cook until the mixture thickens enough to coat the spoon. Pour over the beans and serve immediately. Serves 4.

GREEN BEAN CASSEROLE
(main dish)

1 pound beans, prepared for	3 tablespoons olive oil
cooking (page 91)	1 onion, chopped
1 cup water or stock	2 cloves garlic, chopped

4 large tomatoes, chopped
2 green peppers, seeded and
   chopped
2 stalks celery with leaves, chopped

Basil, oregano, and bay leaf
Coarse salt
Freshly ground black pepper
½ cup grated Parmesan cheese

Start the beans in 1 cup boiling water. When they are half-cooked, about 10 minutes, remove from heat. Drain and reserve liquid.

In a heavy skillet, heat the oil. Cook the onion and garlic over low heat until the onion is clear. Add tomatoes, peppers, and celery and simmer gently. Add 1 cup of the liquid from the beans, the herbs, and seasonings. Bring to a boil, then reduce heat slightly and cook 10 minutes, until liquid is reduced in volume. Combine beans with sauce and pour into a greased, fireproof casserole. Top with cheese. Bake in a moderate oven until the top is browned. Serves 4.

Beets

When you buy beets choose those with their skins intact. If the skin is damaged, the beet bleeds during cooking and loses its color. Leave about 1 inch of the stem on when you are boiling or baking them.

Large beets take from 1 to 2 hours to cook; the smaller ones need ½ to 1 hour. You can slip off the skins when they are done. Baked beets take even longer—about 3 hours in a slow oven. Bake them when you have something else in the oven. They are even more delicious baked than boiled.

Since they take a while to cook and you may not have the time, you can use canned beets for these recipes if necessary (they're not *nearly* as good). Be sure to save the beet juice.

Serve hot with melted butter and parsley, or cold in a Sauce Vinaigrette (page 131).

BEETS WITH SOUR CREAM

This dish is also good heated through and served with brown rice.

4 medium or 2 large cooked beets,
   or 1 can of beets
½ onion, chopped
¾ cup sour cream
2 teaspoons horseradish

Coarse salt
Freshly ground black pepper
1 tablespoon chopped fresh chives
   or parsley

Slice the beets. Place them in a serving dish and scatter the onions over them. Mix the sour cream with horseradish and seasonings. Pour over the beets and garnish with parsley or chives. Serves 4.

Broccoli

Broccoli should be crisp, and the flower buds should be closed and green, not dry and yellow. The smaller the size, the better the taste.

If you boil broccoli in a lot of water, many of the vitamins are lost and the vegetable is rendered limp and lifeless. It should be cooked rapidly in as little water as possible.

Discard the outer leaves and break the broccoli into even-sized flowerets. Stand the broccoli upright in an inch of rapidly boiling water, cover, and steam for about 15 minutes, until the broccoli is tender.

Serve broccoli hot with butter, Lemon Butter Sauce (page 87), or Sauce Hollandaise (page 87), or cold with Sauce Vinaigrette (page 131) or Mayonnaise (page 132).

If you are cooking frozen broccoli, try to steam it with no water at all over very low heat. Add a very little water if necessary.

BROCCOLI AU GRATIN

1 bunch broccoli, steamed
½ cup grated cheese
½ stick butter
   Coarse salt
   Freshly ground black pepper

Preheat oven to 350 degrees. Put the broccoli in a greased casserole. Sprinkle with cheese and dot with butter. Season and bake for about 10 minutes in a hot oven, until it is browned and bubbling. Serves 4.

Brussels Sprouts

Nowadays Brussels sprouts are often sold in containers covered in plastic. Since they always put the good ones on top, you are often in for a surprise when you find what the ones underneath are like. Good sprouts are small, hard, bright green, and crunchy. Big yellow soft sprouts are as bad as stale cabbage.

Sprouts should be cooked only briefly, to retain their bright color and their crunchy texture. To prepare them, remove the wilted outside leaves and trim the stem with a knife. Cook rapidly in not more than 1 inch of boiling water, covered. Add butter and nutmeg and serve. They should not be cooked for more than about 15 minutes.

Frozen Brussels sprouts are not nearly as good as fresh ones, but they are sometimes a better value weight for weight. Add very little water to them, and cook over low heat with the lid tight on the pan. Do not overcook or they will be gray and mushy.

Serve Brussels sprouts with Lemon Butter Sauce or Hollandaise Sauce (page 87), with cooked ham or bacon, Au Gratin (see Broccoli, opposite) with a little cream and nutmeg added, and with boiled chestnuts.

BRUSSELS SPROUTS WITH GARLIC AND HAM
(main dish)

This dish can stand on its own as a supper dish. Serve it with a potato casserole and salad.

1 pound Brussels sprouts, steamed	1 clove garlic, chopped
(opposite)	½ cup breadcrumbs
¼ cup butter (2 ounces)	Lemon juice
1 tablespoon olive oil	Coarse salt
4 slices ham, diced	Freshly ground black pepper

Melt the butter and oil in a heavy skillet. Add the ham and the garlic and stir together for 1 minute. Add the sprouts and sauté for a few minutes. Sprinkle with breadcrumbs, season with lemon, salt, and pepper, and serve immediately. Serves 4.

Cabbage

Until recently, cabbage was a much derided vegetable. No wonder, considering that the only method used to cook it was boiling, and not just boiling for a short time, but for *hours*. The cabbage emerged transformed, a sodden, mushy gray mass bearing no resemblance to the vegetable it once was. A village in England was found to have almost an epidemic of scurvy not long ago even though their diet consisted largely of cabbage. They boiled it so long that there was nothing left of the vitamins and minerals by the time they got around to eating it.

There are several varieties of cabbage on the market. The most common are

green cabbage, which has a firm round head and a bright green color;
Savoy cabbage, which has loose, curly leaves, a dark green color, and a delicate flavor (the outer leaves are delicious for stuffing and the inner ones for stir-frying in the Chinese manner);

white cabbage, which is good for cole slaw, salads, and sauerkraut;

Chinese cabbage, which is long and thinnish with a white stem and light
   green leaves (delicious raw or cooked in the Chinese style; not
   always available); and

red cabbage, delicious in casseroles with prunes, chestnuts, or apples;
   goes well with pork and game. Red cabbage is also good raw in
   salad. Lemon juice or vinegar should be added to it when it is cooking; otherwise it loses its attractive red color and turns purple.

To prepare for cooking, remove the wilted outer leaves, trim the
stem, and cut cabbage in half. Quarter the cabbage or shred it coarsely
(remove the tough core). Wash quickly in cold water.

The best way to cook cabbage is to steam it in the water that clings
to its leaves, with a little oil, as the Chinese do. It is great when stir-fried.

BUTTERED CABBAGE

1 cabbage, prepared for cooking (above)	Coarse salt
	Freshly ground black pepper
1 onion, studded with cloves	Dash sugar
1 stick butter, chopped into small pieces	Dash nutmeg

Preheat oven to 350 degrees. Shred cabbage coarsely. In a large
buttered fireproof casserole, put the cabbage, onion, and butter. Sprinkle
on salt, pepper, and seasonings. Cover and bake for about 1 hour.
Serves 6.

CABBAGE WITH CARAWAY SEEDS

Pork, sausages, or bacon goes very well with this. Use shredded cabbage
here.

1 cabbage, prepared for cooking (above)	sesame oil
	¼ cup butter
1 teaspoon caraway seeds	Coarse salt
Lemon juice, to taste	Freshly ground black pepper
1 tablespoon olive oil, peanut oil, or	

In a heavy skillet with a tight-fitting lid, place cabbage, caraway
seeds, lemon juice, and oil. Steam slowly over low heat, stirring frequently so that it does not burn. Cook for 15–20 minutes, then stir in the
butter until melted. Season. Serves 6.

CABBAGE WITH NUTS AND CHEESE SAUCE
(main dish)

This is a filling dish, but brown rice or mashed potatoes are a good addition for soaking up the sauce. Stewed or baked tomatoes are also good with this.

1 cabbage, shredded	Coarse salt
2 tablespoons olive oil	Freshly ground black pepper
3 tablespoons butter	¼ pound chopped nuts
Juice of half a lemon	Sauce Mornay (page 115)

Heat the oil and butter in a roomy skillet. Add cabbage and stir-fry in the fat over low heat. Cover and simmer for about 20 minutes, checking often to be sure there is enough fat to prevent it from burning. Stir in the lemon juice, seasonings, and nuts. Meanwhile, make the sauce. Pour it over the cabbage and heat until bubbling. Serves 4–6.

See also
CABBAGE IN WHITE SAUCE, page 247

RED CABBAGE WITH SOUR CREAM
(main dish)

Brown rice, baked potatoes, or a green vegetable goes very well with red cabbage. If you wish to serve meat, sausages, pork and ham are the best accompaniments, and if it's a special occasion duck, goose or rabbit is delicious with red cabbage.

To peel the chestnuts, drop them into boiling water and take off their skins while they are hot. It is a tedious business, but the result is so good that it pays off.

This can be cooked for a shorter time on top of the stove, but the flavors will develop to a greater extent when it is baked for the longer period.

1 head red cabbage, shredded	1 teaspoon crushed cardamom seeds
3 tablespoons butter	(optional)
1 tablespoon oil	Dash thyme
1 onion, chopped	Bay leaf
3 cups beef stock or bouillon	1 apple, chopped
3 tablespoons red wine vinegar	Coarse salt
1 tablespoon brown sugar	Freshly ground black pepper
3 tablespoons currants	1 pound chestnuts, boiled and peeled
1 teaspoon grated orange rind	1 cup sour cream

Preheat oven to 350 degrees. Heat butter and oil in a large oven-proof casserole. Sauté the cabbage until slightly limp; you may have to do it in installments, unless you possess an unusually large skillet. When finished, put all cabbage back in the pan and add the onion. Cook for 2–3 minutes. Reserve chestnuts and sour cream, and add all other ingredients to the casserole. Mix well and bake for 3 hours. Add the chestnuts for the last 30 minutes of baking time. Stir in the sour cream just before serving. Serves 6–8.

Carrots

Carrots, as everyone remembers from agonizing childhood meals, are good for you. They are rich in vitamin A which helps the eyesight, particularly at night, and the skin. People who use their eyes a lot (i.e., students) need vitamin A more than other people. It is easier to absorb this vitamin from cooked carrots than raw ones.

Many people do not enjoy cooked carrots, usually because they are served plain boiled. If they are cooked right and served with the right dressing, they are delicious.

When buying carrots, choose small, firm, fresh ones. The big ones are better for soups or stock because the core tends to get a bit woody as they get older. Don't buy soft, pliable carrots.

To prepare for cooking, wash, trim carrot tops and scrape carrots, or peel them with a vegetable peeler if they are old. Young ones should not be peeled unless it is essential. It probably will be essential unless your carrots are organically grown, for chemically grown vegetables may have toxins located in the skin. Unfortunately, most of the vitamins and minerals are also in the skin. After peeling, you may slice or cut lengthwise into matchstick strips (julienne).

Good ways to serve carrots are like Broccoli Au Gratin (page 94), with Lemon Butter Sauce (page 87), and with Sauce Mornay (page 115). A little chopped fresh parsley always improves them.

BRAISED CARROTS

Steaks, chops, and chicken are good with braised carrots. Vegetarians can serve them with green vegetable dishes or as an accompaniment to cheese dishes. They are particularly good with a cheese sauce (see Sauce Mornay, page 115).

1 pound carrots, sliced	1 tablespoon chopped fresh parsley
1 cup stock, bouillon, or water	or chives
1 tablespoon brown sugar	Coarse salt
2 tablespoons butter	Freshly ground black pepper

Put the carrots in a heavy saucepan with the stock, sugar, and butter. Cook gently for 30–40 minutes, or until the liquid has evaporated and the carrots are tender. Season and sprinkle with parsley or chives. Serves 4.

CARROTS FRIED WITH BACON

With toast, this makes a light supper dish. Or serve it with a bean or green vegetable casserole, or a stew.

1 pound carrots, sliced and blanched	Coarse salt
1 tablespoon olive oil	Freshly ground black pepper
1 tablespoon butter	1 tablespoon chopped fresh parsley
4 strips bacon, diced	

Dry the carrots. In a heavy skillet, heat the oil and butter. Fry the bacon, remove, and drain on paper towels. Add the carrots and cook over very low heat for 30–40 minutes, covered, until tender. Season lightly, add the bacon bits, and garnish with parsley. Serves 4.

Note: To *blanch* means to drop the vegetables into rapidly boiling water for one minute. This softens them, and they cook more easily in the fat. Be sure to drain them first, drying thoroughly, before sautéing.

See also
GLAZED OR CREAMED CARROTS, page 249
CARROT AND ONION CASSEROLE, page 248

Cauliflower

Mark Twain is supposed to have described cauliflower as "a cabbage with a college education." It is indeed one of the most attractive members of the cabbage family, along with its close cousin, broccoli. When you buy it, make sure that the head is firm and white and that the flowerets are crisp, not soft, brown, or wilted.

To prepare cauliflower, remove the outside leaves and trim the stalk. Wash and drain. It can be cooked whole or broken into flowerets.

Cooking flowerets shortens the cooking time and ensures that part of the cauliflower will not be overdone. Always undercook rather than overcook cauliflower. It is watery when overcooked.

You can cook cauliflower by the Steam Method or the Milk Method. In the latter case, the liquid can be saved for use in something else, having already whitened the cauliflower, or it can be cooked down into a sauce. Both methods follow.

Steam Method for Cauliflower

1 head cauliflower, broken into
     flowerets
1 inch water

In a saucepan with a tightly fitting lid, heat the water to boiling and stand the flowerets inside with their stems in the water. Cover and cook for 15 minutes, or until just tender. The cauliflower is now ready for a sauce or butter. Serves 4.

Milk Method for Cauliflower

1 head cauliflower, broken into
     flowerets
1 cup milk

Sauce

3 tablespoons butter
1 tablespoon flour (preferably
     wholewheat)
  Nutmeg
  Coarse salt

Freshly ground black pepper, or
     white pepper
Paprika (optional)
Chopped fresh parsley (optional)

Boil milk, drop in flowerets, cover, and cook until tender. Season, drain, and serve. Save cauliflower liquid for another purpose, or make the sauce. In a saucepan, melt the butter, add flour, and cook, stirring constantly, for about 5 minutes without burning. Stir in boiling milk, add nutmeg and seasonings, and cook for 10 minutes, or until thick enough to coat spoon. Pour over cauliflower. Garnish with paprika or parsley if you wish. Serves 4.

Serve plain, cooked cauliflower like Broccoli Au Gratin (page 94), with Lemon Butter Sauce, or with Sauce Hollandaise (page 87). Cooked chopped bacon bits make a good garnish.

SAUTÉED CAULIFLOWER

Partially cook cauliflower by steaming in an inch of water for 7 minutes or boiling in milk for 5 minutes.

Sautéed Cauliflower is good with steaks, chops, green vegetable dishes, tomatoes, or brown rice.

1 cauliflower, partially cooked	Freshly ground black pepper,
¼ cup butter	or white pepper
Juice of half a lemon	1 tablespoon chopped fresh chives
Coarse salt	or parsley, to garnish

Drain and dry the flowerets. Heat butter, without burning it, in a heavy skillet. Add the cauliflower, and sauté it lightly. Squeeze the lemon juice over it, season, and garnish. Serves 4.

NOTRE DAME CAULIFLOWER WITH TOMATOES
(main dish)

Noodles, preferably wholewheat, and green salad are excellent with this Italian dish.

1 cauliflower, broken into
    flowerets
1 cup milk, or more if needed

White Sauce

3 tablespoons butter	Freshly ground black pepper,
2 tablespoons flour (preferably	or white pepper
wholewheat)	Nutmeg
Coarse salt	

Tomato Sauce

1 onion, chopped	1 tablespoon capers
1 clove garlic, crushed	1 tablespoon chopped fresh
3 tablespoons olive oil	parsley
1 tomato, chopped	Dash oregano or basil
2 peppers, chopped	¼–½ cup grated Parmesan cheese
¼ cup black olives, pitted	Paprika

Preheat oven to 350 degrees. Simmer the cauliflower in the milk until almost tender, about 10 minutes. Remove, drain, and set aside in a casserole dish. Reserve cauliflower milk.

Melt butter in a saucepan, add flour, and cook without browning, for about 5 minutes. Bring cauliflower liquid to a boil and add 1 cup to the *roux*. Stir until it coats a spoon, about 10 minutes. Season and set aside.

In a heavy skillet, cook the onion and garlic in the oil until soft. Add the tomato, peppers, olives, capers, and herbs and simmer for 10 minutes.

Pour the White Sauce over the cauliflower. Add the Tomato Sauce. Sprinkle with cheese and paprika and bake for 30 minutes. Serves 4–6.

ALBUQUERQUE CAULIFLOWER CHILI
(main dish)

Beans, especially black or pinto beans, are very good with Cauliflower Chili. See the chapter on Beans for ideas (page 180). This dish is also good with grilled meat.

1 cauliflower, steamed, or parboiled in milk	Dash cinnamon
1 tablespoon olive oil	Coarse salt
1 onion, chopped	Freshly ground black pepper
1 clove garlic, crushed	½ cup grated Cheddar cheese
1 tablespoon chili powder (more or less, according to taste)	½ cup sliced pimiento-stuffed green olives
3 tomatoes, chopped	¼ cup fresh breadcrumbs or wheatgerm
1 tablespoon parsley	Extra oil, as needed
½ teaspoon cloves	

Preheat oven to 350 degrees. Drain the cauliflower and place in an ovenproof casserole. Set aside. Heat the oil in a heavy skillet. Sauté the onion and garlic until the onion is soft. Add the chili powder and cook for 2 minutes, stirring. Add the tomatoes, parsley, spices, and seasonings and cook for about 7 minutes, thickening the sauce. Pour sauce over the cauliflower and sprinkle the cheese on top. Decorate with the olive slices, scatter on the breadcrumbs and, if it looks at all dry, add extra oil. Bake for 30 minutes. Serves 4.

See also
EXTRA-HEALTHY CAULIFLOWER CHEESE, page 250

Celery

Celery is delicious both raw and cooked, and it improves the flavor of most soups, stocks, or stews. It should be crisp and tender. Don't buy celery that is dry, yellowed, or split at the bottom of the stalks.

To prepare it, trim the root and break off the stalks. Wash carefully. Save leaves for stocks and stews.

Celery is best when cooked in a little stock; it evaporates to make a syrupy sauce. Braised Celery is good like Broccoli Au Gratin (page 94), or with a casserole like Notre Dame Cauliflower with Tomatoes (page 101).

BRAISED CELERY

Braised Celery is a good accompaniment for lamb, chicken, or pork.

1 head celery without leaves	1–2 tablespoons stock
1 tablespoon oil	Coarse salt
2 tablespoons butter	Freshly ground black pepper

Chop the celery stalks. In a heavy skillet, heat the oil and butter. Cook the celery over *low* heat for about 15 minutes, so that it softens without browning. Add the stock and cook, covered, until it reduces to a syrupy glaze and the celery is tender. Season lightly. Serves 4.

Corn

There is nothing better than roasted corn in the summer when you bake it in its husk in the ashes of an outdoor fire. It's a flavor that can't be duplicated indoors. But if you have to cook it indoors, boil it in its husk for a short time or bake it in the oven. Don't overcook it. It is great served with melted butter or Lemon Butter Sauce (page 87).

For recipes using corn-off-the-cob, scrape it down as near to the kernel as you can get it and use right away.

CORN-ON-THE-COB

4 ears of corn
  Boiling water, to cover
  Melted butter or Lemon Butter
    Sauce (page 87)

Remove the silk and bad bits from the corn. Plunge into rapidly boiling water and cook for 5–10 minutes for young corn, 15–20 minutes for older corn. Supply plenty of melted butter. Serves 1 (if you're greedy), 2, or 4.

CORN WITH BACON

4 ears of corn
4 strips of bacon

Remove the silk and husks of the corn. Wrap with bacon and grill until the bacon is crisp. Serves 2–4.

BAKED CORN

4 ears of corn

Preheat oven to 375 degrees. Remove silk from ears, then bake the ears of corn in their husks for 15 minutes, or until tender. Foil paper wrapped around them protects the husks from burning, but increases cooking time. Serve with melted butter or Lemon Butter Sauce (page 87). Serves 2–4.

CREOLE CREAMED CORN

Serve this with roasts, chicken, grilled meats or fish, or vegetable stews and casseroles.

3 cups cooked fresh corn (or canned)	**1 cup milk**
	Coarse salt
3 eggs, beaten	**Freshly ground black pepper**
½ cup butter, melted	**Nutmeg**
1 tablespoon brown sugar or honey	

Preheat oven to 350 degrees. Drain the corn (run it under cold water if it is canned). Combine all the ingredients except the nutmeg in a casserole. Sprinkle nutmeg over the top and bake for about 30 minutes, or until set. Serves 3–4.

Cucumbers

Cucumbers are a versatile vegetable. They are most often eaten raw, but there are also many delicious ways to cook them. Choose firm, green cucumbers when you shop. Discard soft or pale ones. If they have a greasy, waxy substance on their skin, this means they have been treated with paraffin wax. This false, commercial shine may contain a carcinogen, so it is very dangerous to eat the waxy skin. If you can't get organically grown cucumbers, or at least unwaxed cucumbers, then *always* peel them.

Cucumbers may be salted and marinated in a little vinegar before they are cooked, to remove their excess moisture. Unless you save the vinegar, however, you are losing many vitamins.

Cooked cucumbers are good with cheese sauce (Sauce Mornay, page 115), and with dill or parsley.

STEWED CUCUMBERS

4 cucumbers, peeled, seeded, and chopped	1 tablespoon brown sugar or honey
2 tablespoons white wine vinegar	Coarse salt
¼ cup butter	Freshly ground black pepper

Soak the cucumbers, salted, in vinegar for 1 hour. Drain and dry. Melt the butter in a casserole or heavy skillet and add sugar and seasonings. Add cucumbers and cook over low heat for about 30 minutes, or until the cucumbers are barely tender. Serves 4–6.

Note: This dish tastes even better if it is baked in a moderate oven for about 45 minutes.

CUCUMBERS BAKED WITH DILL

This is the best way of all to cook cucumbers. The delicate flavor of the dish goes well with chicken and veal. Dill is extremely good with all fish dishes. You must use fresh dill here; dried dill won't produce the same flavor.

4 cucumbers, peeled, seeded, and chopped	¼ cup butter
2 tablespoons white wine vinegar	2 tablespoons fresh dill, chopped
1 tablespoon sugar	Coarse salt
	Freshly ground black pepper

Preheat oven to 350 degrees. Soak the cucumbers in vinegar for 1 hour. Remove and dry on paper towels. Place in a casserole and sprinkle with the sugar. Cut up the butter into small pieces and put it on top. Add the dill and seasonings. Cover and bake for about 45 minutes. Serves 4–6.

COOKED CUCUMBERS WITH YOGHURT

4 cucumbers, baked or stewed   Coarse salt
   (page 105)   Freshly ground black pepper
1 cup yoghurt   Chopped fresh dill or parsley
1 egg, beaten   (optional)

Add the yoghurt and egg to the cooked cucumbers. Correct seasoning and heat through (do not scramble the egg). Serve garnished with
extra dill or parsley. Serves 4–6.

STUFFED CUCUMBERS

Use the skins *only* if the cucumbers have not been waxed. Otherwise,
peel them.

Brown rice, vegetable casseroles, fish, and lamb are particularly good
with stuffed cucumbers. Cheese sauce (Sauce Mornay, page 115) is excellent
if poured on the cucumbers for the last 10 minutes of cooking.

4 cucumbers, halved and seeded
  Coarse salt
2 tablespoons vinegar

Stuffing

2 tablespoons butter   Coarse salt
1 onion, chopped   Freshly ground black pepper
¼ cup wholewheat breadcrumbs   ¼ cup ground nuts
  Milk, to cover   ¼ cup cream cheese
  Sage

Preheat oven to 350 degrees. Salt the cucumbers and pour the
vinegar on them. Let them stand for about 30 minutes, to remove excess
moisture. Drain and dry them. Meanwhile, prepare the stuffing. Soften
the onion in the butter. Soak breadcrumbs in milk with sage and seasonings. Add onions to breadcrumbs and combine with nuts. Stuff the cucumbers and cover them with the cheese. Bake about 45 minutes. Serves
4.

CUCUMBER FLAN
(main dish)

Make your own wholewheat pie crust (page 197), or use a frozen pie
crust. The wholewheat crust will be much better, if you have the time.

This is a filling dish and can be served with tomatoes, peppers, green beans, or peas for dinner. If you want meat, it is very good with grilled chops, liver, or fish. If you are serving it with fish, put some dill in it, if possible.

4 cucumbers, stewed or baked
    (page 105)

Béchamel Sauce

2 tablespoons butter	1 egg, beaten
2 tablespoons flour	Nutmeg
2 cups hot milk	1 baked pie crust
Coarse salt	Cooked, chopped bacon (optional)
Freshly ground black pepper	

Preheat oven to 350 degrees. Cook cucumbers and drain thoroughly. While the cucumbers are cooking, make the sauce. Gently melt the butter in a saucepan and add the flour. Cook, stirring, without burning, for 5 minutes. Gradually add the milk and bring to a boil again. Season and cook until thickened to consistency of heavy cream. If the sauce is too thick, add more milk, a little at a time, until it thins out. If it is too thin, boil it down over high heat, stirring constantly. (In an emergency, make a paste of a little butter and flour and add it gradually, stirring all the time.)

Remove from heat and cool slightly. Add a little of the sauce to the egg, in another bowl, stirring constantly. Then very gradually add egg mixture to sauce, stirring until thickened. Mix in cucumbers and pour into pie shell. Sprinkle with nutmeg and bake for 15–20 minutes. Garnish with bacon, if desired. Serves 4–6.

Eggplant

The eggplant, also known as *aubergine,* has been known in the Middle East and Mediterranean area for centuries. It is superb with lamb, eggs, and chicken, and eggplant casseroles are delicious hot or cold. Eggplant is even better when reheated.

It is a beautiful vegetable, with shiny purple skin and dark green leaves clustered at the top. Buy smooth-skinned eggplants. If the skin is wrinkled and dry, the eggplant is old. Luckily, eggplant is very cheap.

Do not peel them. The skin contains flavor and vitamins and helps to retain the eggplant's shape while cooking. Eggplant should be salted and allowed to stand for about 30 minutes before cooking, to remove excess moisture. Otherwise, your dish may be too watery.

STEWED EGGPLANT
(main dish)

You need serve only brown rice or noodles with stewed eggplant. It is a very filling dish. Serve it hot or cold, or reheated. If you are entertaining, cook it the night before and reheat it. You can do this dish successfully in an electric skillet.

Stoned black olives, anchovies, and slices of lemon can be used to garnish the stew.

3 medium-sized eggplants, cubed	Dash allspice
½ cup olive oil	¼ cup currants, soaked in water
1 onion, chopped	(optional)
2 cloves garlic, crushed	Coarse salt
1 pound tomatoes, chopped	Freshly ground black pepper
Dash oregano	1 tablespoon chopped fresh parsley,
Dash basil	to garnish (optional)

Salt the eggplant and let it stand for 1 hour. Dry with paper towels. Heat the oil in the skillet and brown the eggplant on all sides. Remove and drain on paper towels. Soften the onion in the oil, add the garlic and tomatoes and cook for about 5 minutes. Add the remaining ingredients, together with the eggplant, cover, and stew for 1 hour. Garnish as desired. Serves 6–8.

FRIED EGGPLANT

This is a delicious dish served with meat, especially lamb. Nothing else is needed except, perhaps, a salad. If you like garlic, you'll love it. Omit the garlic if you'd rather.

If you use an electric skillet, you can cook chops with the garlic and herbs.

1 medium-sized eggplant	Fresh basil or marjoram (if
Olive oil	available), chopped
2 cloves garlic, crushed	Coarse salt
2 tablespoons chopped fresh parsley	Freshly ground black pepper

Cut eggplant into thinnish slices, salt, and let stand 30 minutes. Pat dry. Heat plenty of oil in the skillet, add the eggplant, and fry over high heat for about 15 minutes. Remove and drain. Add the garlic and herbs and cook for 2 minutes. Pour over the eggplant. Serves 4.

EGGPLANT PARMIGIANA
(main dish)

This is the famous Italian dish. It is good with spaghetti or noodles, or by itself.

3 medium-sized eggplants
  Coarse salt
2 tablespoons olive oil
2 onions, chopped
2 cloves garlic, crushed
4 tomatoes, chopped
  Dash basil
  Coarse salt

Freshly ground black pepper
1 beaten egg
2 tablespoons flour (preferably wholewheat)
  Olive oil
1 cup grated Parmesan cheese
1 can anchovies, drained (optional)
1 tablespoon chopped fresh parsley

Preheat oven to 350 degrees. Cut the eggplant into slices, salt, and let stand for 1 hour. In a heavy skillet, heat the oil and soften the onion. Add the garlic and tomatoes with basil and seasonings and cook over low heat for about 30 minutes.

Pat the eggplant slices dry. Dip them into the egg, then the flour, and fry them in hot olive oil until brown.

In a casserole put the eggplant in layers with the tomato sauce. Top with the cheese and anchovies, if desired. Bake for 30 minutes. Top with parsley. Serves 6–8.

MEAT-STUFFED EGGPLANT
(main dish)

Nothing more than a salad is needed with this dish. Leftover ground meat can be used for the stuffing.

3 medium-sized eggplants
  Coarse salt
3 tablespoons olive oil
2 onions, chopped
1 clove garlic, crushed
½ pound ground beef or lamb
½ cup wholewheat breadcrumbs or cooked rice

2 tablespoons chopped pine nuts (optional)
1 beaten egg
  Dash cinnamon
  Dash oregano
1 tablespoon chopped fresh parsley
  Coarse salt
  Freshly ground black pepper

Preheat oven to 350 degrees. Cut the eggplants in half and scoop out the flesh. Chop into small cubes and salt. Leave the skin intact, but salt it too. Let stand for 1 hour. Pat dry. Heat the oil in a skillet. Soften the onion in the oil. Add the garlic and eggplant and brown. Add the beef and cook for a few minutes. In a bowl combine all the remaining ingredients. Combine with onion, eggplant, and meat and stuff into the eggplant shells. Bake for about 45 minutes. Serves 6.

Fennel

Fennel as we know it on the market is a white bulbous vegetable, somewhat similar in appearance to celery. It is a delicious vegetable with a slight taste of aniseed. It can be eaten raw or cooked and goes particularly well with fish.

Choose fresh white heads of fennel; don't buy them if they are brown or very split at the ends. Naturally, the smaller heads are the best.

BRAISED FENNEL

Serve this with fish, grilled meat, and sausages, or with vegetarian beans, pasta, or potato dishes.

1 head fennel, if large, or 4 small ones	Lemon juice
	Coarse salt
2 tablespoons butter or oil	Freshly ground black pepper
¼ pint stock or bouillon (chicken or vegetable)	1 tablespoon chopped fresh parsley

Trim the fennel stalks and cut the bulb in half if small, in quarters if large. In a heavy skillet heat the butter or oil. Add the fennel, stock, and lemon juice. Simmer for 20–30 minutes, adding more stock if necessary, until the liquid has evaporated and the fennel is tender. Season, and serve garnished with chopped fresh parsley. Serves 4.

FENNEL AU GRATIN

Fennel, braised (as above)	breadcrumbs
½ cup Parmesan cheese, grated	1 tablespoon butter, diced
¼ cup wheatgerm or wholewheat	

Preheat oven to 375 degrees. Put the fennel in a casserole dish and cover with the cheese, wheatgerm, and butter. Bake until the cheese is melted and bubbling. Serves 4.

Greens

Green, leafy vegetables are high in vitamin and mineral content. Some of the best-known greens are escarole, Swiss chard, beet greens, turnip greens, collard greens, kale, mustard greens, cabbage, dandelion greens, and spinach. Greens should be young and fresh, not wilted; tender young greens take less time to cook than older, tougher greens.

Wash all greens, especially spinach, in several changes of water to get the grit out. Pay no attention to claims that packaged fresh spinach has been washed. All yellow, wilted leaves and tough stalks should be removed. Allow ½ pound of greens per person.

Greens should be cooked in only the water that clings to their leaves after washing. They are useful for last-minute meals since they require so little time. The most common fault in cooking greens, and the reason they are often disliked, is that they are boiled until bitter, then served up mushy and lacking in the vitamins and minerals they had before. One caution: don't cook or keep spinach in an iron or aluminum pan. There is some sort of chemical reaction, especially with aluminum, that results in a toxic taste you'd be wise not to try.

To steam greens, put them in a heavy-bottomed pot with no extra water or salt. Keep stirring them if they show signs of sticking to the bottom. When they are tender, stir in a little butter, season, and serve. Another excellent method is Basic Stir-Fried Greens (page 112), the Chinese way.

Frozen greens, though not as good as fresh ones, are usually of good quality and save you the time of cleaning and trimming. Do not add extra water to frozen greens; there will be enough in the thawing. If they are to be stir-fried, they must be thawed and thoroughly dried first.

Most greens can be cooked like spinach, and the following recipes, except where noted, are interchangeable. When greens have been steamed they are delicious stirred with fresh cream, with butter, with Sauce Mornay (page 115), Sauce Hollandaise (page 87), or Sauce Béchamel (page 107), and au gratin (page 94). They are good with fish, eggs, chicken, and roasts and can also be used in fillings for pancakes and omelettes, where a small amount goes a long way.

BASIC STIR-FRIED GREENS

This recipe can be used for all young greens. Wash thoroughly and remove woody stalks or bad pieces before you begin. Make sure the leaves are dry before you fry them.

Cooked this way, they are a bright appetizing green, crisp and full of flavor.

2 pounds greens, washed, dried, and chopped	(optional)
3 tablespoons sesame, peanut, or vegetable oil	1 clove garlic, chopped (optional)
2 scallions, chopped	Coarse salt
1 tablespoon fresh ginger, chopped	Freshly ground black pepper
	Soy sauce, to taste

In a large heavy skillet, heat the oil. Add the scallions, ginger, and garlic, and stir-fry for about 3 minutes. Add the chopped vegetables and stir-fry for 10–20 minutes, until they are cooked. Season with soy sauce or salt, add pepper, and serve immediately. Serves 4.

TURNIP GREENS SOUTHERN STYLE

Greens don't have to be boiled for an hour to be good, as this version of Southern style greens proves. Use any kind of greens. Serve with pork, sausages, liver, or fried chicken.

2 pounds turnip greens, or other greens, washed and chopped	1 tablespoon brown sugar
1 tablespoon water	2 scallions, chopped
3 tablespoons vinegar	Coarse salt
	Freshly ground black pepper

Steam the greens until they are tender (about 20–30 minutes) in a tightly covered heavy-bottomed saucepan (see page 111). Add a tiny bit of water if greens are sticking to pan. In a small pan, combine the remaining ingredients and boil to a syrup. Pour over the greens. Serves 4.

GREENS WITH SALT PORK OR BACON

This is good with rice, eggs, sweet potatoes, liver, kidneys, and vegetable casseroles. Classic accompaniments are slices of fresh onion and cornbread.

2 pounds greens, washed, chopped and dried	3 tablespoons bacon fat, or drippings from 2 slices of fried salt pork

1 onion, chopped
2 tablespoons pine nuts (optional)
2 tablespoons soaked raisins
   (optional)

Dash nutmeg
Coarse salt
Freshly ground black pepper

In a heavy skillet, melt the fat or cook the salt pork. Add onion and cook until soft. If using salt pork, remove it now. Add the greens with the nuts and raisins and fry for 5–15 minutes, or until tender. Season (not too much salt), add the nutmeg, and serve at once. Serves 4.

BRAISED GREENS

This recipe is particularly good for escarole. Serve it with roasts or casseroles that are being cooked in the oven at the same time.

2 pounds greens, washed and dried
¼ cup olive oil
1 clove garlic, crushed
3 tablespoons butter

3 tablespoons orange or lemon juice
Coarse salt
Freshly ground black pepper

Preheat oven to 350 degrees. Put the oil and garlic in a casserole. Add the leaves, chopped if necessary, and dot with butter. Add the orange or lemon juice and braise, covered, for 20–40 minutes, depending on the greens used. Season. Serves 4.

CREAMED GREENS

Spinach is superb cooked like this, and the more butter the better.

2 pounds greens, steamed (page
   111), and drained
¼ cup butter
Coarse salt

Freshly ground black pepper
Dash sugar
Dash nutmeg
½ cup hot cream

Melt the butter in a saucepan. Add the greens, well chopped. Stir well and season. Heat the cream and pour over the greens. Heat thoroughly and sprinkle with nutmeg. Serves 4.

See also
SPINACH PANCAKES, page 220
SPINACH CROQUETTES, page 212

Leeks

Since they are usually quite expensive, we shall give only the basic leek recipe here, in the hope that you will be able to try it at a time when leeks are low in price at the market.

The worst part about preparing leeks is cleaning them. You think you have them clean, but when you sit down for your first taste you get a mouthful of grit. To be sure they are absolutely clean, cut them almost in half, leaving them joined at the bottom. Hold them under running water, pulling each section back. Letting them soak for a while in water also helps the grit to seep out. French restaurants always serve miraculously perfect leeks, whole without cuts, and with no grit. Their method is to cut a cross at the bottom of the leeks, then hold them under cold running water. It works, but to be absolutely sure, cut them down the side.

Once cleaned, leeks take little time to prepare. They are a very important ingredient in many soups and stews and are delicious braised, or chilled and served with a Sauce Vinaigrette (page 131).

BRAISED LEEKS

8 leeks, prepared for cooking
  Water, stock, or bouillon
3 tablespoons butter
  Coarse salt
  Freshly ground black pepper

Put the cleaned leeks into a pan and fill with water or stock to cover about two-thirds of the leeks. Add the butter and simmer for 20–30 minutes, depending on the thickness and age of the leeks. Most of the liquid will evaporate. Season. Serves 4.

BRAISED LEEKS WITH SAUCE MORNAY

Sauce Mornay is the basic white sauce (Sauce Béchamel) with cheese. It is delicious on leeks, and this dish goes well with delicately flavored meats such as chicken or veal.

8 leeks, braised (see Braised Leeks,
  above)

Sauce Mornay

2 tablespoons butter	Coarse salt
2 tablespoons flour	Freshly ground black pepper
2 cups milk or stock	⅓ cup grated Swiss or Parmesan
1 egg yolk	cheese
2 tablespoons cream	Nutmeg

Preheat oven to 350 degrees. Melt the butter in a saucepan. Add the flour and cook for 3 minutes, stirring, without browning. Meanwhile, heat the milk or stock. Gradually add it to the butter-flour mixture and stir until thickened. Beat together the egg yolk and cream. Add a very small amount of the sauce to the egg yolk mixture and stir constantly. Then return this mixture to the sauce, always stirring, and heat it through. Add the cheese and stir until the cheese melts and the sauce has thickened. Season and pour over the leeks in a casserole. Sprinkle with nutmeg and bake in the oven or under a grill until bubbling. Serves 4.

Mushrooms

Apart from their use as a flavoring for sauces, stuffings, and other recipes, mushrooms are delicious by themselves. They are said to provide the same nutrition as lean beef, and when served as a main course are a cheap, quick, and nourishing supper dish.

Choose smooth, light, unspotted mushrooms. If they are dark and wrinkled and their gills are exposed, they have been around for a while.

If they are fairly clean and not too sandy, wipe them with a damp cloth. If they are dirty, wash them in plenty of water and dry them immediately. Avoid peeling, if possible, for most of the flavor is in the skin. Save the stems for stock or sauces.

Mushrooms should never be overcooked. If they are, they lose much of their flavor and their texture. They should be sautéed quickly in butter and lemon juice. They will absorb the butter in 3–5 minutes and be ready to serve. If you must hold them, do not cover, or the juices will be drawn out again. If you are putting them in a sauce, cook them separately and add them at the end. Light-colored mushrooms should not be cooked in an aluminum pan; it will darken them.

Mushrooms are unbelievably good when marinated overnight in oil and served raw as a salad (see page 137). Cultivated mushrooms sometimes have more flavor eaten this way than they do when they are cooked.

MUSHROOMS PROVENÇALE

Mushrooms cooked this way have a strong garlic flavor. They are delicious as a side dish with meat or chicken, or served with brown rice and tomatoes.

1 pound mushrooms
3 tablespoons olive oil and/or butter
2 cloves garlic, crushed
2 tablespoons chopped fresh parsley
or basil
Coarse salt
Freshly ground black pepper

Dry the mushrooms and slice them, leaving their stalks on if you wish. Heat the oil or butter (or a mixture of both) and sauté the garlic and mushrooms for about 5 minutes. Add the herbs and seasonings. Serves 4–6.

MUSHROOMS WITH SOUR CREAM ON TOAST
(main dish)

Mushrooms cooked with cream and served on toast are a delicious supper dish. If you want a more substantial meal, have kidneys, liver, or bacon, too. Or serve the mushrooms on the side with a casserole dish.

1 onion, chopped
3 tablespoons butter
1 pound mushrooms, chopped
Squeeze of lemon
Coarse salt
Freshly ground black pepper
½ cup sour cream or heavy cream
Paprika
Buttered toast

Fry the onion in the butter, without browning, until soft. Add the mushrooms and a squeeze of lemon juice. Cook for 3–5 minutes. Season and add the sour cream. Heat through without boiling and spread the mixture on buttered toast. Sprinkle with paprika. Serves 4–6.

See also
MUSHROOMS ON TOAST, page 226

Okra

Okra is the basis of the famous Louisiana gumbos, where it helps to thicken the sauce. It is good with tomatoes and peppers, or by itself with plenty of melted butter.

Always choose small tender pods. They should be bright green and not more than two inches long. The large pods are rather tough but can be used if sliced into 1-inch pieces. Trim off the stems. Frozen okra, although not as good as fresh, is very good.

Okra should not be overcooked. Use as little water as possible and don't boil it for more than 8 minutes. Serve hot with lemon and melted butter, or try it cold with Sauce Vinaigrette (page 131) or Mayonnaise (page 132).

OKRA AND CHEESE CASSEROLE
(main dish)

You can make this equally well in an electric skillet. Serve with lamb, beef, chicken, or seafood. It can also be served with eggs, rice, or wholewheat spaghetti.

¼ cup butter, or 3 tablespoons bacon fat	2 pounds tomatoes, peeled and sliced
3 whole scallions, chopped	1 clove garlic, crushed (optional)
1 pound fresh okra, or 2 packages frozen okra	Coarse salt
	Freshly ground black pepper
4 ears of corn, or 1 can corn	½ cup Swiss or blue cheese, diced

Preheat oven to 350 degrees. Melt the fat and sauté the scallions without burning them. Trim okra stems. Add okra to scallions and cook for about 2 minutes, stirring. In a casserole or heavy skillet arrange layers of okra, corn (scraped off the cob or canned), tomatoes, and seasonings. Bury the garlic in the middle of the layers. Top with cheese and bake or simmer in skillet for 45 minutes to 1 hour. Serves 4.

Onions

Besides their obvious and excellent use as flavorings for stews, soups, stocks, sauces—almost everything—onions are extremely good on their own. They are also very cheap. An onion tart costs next to nothing and provides a nourishing, delicious, and filling meal. Stuffed onions are a good way to use up leftovers. Onions creamed, glazed (see page 117) or fried go well with almost every dish. And, what is more, onions keep for a long time and don't need refrigeration.

There are several different kinds of onions besides the usual white ones. Spanish onions are large and quite good for boiling, braising, and frying. Shallots, often used in French cooking, are very small onions with a delicate but pronounced flavor. They are more expensive than the common garden variety.

To peel small onions, drop them for a few minutes into boiling water. The peel slips off and you don't cry. Large onions must be parboiled before baking, and the skin can be removed after parboiling.

GLAZED OR CREAMED ONIONS

This basic recipe for onions is much better than plain boiled onions, and after being cooked this way they can be sprinkled with parsley and covered with Sauce Béchamel (page 107) or Sauce Mornay (page 115).

These onions are delicious with roasts, steaks, hamburgers, chicken, lamb, or veal, and with bean dishes or vegetable casseroles.

About 18 small white onions	Dash thyme
Boiling water	Bay leaf
¼ cup butter	1 tablespoon chopped fresh parsley
Stock or water, to cover	Coarse salt
1 tablespoon sugar	Freshly ground black pepper

Sauce Mornay (page 115), or Sauce
    Béchamel (page 107), if you
    want creamed onions

Drop the onions for a few moments into boiling water. Drain and slip off their skins. Melt the butter in a saucepan. Toss the onions in the butter until they are golden. Add the water or stock barely to cover. Add the sugar, herbs, and seasonings and simmer for 40–50 minutes, or until the onions are tender and the sauce has reduced to a caramel glaze. For creamed onions, add Sauce Mornay or Sauce Béchamel and heat through without boiling. Serves 4.

ONIONS WITH SOUR CREAM

For a vegetarian meal, serve these over wholewheat noodles and have a green vegetable. They also go well with veal, chicken, pork, kidneys, or liver.

4 large onions, chopped	1 cup sour cream
¼ cup butter	Coarse salt
Dash oil	Freshly ground black pepper
Dash mace	Dash nutmeg

Sauté the onions in the oil and butter until clear. Add the remaining ingredients and heat through without boiling. Serves 4.

STUFFED ONIONS
(main dish)

This is an ideal way to use up leftover vegetables, bacon, fish, meat, or sauces. Your leftovers may be enhanced by the addition of raisins, currants, nuts, cinnamon, cloves, sage, or parsley, all of which make delicious combinations with onions.

Stuffed onions alternated with stuffed tomatoes look attractive. Serve them with potatoes or rice and a green vegetable. They are also good with grilled meat or fish, or they can be baked in the oven at the same time you are doing a roast.

Sauce Mornay (page 115) or Sauce Béchamel (page 107) can be poured on after baking.

6 large onions, peeled	Dash thyme
Boiling water, to cover	Dash ground cloves (optional)
¼ cup butter or 4 tablespoons	¼ cup raisins (optional)
bacon fat	Coarse salt
½ cup wholewheat breadcrumbs	Freshly ground pepper
¼ cup chopped or ground nuts	Dash nutmeg
½ cup Cheddar, Swiss, or cream	1 tablespoon chopped fresh parsley
cheese, chopped	1 egg, beaten
1 tablespoon brown sugar	

Preheat oven to 350 degrees. Boil the onions for fifteen minutes and drain. Scoop out the insides of the onions and chop them coarsely. Reserve onion shells. Sauté chopped onions in the butter or bacon fat until soft. Remove them and combine in a mixing bowl with all the remaining ingredients. Season and stuff into the onion shells. Bake for about 1 hour, or until tender. Serves 4–6.

ONION TART
(main dish)

There are many variations on this tart, which originates in the south of France. It is very filling and constitutes a hearty dinner when served with a green vegetable and a salad.

You can vary the recipe somewhat to suit your taste and the ingredients on hand. For instance, use twice as many onions and omit the eggs. Or combine onions and tomatoes and delete the eggs. Garnish your tart with pitted black olives, chopped bacon, chopped fresh parsley, or anchovies arranged like wheel spokes on the top. Whatever you do, the tart should emerge as a particularly attractive dish, and no one will guess how easy and inexpensive it was to make.

1 pie shell, frozen or homemade (page 197), baked	2 eggs, beaten Coarse salt
3 pounds onions, chopped	Freshly ground black pepper
1 clove garlic, crushed (optional)	Dash thyme
4 tablespoons butter or bacon fat	¼ cup grated cheese (optional)

Preheat oven to 325 degrees. Gently fry the onions with the garlic in the fat, without browning, over low heat. This will take about 30 minutes. Remove from heat and stir in the eggs and seasonings. Fill the pie shell, sprinkle cheese over the top, and bake for 20–30 minutes. Serves 4–6.

Peas

When peas were first introduced to the court of Louis XIV they became the rage. They were considered as much a delicacy as truffles are nowadays. Princes and princesses were said to have gone home and eaten a plate of peas before retiring, after having already dined lavishly with the king. The delicate peas that they knew then are only available here to people who grow their own. But frozen peas have become so good and are so easy to prepare that they are almost better than some of the fresh ones you see on the market.

Peas should be bright green with well-filled, velvety pods. They should be tender and sweet. Old peas are larger and tougher, but they too can be cooked successfully. One pound of podded peas will yield about 1 cup of hulled peas; allow ½ cup per serving.

Peas go with just about everything, and they always look good. If you are cooking frozen ones, thaw them out a little first and gently cook them in butter. Try not to use any water. Chopped, sautéed scallions can be added for extra flavor, and if you must use liquid, try a small amount of chicken bouillon. Serve peas as soon as possible after cooking them.

BUTTERED PEAS

Use plenty of butter and almost no water.

1 pound of pea pods, or 1 package
    frozen peas
A little water or chicken stock, as
    needed
3 tablespoons butter

Dash sugar
Coarse salt
Freshly ground black pepper
1 tablespoon chopped mint or chives
    (optional)

If using frozen peas, partially thaw them. Put them in a heavy-bottomed pan with the butter. Add liquid if necessary. Add the sugar and cook gently for about 10 minutes. Season and add the herbs, if desired. Serves 2.

CHINESE SNOW PEAS

These are young, very tender pea pods. Frozen snow peas are more readily available than fresh ones. They should be thawed and dried, if possible, then sautéed very quickly in oil. They are great for last-minute meals.

1 package frozen pea pods, or
    1 pound fresh pea pods
2 tablespoons sesame, peanut, or
    vegetable oil
1 clove garlic (optional)

1 tablespoon chopped fresh ginger
    (optional)
2 scallions, chopped (optional)
Coarse salt, or soy sauce
Freshly ground black pepper

Dry the pea pods. Heat the oil in a heavy skillet. Add the garlic, ginger, and scallions, if desired. Stir-fry for 2 minutes. Add the pea pods and stir-fry for 3 minutes. Remove and serve immediately. Serves 2-4.

Peppers

Not all peppers are hot, as their name implies. There are endless varieties, ranging from sweet green bell peppers to the small hot red peppers. Large green peppers often turn red or yellow when very ripe, but they are not hot. The very small green peppers may be fiery hot. Those that you will probably use most in cooking or for stuffing are the beautiful green ones found in most markets, the bell peppers. They are rich in vitamin C.

Choose fresh, shiny, unwrinkled peppers. Beware of greasy skins; that false shine, as with cucumbers, is a commercial preparation, and you will have to peel them. This is tedious but best done by holding them over a flame or turning them under the broiler until the skin blisters. Wrap them in a cloth for a few minutes and slip the skin off. Try to get organically grown peppers. The seeds and fibrous dividers inside should all be removed and discarded before you use the peppers.

Peppers are cheap, and stuffed peppers make a filling and nourishing meal.

PEPERONI

These stewed peppers go well with lamb, fish, or chicken. Rice or a potato casserole is a good vegetable accompaniment.

2 red peppers	About 4 tablespoons olive oil
2 green peppers	Coarse salt
1 onion, chopped	Freshly ground black pepper
1 clove garlic, crushed	

Cut the peppers in half and remove the top, seeds, and fibrous portion. Slice them. Combine peppers, onion, and garlic in a heavy skillet and stew in the oil until tender. Season well. Serves 4 as a side dish.

STUFFED PEPPERS
(main dish)

The best stuffings are made up from combinations of the leftovers you have on hand. You can use almost anything—leftover ham, shrimp, fish, chicken, or other meat; mushrooms or mushroom stems; tomatoes; bread or rice; herbs and spices. There are few better ways of using up leftovers. Just don't fill the peppers too full.

A light vegetable dish or a salad goes well with the peppers.

4 large green peppers	Dash thyme
1 onion, chopped	Squeeze of lemon
2 tablespoons butter or oil	1 clove garlic, crushed
1 small cup cooked rice or	Coarse salt
breadcrumbs	Freshly ground black pepper
1 small cup leftover meat (veal,	1 cup stock, bouillon, oil, or
beef, pork, or lamb), chopped	Tomato Sauce (page 166)
1 tablespoon chopped fresh parsley	¼ cup grated cheese (optional)

Preheat oven to 350 degrees. Cut tops off peppers and carefully remove seeds and fibrous inside, taking care not to break them. Sauté onion in butter until soft. Combine in a mixing bowl with the rice or breadcrumbs, meat, parsley, and seasonings. Mix thoroughly and stuff the peppers. Place in a baking dish and add Tomato Sauce or other liquid to a depth of about ¼ inch. Sprinkle tops of peppers with grated cheese, if desired. Bake from 45 minutes to 1 hour. Serves 4.

Squash

There are two basic kinds of squash, although there are several varieties in each category: summer squash, which has a thin and usually edible skin; and winter squash, which has a very thick skin too tough to eat. Both are very cheap in season.

Winter squash is delicious cooked with honey, brown sugar, or molasses, and it goes with pork, ham, or sausages. Acorn, Hubbard, Butternut, Turban and pumpkin are among the varieties available. Summer squash is superb when cooked in butter, or with peppers, tomatoes, or cheese in casseroles. Besides the common yellow crookneck or straight-neck, try cooking the pretty white pattypan. Its scalloped edges make it especially attractive when stuffed.

BAKED SQUASH

During the winter months this makes a good meal with turkey, ham, or pork. It is also good with vegetable casseroles and stews.

1 large winter squash or 2 small squash	Dash nutmeg or ginger
4 tablespoons butter	Dash mace or sesame seeds (optional)
2 tablespoons honey, dark molasses, or brown sugar	Coarse salt
Dash cinnamon	Freshly ground black pepper
	A little water or sherry

Preheat oven to 375 degrees. Cut the squash into quarters or thick slices. Remove seeds and stringy portions. Place in a greased baking dish and dot with butter. Add the honey, spices, and seasonings. Pour in a little sherry or water to keep them from sticking to the bottom of the dish. Cover and bake for about 45 minutes, uncovering for the last 15 minutes to allow the squash to brown. Serves 4.

Note: You can steam the squash first in a small amount of boiling water until tender and then brown under the broiler with the butter and spices.

STUFFED SQUASH
(main dish)

Leftover peas, chopped ham, chicken or other meat, etc., can be used here. Using this recipe as a guide, invent your own stuffings.

Don't serve anything too heavy with this dish. A green vegetable or salad would be plenty.

2 medium-sized winter squash
1 small cup cooked rice, noodles, or
    breadcrumbs
1 small cup sausage meat or chopped
    cheese
Dash sage
1 teaspoon crushed juniper berries
    (optional)

1 teaspoon dark mustard
2 tablespoons honey, dark molasses,
    or brown sugar
1 tablespoon chopped fresh parsley
Coarse salt
Freshly ground black pepper
A small amount of water

Preheat oven to 375 degrees. Cut the squash in half and scoop out the seeds. In a bowl, combine the remaining ingredients. Stuff into the squash. Put a little water in the bottom of a greased baking dish and bake the squash, covered, for 45 minutes to 1 hour. Uncover for the last 10 minutes to brown. Serves 4.

SUMMER SQUASH WITH CHEESE
(main dish)

Rice or potatoes go well with this dish. Leftover meat can be chopped and added to the casserole.

Zucchini can be used here instead of summer squash.

1 pound summer squash, sliced
2 green or red peppers, seeded and
    chopped
1 onion, chopped
1 clove garlic, crushed
3 tablespoons butter or oil
3 tomatoes or 1 medium can

    tomatoes, chopped
1 teaspoon brown sugar
Dash basil
Coarse salt
Freshly ground black pepper
½ cup grated cheese

Preheat oven to 350 degrees. Sauté the peppers, onion, and garlic in oil or butter until limp. In a greased casserole or baking dish layer the squash, the pepper-onion mixture, and the tomatoes, seasoning as you go. If you are using canned tomatoes, add some of the juice. If you are using fresh ones, add a little water to the bottom of the dish to keep the squash from sticking. Top with the cheese and bake for about 20 minutes, or until the squash is tender. Serves 4.

Note: This dish is good cold.

Tomatoes

Without tomatoes, which Cortés discovered on his conquest of Mexico (probably the only good thing he did in the New World), the whole of cookery would be different—and much the worse for it. They go with almost everything and are as versatile and basic as onions.

Serve them with or in fish, poultry, meat, vegetables, rice, pasta, and eggs. Fresh and dried herbs (particularly basil, thyme, and tarragon) go very well with them.

To peel tomatoes easily, either run them over a gas flame or drop them into boiling water for a few minutes until their skins loosen and can be slipped off readily.

TOMATOES PROVENÇALE

Serve this dish with meat, fish, or poultry and a potato casserole. It also goes well with vegetable casseroles lacking tomatoes.

4 medium-sized tomatoes	1 clove garlic, crushed
¼ cup breadcrumbs	2 tablespoons chopped fresh parsley
Coarse salt	About ¼ cup olive oil
Freshly ground black pepper	

Preheat oven to 350 degrees. Cut the tomatoes in half. Combine the breadcrumbs, seasonings, and parsley. Spread the mixture on the top of each tomato half and press down firmly. Coat tomatoes with olive oil. Brown slightly in the broiler, then bake for 15–20 minutes. Serves 4.

STUFFED TOMATOES
(main dish)

Tomatoes make excellent cases for using up bits and pieces and leftovers. Try any or several of the following suggestions: leftover lamb, beef, chicken, fish; chopped liver, kidneys, bacon; peas, beans, carrots, mushroom stems, currants; curry powder or curried leftovers; breadcrumbs, wheatgerm, chopped noodles, etc. See Rice-Stuffed Tomatoes (below) for general guidelines and instructions.

RICE-STUFFED TOMATOES

This is a basic recipe and can be changed around as you wish. Green vegetables, salad, and grilled meat go well with this dish. It is particularly good with lamb.

4 large tomatoes	Dash oregano or basil
4 tablespoons olive oil	1 teaspoon tomato purée
1 clove garlic, chopped	(optional)
1 onion, minced	Coarse salt
½ cup rice	Freshly ground black pepper
1½ cups chicken broth	

Preheat oven to 350 degrees. Make a little hole in the top of the tomatoes and, with a teaspoon, carefully scoop out the flesh without damaging the skin. In a skillet, heat the oil. Add the onion and garlic and cook until the onion has softened. Add the rice and cook, stirring, for 3 minutes. Add the chicken broth and simmer without stirring until the broth is almost absorbed and the rice is almost cooked, about 20 minutes. Add the herbs, season well, and stuff the mixture carefully into the tomatoes. Add a small amount of water to the pan to keep the tomatoes from scorching. Bake for 20–30 minutes. Serves 4.

VEGETARIAN STUFFED TOMATOES

Serve these with rice or noodles and a green vegetable.

12 medium-sized tomatoes	2 tablespoons raisins
3 hard-boiled eggs, chopped	1 cup cream cheese or sour cream
¼ pound ground or chopped nuts	Dash basil
1 onion or 2 scallions, including	Coarse salt
green part, chopped	Freshly ground black pepper
3 tablespoons butter	1 tablespoon chopped fresh parsley

Preheat oven to 350 degrees. Cut holes in the tops of the tomatoes and carefully scoop out the pulp with a spoon. Put pulp in a mixing bowl with the eggs and nuts. Sauté the onion in butter until soft. Add it to the bowl. Add raisins, cream cheese or sour cream, and seasonings. Mix well and correct seasoning. Stuff the tomatoes and place them in a greased baking dish. Add a small amount of water. Bake for 25–30 minutes. Serves 4.

See also
TOMATOES ON TOAST, page 227
TOMATO AND EGG CASSEROLE, page 213

FRIED GREEN TOMATOES

Sometimes green tomatoes appear on the market. They are usually cheap and have a delicious, slightly tart taste.

Serve them with meat dishes, fish, or chicken, but serve them hot and crisp. If they wait around for long, they'll be soggy.

You will get a different and exotic flavor by dipping them in soy sauce, Worcestershire sauce, or Tabasco before dredging them in flour.

Add extra spices and seasonings to the flour that you roll them in. Turn them just before you cook them, to prevent flour from getting moist.

6 medium-sized tomatoes, sliced	**Thyme, basil, dry mustard, or**
Soy sauce, Tabasco, or Worcester-	**cayenne pepper, mixed with the**
shire sauce (optional)	**flour**
Freshly ground black pepper	**Oil for frying (to cover bottom**
Flour for dredging (preferably	**of pan)**
wholewheat)	**Coarse salt**

Heat the oil in a skillet. Dip tomatoes in sauce if you like, and then into the seasoned flour. When the oil is smoking in the skillet, add the tomatoes and fry them on both sides until crisp and brown. Do not crowd them in the skillet. Salt and serve. Serves 4.

Turnips

When they are cooked properly turnips are a delicious vegetable. There are two kinds of turnips on the market: the white turnip (which is most suited to these recipes) and the yellow turnip, or rutabaga. It is tougher than the white and should be boiled 30 minutes or longer; it can then be sautéed or browned with roasts. Young white turnips may be steamed for 20–30 minutes and seasoned. Old ones might be blanched first, then boiled or glazed.

They are also very good raw, sliced thin or shredded in salads.

To prepare turnips, remove the tops and peel turnips with a paring knife. If tender, the tops of white turnips can be cooked as greens.

Instead of boiling them in water, try boiling them in milk, which can then be used for a Béchamel Sauce (page 107) or Sauce Mornay (page 115).

See Glazed Carrots (page 249) for tips on glazing turnips.

Cooked turnips are particularly good with roasts or fowl (duck, goose, ham, pork, beef), with sausages, and with vegetable casseroles. They absorb fat easily and come out succulent and well-seasoned when roasted with meat or poultry. Sometimes they are just sautéed in butter after boiling.

BRAISED TURNIPS

Braised turnips can be served as they are, or with Béchamel Sauce (page 107), Sauce Mornay (page 115), or Tomato Sauce (page 166). The addition of chopped fresh parsley, diced ham, chives, diced bacon, sour cream, or caraway seeds also improves them.

Serve with meat dishes or a vegetable casserole.

1½ pounds white turnips, peeled and cubed	Coarse salt
4 tablespoons butter	Freshly ground black pepper
Chicken stock or bouillon, to cover	Chopped fresh chives or parsley (optional)

Sauté the turnips lightly in the butter and add stock to cover. Cover pan and cook for about 30 minutes, until the stock has evaporated and the turnips are tender. Season, and add herbs, if desired. Serves 4.

FRIED TURNIPS

Turnips are very good cooked like this. They absorb the taste of the bacon without becoming greasy, and they're not as fattening as potatoes, although it's hard to distinguish them from potatoes in appearance.

Use only tender white turnips for this recipe. Serve with meats and casseroles in place of the ubiquitous potato.

If you have a roast or casserole in the oven, you can start the turnips by sautéing them in the bacon fat, then transferring them to a baking dish and letting them finish cooking in the oven along with the roast.

1½ pounds turnips, peeled	Coarse salt
About 3 tablespoons bacon fat, or 4 strips of bacon	Freshly ground black pepper
	1 tablespoon chopped fresh parsley

Either slice turnips thinly, or chop into long strips like French fries. Dry thoroughly. Heat about three tablespoons of bacon fat, or the bacon, in a skillet. When fat is smoking, add the turnips and cook over low heat until brown and tender. Drain turnips, season, and sprinkle with parsley. Serves 4.

Zucchini

These are delicate, smooth-skinned baby marrows (and have much more taste than full-grown marrows). Choose firm, small zucchini. Don't buy the ones with wrinkled skins or those that are soft and squashy to the touch.

They are delicious served with all kinds of meat dishes, fish, and eggs. After they have been tossed in butter they can be served with Sauce Béchamel (page 107), Sauce Mornay (page 115), or Tomato Sauce (page 166).

They go very well with tomatoes and eggplant and can be substituted for summer squash in many recipes.

To stir-fry zucchini Chinese style, drop into boiling water for 5 minutes, slice, then stir-fry in oil according to Basic Stir-Fried Greens (page 112).

ZUCCHINI STEWED IN BUTTER

This dish is particularly good with grilled or roasted meat. You can, if you like, add a chopped clove of garlic to the pan. You might coat the zucchini with a little fresh cream or sour cream when they have been cooked, or serve them with a cream sauce.

1½ pounds zucchini	Freshly ground black pepper
3 tablespoons butter	1 tablespoon chopped chives or
1 tablespoon oil	parsley (optional)
Water or stock if needed	Squeeze lemon juice (optional)
Coarse salt	

Slice the zucchini. Heat the butter and oil in a skillet and add the zucchini, cooking gently over a low flame, covered. Watch to see that they don't get too dry, and add a little water or stock if necessary. When browned and tender, season and sprinkle with herbs and lemon juice. Serves 4.

Salads

The salads in this chapter are divided into main salads, enough for a whole meal, and side salads. Hot garlic bread, cheese and a salad make one of the best meals there is. It doesn't take much more time to prepare a salad than a sandwich, and for a quick meal when you're working hard, or a summer lunch or dinner, nothing could be better. Raw vegetables have a high mineral and vitamin content—particularly vitamin C, which wards off colds.

If you're trying to lose weight it is a good idea to have a salad before your meal. It will fill you up and you'll eat less. In France salad is served after the main course because the vinegar in the dressing spoils the taste of a good wine.

Nothing is better for you than to eat a salad at every meal (except breakfast, heaven forbid). Fruit salads coated with mayonnaise or elaborate mixed salads are fine on their own, but they don't go with a full meal. The simple salad is the best.

When you buy vegetables for salad, choose those that are fresh and that have been trimmed the least. Remove any wilted leaves and wash the lettuce. Dry it thoroughly with a towel, leaf by leaf, so that it will hold a coating of salad dressing. If you don't your salad will be watery. When you've dried the lettuce, put it in a pastic bag in the refrigerator until you are ready for it. This applies to all salad ingredients. Vegetables left in the light and at room temperature start to lose their vitamins.

It would be great to be able to wipe the vegetables instead of washing them, but unless you have an organic garden this is impossible. Vegetables are sprayed so much now that it is scarcely safe to eat the outside leaves and the peel. In any event, they must be washed thoroughly.

Tear lettuce into strips; leave watercress in sprigs. Cut other vegetables into pieces of the same size—cubes, strips, and so on. Use a wooden salad bowl if possible and wipe it out well with paper towels each time you use it.

Salad Dressing

A good salad can be ruined by a bad dressing. Bottled dressings on the whole are appalling, and it is hard to imagine why people insist on buying them when an oil and vinegar dressing is not only cheaper but much better. You should use a good olive oil for dressing. If that seems too expensive, use peanut, soy, sesame, or vegetable oil, but *don't* use corn oil.

If you soak some fat ripe olives in inferior olive oil for a few days, it will improve the taste of the oil.

Cottonseed oil is dangerous since it is contaminated by the poison sprays used to kill the boll weevil. Watch for it when buying canned sardines.

Vinegar can be improved by the addition of fresh herbs. Allow them to stand in the bottle for several days. Tarragon, particularly, will transform cider or white vinegar.

When leafy vegetables have been washed and dried, coat them with a tablespoon of oil (if you are going to serve them soon). Toss them so that every leaf is coated. This will stop moisture from getting in and prevent wilting. Mix the rest of the dressing and pour it on just before you are ready to eat.

Moist vegetables, however, such as tomatoes and mushrooms, are good when marinated in the dressing for an hour or so.

SAUCE VINAIGRETTE
(French Dressing)

This is the basic salad dressing, along with Mayonnaise (page 132). It can be varied by the addition of different fresh herbs. You can mix the dressing right on the salad, adding the oil first, or you can mix it in a bowl or shake it in a bottle and pour it on.

2 tablespoons tarragon, white, or
   red wine vinegar
6 tablespoons olive oil, or a
   substitute (see Salad Dressing,
   above)
¼ teaspoon mustard

Pinch of fresh herbs (optional)
1 garlic clove, crushed into the oil
   and removed before serving
   (optional)
Coarse salt
Freshly ground black pepper

Mix the ingredients together and pour over the salad just before serving. Gently toss to coat the leaves. Makes about ½ cup.

Note: Lemon juice can be used instead of or with the vinegar.

SAUCE RAVIGOTE

This is made by adding a tablespoon chopped capers, a tablespoon chopped onion or scallion and some chopped fresh herbs to Sauce Vinaigrette.

MAYONNAISE

For some reason the idea of making mayonnaise strikes terror into the hearts of even the most accomplished cooks. It is not nearly as difficult as people have been led to believe. It merely requires a little patience, and it is so much better than the bought kind that it is well worth the effort. The trick is to get the oil absorbed into the egg yolks without curdling. If it curdles you have either added too much oil or added the oil too quickly. All you need to do in this case is to add another egg yolk and continue beating until the mixture is smooth.

1 egg yolk	if you have no cayenne
¼ teaspoon dry mustard	Up to 1 cup olive oil
Coarse salt	Lemon juice or vinegar to taste
Cayenne pepper, or black pepper	

Put the egg yolk in a bowl and beat with a fork until it is thick and sticky. Add the mustard, salt, and pepper, beat in, and add the oil one drop at a time to start with, gradually increasing the amount but never pouring it all in in a hurry. When the mayonnaise has reached the right consistency, add the remaining ingredients. If it is too thin, add more oil. If it is too thick, add a little extra lemon juice or vinegar. Makes about 1 cup.

SOY DRESSING

This is especially good for watercress, spinach, avocado, endive, radishes, and tomatoes, as well as for Chinese salads.

6 tablespoons sesame, peanut, soy, or vegetable oil	Freshly ground black pepper
1 teaspoon sugar	1 tablespoon chopped fresh ginger (optional)
2 tablespoons lemon or orange juice	1 clove garlic, crushed (optional)
1–2 teaspoons soy sauce, to taste	1 scallion (including green part), chopped (optional)

If you are using this on a leafy salad, first coat the leaves thoroughly with a couple of tablespoons of the oil. In a small bowl, mix the remaining ingredients. Pour over the salad and toss gently. Makes about ½ cup.

YOGHURT DRESSING

This goes particularly well with cucumbers, beets, mushrooms, and tomatoes.

1 cup yoghurt

3 tablespoons peanut, olive, or
    sesame oil

1 tablespoon lemon juice or vinegar

1 clove garlic, crushed (optional)

Coarse salt

Freshly ground black pepper

Dash soy sauce (optional)

Mix all the ingredients together thoroughly, cover, and refrigerate until needed. Remove the crushed garlic clove before combining dressing with the salad. Makes about 1½ cups.

SIDE SALADS

AVOCADOS

There are two kinds on sale: the tough-skinned, dark ones during the summer and the green-skinned ones during the winter. They are much the same inside. Buy avocados when they're still hard (and cheap), and let them ripen on the windowsill. Ripe ones, unless they're overripe, are usually expensive.

A New York Italian greengrocer was recently heard yelling at a customer who was testing an avocado to see if it was ripe. "Don't press so hard. Squeeze it gently, like a woman; it bruises easy." Avocados are ripe when they are soft at the narrow end as well as at the fat end. Don't refrigerate them until they are ripe, and even then don't bother unless you are storing them. They taste better at room temperature.

Avocado seeds can grow into splendid house plants and they are easy to start. First, spear the seed with 3 or 4 toothpicks around the middle; hang the toothpicks on the rim of a large-mouthed jar or glass, with the widest end of the avocado seed inverted. Fill the glass with water, up to and covering the bottom of the seed. In 2 or 3 weeks it will sprout roots and you can plant it in a pot. Keep it well watered and you will soon have a lovely plant with broad, smooth leaves.

The best way to serve avocado is with Sauce Vinaigrette (page 131). Cut it in half, remove the stone, squeeze some lemon juice over the flesh to keep it from browning when exposed to the air, and fill with the dressing. If it is a particularly good avocado, it will need no more than lemon juice.

Avocados are very good sliced in salads.

CABBAGE AND RADISH SALAD

This is a good salad for parties because a cabbage head is cheap and goes a long way. If you don't need all of it, cut off what you need and wrap the remainder in plastic and refrigerate it. Use the large heads of white cabbage.

1 head cabbage, shredded	¾ cup olive oil
1 bunch radishes, sliced	Salt
Juice of a garlic clove	Freshly ground black pepper
Juice of 1 lemon	

Wash and dry cabbage. Shred it finely against the grain and put it in a large salad bowl. Add the sliced radishes. In a separate small bowl, mix the dressing. Squeeze the juice from a clove of garlic into the bowl, or, if you don't have a garlic squeezer, crush it with a fork so that the juices are squeezed out. Remove the clove. Add remaining ingredients and mix well. Pour the dressing over the cabbage and radishes and toss well, correct seasoning, and serve. A head of cabbage makes enough salad for about 10 people.

COLE SLAW WITH CARAWAY SEEDS

Sausages, cold ham, and cold pork are particularly good with this salad.

Shred a firm head of white cabbage against the grain. Finely chop an onion and a green pepper or two. Make a Sauce Vinaigrette (page 131), or Mayonnaise (page 132), and to the sauce add a little dark mustard, a dash of brown sugar and a tablespoon of caraway seeds. You can, if you wish, add some chopped fresh parsley. Toss in a bowl, correct seasoning and serve. Serves 6–8.

Note: For a single-person salad or to serve fewer people, shred the amount of cabbage you want and wrap the rest in plastic. It will keep for several days in the refrigerator and can be cooked or used for other salads. (See vegetable section.)

RAW CARROT SALAD

This salad is good with buttered toast. It also goes well with curry, pasta, and chicken, pork, or veal.

Shred three or four carrots, a couple of apples (with their skins on) and some radishes (use the big Japanese icicle radish if you can find it). Soften 2 tablespoons raisins in a little warm water and dry them before you add them to the salad. Grate about half a pound of mild hard cheese and combine it in a salad bowl with the other ingredients. Toss in 6 tablespoons oil and add the juice of half a lemon mixed with a table-spoon of mustard. Season and serve. Enough for 4.

Note: To prevent the apple from turning brown, squeeze some lemon onto it while preparing the other ingredients.

See also
RAW CARROTS IN LEMON JUICE, page 248

CELERY AND BEET SALAD

A good winter salad, when lettuce is expensive, this goes well with meat, chicken, turkey, or pasta.

Make a mayonnaise (page 132). Cut about 6 stalks celery into thin strips about 3 inches long. Slice 2 cooked beets. Put the mayonnaise into a salad bowl. Add the beets and, if you like, squeeze a little garlic on them. Add celery and a squeeze of lemon and toss the whole thing. It will turn quite pink. Serves 4.

Note: This is a good single-person salad. Since it is a bother to make the mayonnaise just for one, use the bottled kind (if you can stand it) or mix together a little oil, vinegar and lemon juice and use that instead. We'd prefer the latter.

See also
SALAD APHRODITE, page 247

CUCUMBERS IN YOGHURT

Popular throughout the Middle East and the Mediterranean, this is a cool and refreshing summer salad. It is particularly good with curry. If you can use Homemade Yoghurt (page 237), it will be superb.

2 cucumbers, peeled and sliced	Coarse salt
½ cup yoghurt	Freshly ground black pepper
1 tablespoon white wine vinegar	Chopped fresh mint, basil, or
or lemon juice	dill (optional)
1 clove garlic, crushed	

Peel and slice two cucumbers. If you have the time, salt the cucumbers and leave them for half an hour to remove the excess moisture. Pat them dry. Combine yoghurt with vinegar or lemon juice, a crushed clove of garlic, salt and pepper. If you like, sprinkle the mixed salad with fresh herbs. Serves 4.

ENDIVE AND WATERCRESS SALAD

A lot of endive is expensive, but one isn't. Serve this with meat (especially lamb), chicken or fish. You can use one of two dressings here, either a Sauce Vinaigrette (page 131) with a garlic clove crushed in it (if you like) or Soy Dressing (page 132). The Soy Dressing is good with lamb, rice, fried foods and Chinese dishes.

1 bunch watercress	1 clove garlic, crushed (optional)
1 endive	Coarse salt
Sauce Vinaigrette (page 131) or	Freshly ground black pepper
Soy Dressing (page 132)	

Wash and dry a bunch of watercress. Pull apart and dry the leaves of the endive. If they are very big, tear them in half. Put them in a salad bowl and add the dressing, coating them with oil first. Correct seasoning. Serves 4.

Note: For one person, buy just the endive and make a little dressing. A whole bunch of watercress would be too much and it doesn't keep that well.

GREEN SALAD

A green salad is a green salad is a green salad. Nothing else. It should be plain and simple and it is best served after the main course. It should consist of fresh green leafy vegetables (the brightest green possible) such as lettuce (not iceberg—it is best shredded in other salads since it is rather tasteless on its own), spinach leaves, endive, watercress, or young dandelion leaves. Occasionally diced green peppers, celery, or fennel may be added. Fresh green herbs such as basil, tarragon, mint, chives, or parsley are also good. Dried straw from an ancient bottle of old herbs *won't* do. Leave out the herbs if that's all you have on hand.

Keep the salad green. Don't add other vegetables. And remember that green salad is supposed to be a light, digestive salad, not one that you can't finish, so don't serve it with mayonnaise.

The leaves *must* be dry, or the salad will be watery and the dressing diluted. Wash the leaves, drain them in a colander, shake them out, then *dry them one by one.* Don't use paper towels. It's a waste—you use too much because they get so wet. Drying the leaves is boring, but it shouldn't take more than ten minutes and it really is worth it.

When the leaves are dry, tear them into more or less uniform pieces. Put them in a salad bowl, add a tablespoon or two of oil, and toss the leaves with a salad spoon and fork until every leaf is coated. The oil forms a protective film and prevents the leaves from wilting.

Then make the dressing, Sauce Vinaigrette (page 131), reducing the oil called for according to how much you have used in coating the leaves. Add a crushed clove of garlic if you like. When ready to serve, coat the salad with the dressing. Your salad should be fresh, crisp, and green, with the leaves shiny under the delightful dressing you have made.

MARINATED MUSHROOMS

The mushrooms that you find on the market seem to retain their flavor and texture much better raw than when they are cooked. Marinated overnight, they absorb all the sauce and are absolutely delicious the next day. Serve these marinated, raw mushrooms alone or with rice dishes, pasta, meat, or chicken. A main-dish salad can be made by adding hard-boiled eggs, sliced tomatoes, peppers, pitted olives, capers, and lettuce, all tossed with Sauce Vinaigrette (page 131). Fresh French or Italian bread, red wine, and cheese make a meal.

ITALIAN PEPPER SALAD

This salad is great with steaks or hamburgers. To make it the true Italian way you should char the skins of the whole peppers over a gas flame and scrape the skin off. It is not really necessary, but it does give the peppers a delicious roasted flavor, and it helps them to absorb the dressing more easily. Anchovies and lettuce leaves are good with the peppers. If the peppers have been roasted, you can keep them in a tightly sealed jar for several weeks in the oil.

Choose three or four fresh red, green or yellow peppers (a mixture will look attractive). Char them if you wish. Slice them and pour about 5–6 tablespoons good olive oil on them. Add a little vinegar to taste (about a tablespoon). Season them and serve. Enough for 4.

RADISH SALAD

Radishes are delicious served raw with coarse salt and unsalted butter. They are also good in a sour cream dressing on toast, or served in an oil-and-vinegar dressing with vegetable casseroles, fish, and grilled or roasted meat.

For the sour cream version, trim the ends off a bunch of radishes and leave them whole, unless they are big, in which case slice them. Mix together half a cup of sour cream and a teaspoon of sugar, a tablespoon of vinegar and a small onion, chopped. Season and add a little chopped fresh parsley if desired. Serve on hot buttered toast.

Or, slice the radishes and marinate them in a combination of 5 tablespoons oil, 2 tablespoons vinegar, 1 tablespoon capers, dash of chili powder and salt and pepper. Leave them for about half an hour and serve. Both recipes are enough for 4 people.

POTATO SALAD

Homemade Potato Salad is delicious with your own Mayonnaise (page 132) or with the dressing below. Serve hot with sausages, or cold with chicken and most other meats. Chopped cooked bacon is good crumbled into the salad.

1½ pounds potatoes, boiled in their
    skins
Mayonnaise (page 132) or
3 tablespoons white wine or stock
2 tablespoons white wine vinegar
    or tarragon vinegar

1 teaspoon dark mustard
Coarse salt
Freshly ground black pepper
6 tablespoons olive oil
3 scallions, chopped

While boiling potatoes, make Mayonnaise or this dressing: Combine white wine or stock with vinegar. Add dark mustard and season. Very slowly beat in the olive oil, starting with just a few drops.

Slip potatoes out of their skins, and slice. The potatoes should be warm to absorb the dressing properly. Put in a large bowl with the scallions and coat thoroughly with the dressing. Serves 4–6.

RICE SALAD

This substantial salad is good by itself or with seafood, cold chicken, veal, or lamb. Chopped canned pimientos, cooked green peas, diced mushrooms, olives, or cucumbers are good additions.

½ pound cooked rice, hot
Sauce Vinaigrette (page 131)
4 tomatoes, peeled and chopped
2 green peppers, chopped

1 tablespoon chopped parsley or
    chives
3 hard-boiled eggs, sliced
Paprika

Combine rice with Sauce Vinaigrette and add tomatoes, peppers, and herbs. Toss all together. Arrange sliced eggs on top and sprinkle with paprika. Serves 4–6.

SPINACH SALAD

A couple of armfuls of spinach are often reduced to a paltry cupful when cooked, and if you're cooking for other people it can be a very embarrassing moment when you hand round the spinach with a tea-spoon. If spinach is young and fresh it can be delicious served raw in a salad, and it goes a long way. A great dressing to put on it is Roquefort Dressing. We do not mean the stuff that comes in bottles and tastes like library paste. We mean the cheese, mashed in a bowl with oil and vine-gar and poured onto the spinach. It makes a lovely thick creamy sauce. Since Roquefort cheese is expensive, blue cheese can be a substitute.

Cooked, sliced potatoes and whole baby tomatoes are good in this salad, and it goes well with lamb, beef, pasta, chops, and grilled meats. It is best served after the main course. Raw spinach is also good with sliced oranges and Soy Dressing (page 132).

For 4 people use 1 pound of spinach.

Half a cup of heavy cream mixed with a few tablespoons of oil, beaten in gradually, a squeeze of lemon, and salt and pepper also makes a good dressing for spinach. A dash of nutmeg can be added, too.

ROQUEFORT OR BLUE CHEESE DRESSING

½ cup Roquefort or blue cheese, at room temperature
4 tablespoons olive oil

1 tablespoon white wine vinegar
Coarse salt
Freshly ground black pepper

Mash the cheese in a mixing bowl. Slowly add the oil and beat well. Add the vinegar and seasonings, mix thoroughly and pour over the spinach. This will keep for a couple of weeks in the refrigerator. If you make it with blue cheese, it is called Blue Cheese Dressing, not Roque-fort.

The spinach must be thoroughly washed (at least three or four times to get the grit out) and dried with a towel. If it is wet the dressing won't stick to it and the salad will be watery.

TOMATO SALAD

Whether served with another dish or on its own after the main course, or even as a starter, this salad seems to go with almost any meal that doesn't include a lot of tomatoes.

Tomatoes are good sliced and sprinkled with a little sugar, some chopped herbs such as mint, parsley or basil, and salt and pepper. They are also delicious sliced with a couple of chopped scallions (including the green part), some chopped dill, parsley or basil, and Sauce Vinaigrette (page 131).

Allow about one large tomato per person.

For a single-person meal, slice a tomato, add a tablespoon of oil, a dash of vinegar and a few chopped fresh herbs if you have them.

Tomatoes benefit from sitting in the dressing for a while before they are served. This is not the case with leaf vegetables, nor should tomatoes be mixed into a leaf salad until you are ready to serve it. Their juice can make the leaves start to wilt.

WATERCRESS AND RADISH SALAD

This salad is particularly good with lamb chops. It also goes with Chinese food, steak, chicken, and fish.

Wash and dry thoroughly a bunch of watercress, using a towel to dry the leaves. Trim the tops of a bunch of radishes, wash and dry them, and unless they are very big leave them whole or cut them in half. Make a Soy Dressing (page 132) with orange juice and a clove of garlic. Remember to toss the cress well in a little of the oil before you add the rest of the dressing. Serves 4.

Note: Dandelions and endive are very good in this combination.

CHICK PEA SALAD

This is a good party dish. It is cheap and attractive and it goes a long way. Particularly good with curries, it is also great with cold lamb, chicken, ham, and tongue. It can be served on oiled lettuce leaves, and you can add diced canned pimientos, green peppers, diced celery, and a teaspoon of horseradish combined with the dressing. Try a garnish of sliced tomatoes.

1 cup cooked or canned chick peas, heated

3 tablespoons olive, sesame, or peanut oil

1 tablespoon white wine vinegar

1 clove garlic, crushed (optional)

1 onion, chopped

1 tablespoon chopped fresh parsley

Dash cayenne

Squeeze of lemon

Coarse salt and freshly ground pepper

Combine oil, vinegar, and garlic, if desired. Coat chick peas with the mixture and marinate for 1 hour, or overnight if possible. Warm peas absorb the dressing more readily.

Before serving, sprinkle onion and parsley over the peas. A dash of cayenne and a squeeze of lemon are nice if you like. Serves 3.

LENTIL SALAD

Lentils are cheap and very good for you. Unlike dried beans, they don't take hours to cook. They should be warm when the dressing is added, and they improve if allowed to marinate for a while. This dish goes well with cold pork, ham, tongue, chicken, and turkey. Lentils can also be prepared like White Bean Salad (below).

1 cup cooked lentils, warm
4 tablespoons olive oil
1 tablespoon vinegar or lemon juice
1 tablespoon mustard
1 tablespoon chopped fresh parsley
   Coarse salt
   Freshly ground black pepper

1 small onion, chopped
4 anchovies, chopped (optional)
8 Italian or Greek olives, pitted
   (optional)
2 tomatoes, quartered, or 8 cherry
   tomatoes, halved

Combine olive oil, vinegar or lemon juice, mustard, and parsley. Add to the lentils, season (go easy on the salt), and toss well. Set aside to marinate for 1 hour or more.

Mix chopped onions and anchovies and olives, if you like, with the lentils. Check the seasoning and garnish with tomatoes. Serves 3–4 as a side salad.

WHITE BEAN SALAD

This is great with cold lamb, pork, or ham. The beans should be warm when they're coated with the dressing, then marinated for several hours before you serve them. This is a good salad to make a day in advance. If you are using canned beans, warm them through and drain them well.

1 cup white beans, cooked and
   drained
4 tablespoons olive oil
1 tablespoon white wine vinegar
   or lemon juice
1–2 cloves garlic, crushed
   Coarse salt
   Freshly ground black pepper

1 small onion or 3 scallions (with
   tops), chopped
1 tablespoon chopped fresh dill,
   basil, mint, or parsley
2 hard-boiled eggs, halved
   (optional)
1 tomato, sliced

Combine olive oil, vinegar or lemon juice, and garlic. Mix with beans, season with salt and plenty of freshly ground black pepper, and marinate.

Mix the onion with the beans and herbs, and garnish, if you wish, with eggs and sliced tomatoes. Serves 2–3.

Note: White beans can be substituted for red ones in Kidney Bean Salad (page 148).

ANTIPASTO

Although this dish is traditionally eaten before the spaghetti or other pasta is brought on, it is so filling and good that it stands on its own. If you are entertaining, it makes a cheap and simple last-minute meal. Make the dish look attractive; it can be served in a salad bowl, but it looks prettier on a plate. Serve it with plenty of Italian or French bread and red wine.

On a large flat dish arrange a bed of lettuce leaves which have been washed, well dried and tossed in a tablespoon of oil. Then look around and see what you have. There are no hard and fast rules about this dish. Here are the basic ingredients: Slices of salami (choose good red salami with white fat; if the skin is dry and cracked don't buy it); slices of ham; a can of tuna or sardines; a couple of hard-boiled eggs cut into quarters; about 3 tomatoes, quartered; a small can of artichoke hearts, if you like; a small can of pimientos, sliced; some small whole radishes; some green or black olives; some Marinated Mushrooms (page 137); and some small slices of good Italian cheese.

Then mix together about 6 tablespoons olive oil, 2 tablespoons vinegar (red wine, if possible), a tablespoon of dark mustard, squeeze of lemon juice and a crushed clove of garlic (optional), salt and pepper. Pour it over the salad and sprinkle with chopped fresh parsley. Enough for 4–6, depending on how generous you were with the ingredients.

EGGS MAYONNAISE

One of the simplest and most attractive salads there is. It can be served as an hors d'oeuvre. Since it is extremely filling you can serve it plain for lunch or dolled up with diced cucumbers and tomatoes, black olives, anchovies, celery cut in strips, and strips of canned pimiento arranged over the top—or whatever you like for a summer dinner. Serve the eggs with thinly sliced toast.

Allow three halves of egg per person for lunch and at least two eggs each for dinner. To find out how to boil an egg, see page 149. Meanwhile, make the Mayonnaise, page 132.

Peel the eggs, cut them in half, pour the mayonnaise on them and scatter a little fresh parsley on top. A sprinkle of Cayenne or paprika looks good.

It is probably easier to serve these on individual plates rather than transferring the eggs from a serving dish, which can be a rather messy business.

MAIN SALADS

BEEF SALAD

This is good food for a party. It looks attractive, and by adding other leftovers you can stretch it. Cooked beans, beets, potatoes, broccoli, zucchini, cauliflower, and so on can be added. It can also be made in advance and it improves if it is marinated in the dressing. Use rare roast beef or leftover steak. Well-done meat is best saved for stuffed cabbage or a bean dish.

Cut the meat into thin strips. Place in a large bowl. Add 3 chopped scallions (including green part), 4 chopped pickles, 4 chopped tomatoes, 2 tablespoons chopped parsley, 2 tablespoons capers.

Make a Sauce Vinaigrette (page 131), and add 2 tablespoons dark mustard to it. Mix it thoroughly with the ingredients in the salad bowl and leave it until you are ready.

Put 3 eggs on to boil.

Wash and thoroughly dry a head of lettuce or watercress (or both).

Tear the lettuce leaves into smaller pieces and coat them thoroughly with a tablespoon of oil.

Slice the eggs.

When ready to serve, toss in the lettuce or watercress and taste for seasoning. Decorate with hard-boiled egg slices and sprinkle with a little chopped fresh parsley. Serves 4–6, depending on the amount of meat.

CHICKEN SALAD

Use leftover cooked chicken for this recipe. Cooked potatoes, cooked peas, or other suitable leftover vegetables can also be added, as can tuna fish, chopped ham or tongue.

Put 3 eggs on to boil. Slice the chicken meat. Wash and thoroughly dry a head of lettuce. Tear lettuce leaves into pieces and put them in a salad bowl. Toss well in a tablespoon of oil.

Cut 4 tomatoes into quarters (or smaller if they are very big), chop up 3 or 4 stalks of celery and put in the salad bowl, together with the chicken.

Make a Mayonnaise (page 132). The eggs should be ready by now. Cut them into quarters and set them aside. Toss the salad ingredients well in the mayonnaise. Arrange the eggs on the top, sprinkle with paprika, and serve. Enough for 4–6, depending on how much chicken you have.

FISH SALAD

This is an excellent way to use up any kind of cold leftover white fish. Serve with garlic bread and white wine or beer.

1 bunch watercress, washed and dried	2 tablespoons horseradish
1 tablespoon oil	2 tablespoons oil
1 pound cooked white fish, picked over for bones, and chopped	Squeeze of lemon
	Coarse salt
4 tomatoes, chopped	Freshly ground black pepper
1½ tablespoons capers	1 tablespoon chopped fresh dill or parsley (optional)
½ cup sour cream	2 hard-boiled eggs, sliced

Place watercress in a bowl and coat with oil. Add fish, tomatoes, and capers.

In a small bowl, mix sour cream, horseradish, oil, a good squeeze of lemon, and salt and pepper. Add chopped fresh dill or parsley if you like.

Pour over the salad, mix well, and garnish with slices of egg. Serves 2–3.

HERRING SALAD

This is a ten-minute meal. Put a couple of eggs on to boil when you come in. Herring goes with beer and wholewheat or black bread spread thickly with unsalted butter.

2 hard-boiled eggs, quartered	½ cup chopped cooked or canned beets
1 jar creamed herring	
3 pickles, chopped	1 onion, chopped

1 apple, chopped
Lemon juice
Extra oil, as needed
Vinegar, if needed
Coarse salt

Freshly ground black pepper
1 head lettuce, washed and dried
1 tablespoon oil
Chopped fresh parsley or dill, to
garnish

Cut the herring into small pieces and put it in a small bowl with its cream. Add pickles, beets, and chopped onion. Chop apple and squeeze a little lemon juice on it to prevent discoloration. Add to other ingredients.

Coat lettuce leaves thoroughly in the oil and arrange them around the sides of a large salad bowl.

Add a little oil, vinegar, and seasonings to herring mixture and pour into the center of the lettuce leaves.

Arrange the hard-boiled eggs in a wheel shape over the herring. Sprinkle with fresh herbs if desired. Enough for 3–4.

SARDINE-STUFFED TOMATOES

For people trying to lose weight this makes a good lunch. It's as easy to prepare as a sandwich, and is much better for you. Suitable leftovers (ham, vegetables, etc.) can be chopped and added to the stuffing.

Omit the rice if you're dieting.

2 large tomatoes
¼ pound cream cheese
1 chopped scallion (or chopped
chives)
1 can sardines, with their oil

Leftover cold rice (optional)
Coarse salt
Freshly ground black pepper
Dash curry powder

Cut the tomatoes in half and scoop out the seeds. In a bowl, combine the cream cheese, scallion, sardines (with their oil), rice and seasonings. Taste, and stuff into the tomatoes. Sprinkle a little curry powder over the top. Serves 2.

FRANKFURTER AND CABBAGE SALAD

This is quite economical and good for entertaining. Dark bread and beer are all you need with it.

Cold cooked frankfurters can be used here, and chopped cooked ham can be added, too. A tablespoon of caraway seeds is a delicious addition.

Kosher frankfurters are the best. Be sure to read the ingredients when you buy franks, and if the chemistry involved in their preparation horrifies you too much, settle for pork sausage. Some health food shops now carry additive-free frankfurters.

4 tomatoes, chopped	mustard
2 red or green peppers, chopped	1 teaspoon tomato purée
6–8 cooked frankfurters, sliced	(optional)
1 head white cabbage, shredded	1 tablespoon caraway seeds
Sauce Vinaigrette (page 131),	(optional)
plus 1 tablespoon dark	

Put chopped tomatoes and peppers in a salad bowl. Add frankfurters and shredded cabbage.

Combine Sauce Vinaigrette, mustard and tomato purée. Mix well, pour over the salad, and toss thoroughly. Serves 6.

HAM SALAD

Tongue or chicken can be added or substituted here. You may also use leftover cooked potatoes, but they are better cooked fresh and coated with the dressing while they are still warm. Toast or dark bread is good with this salad, along with beer.

Make a Mayonnaise (page 132) and add a tablespoon of dark mustard to it.

Put about 1½ pounds cooked, sliced potatoes in the salad bowl with a half a pound of diced, cooked ham. Coat with the mayonnaise. Chop a couple of scallions (including the green part) and cut 3 stalks of celery into thin strips about 3 inches long. Put them in the bowl. Add about half a cup of chopped mild cheese, toss well, correct seasoning and serve. Serves 4.

CHEESE AND WATERCRESS SALAD

Use a mild Cheddar or similar semi-soft cheese.

This is good with cold meat or chicken, or on its own with buttered toast and beer.

Wash and thoroughly dry a bunch of watercress. Toss in a salad bowl in a tablespoon of oil. Add half a pound of diced cheese, 2 diced green peppers, and about 8 pitted black olives (the good Greek or Italian kind).

Mix 5 tablespoons oil with 1 tablespoon dark mustard and 2 tablespoons red wine vinegar. Add a crushed clove of garlic, if you like. Season with coarse salt and freshly ground black pepper. Serves 4.

RICE AND MEAT SALAD

This is a spicy salad and is very good for parties or large groups. Try to get the dressing on the rice while the rice is hot. You can use leftover cooked lamb, veal, chicken, ham, pork, or rare beef. If you like curry, put in plenty of curry powder.

2 cucumbers, peeled, seeded, and
   chopped
½ pound meat, cut into thin strips
½ pound cooked rice
   Yoghurt Dressing (page 132)
1 tablespoon curry powder
1 teaspoon ginger
   Dash nutmeg
   Dash cinnamon

4 stalks celery, cut into thin strips
3 apples, chopped
   Squeeze of lemon
   Small can anchovies, drained and
      chopped
¼ pound mixed peanuts and
   almonds, chopped
2 hard-boiled eggs, chopped, to
   garnish

Marinate the meat and cooked rice in Yoghurt Dressing (page 132) to which spices have been added. Salt cucumbers and set aside to drain. Add celery and chopped apples which have been sprinkled with lemon juice to prevent browning. Add anchovies, chopped nuts, and cucumbers. Taste for seasoning, and garnish with chopped eggs, if desired. Serves 4–6.

WALDORF SALAD

This is the famous apple and celery salad said to have been created at the Waldorf Hotel in New York. The basic recipe given here comes from *The Cook Book by "Oscar" of the Waldorf*, by Oscar Tschirky. He was chef resident there and wrote this book in 1896. Unfortunately it is now out of print. The list of ingredients in the market, which includes green turtles, frogs, peacock, buffalo, gooseberries, greengage plums, and twelve kinds of oysters and clams (which you are supposed to tick off as you get them in supply), is enough to drive you wild. What happened to all those fruits and vegetables, not to mention the meat and fish? Steak and potatoes had certainly not yet taken over then.

"Peel two raw apples and cut them into small pieces, say about half an inch square, also cut some celery the same way and mix it with the apple. Be very careful not to let any seeds of the apples be mixed with it. The Salad must be dressed with a good mayonnaise."

The salad is improved by the addition of about 2 tablespoons chopped walnuts, and perhaps some leftover cooked green peas. To stretch it, lettuce leaves coated with a little oil can be arranged around the salad. Use homemade Mayonnaise (page 132).

Serve wholewheat bread and butter and beer or white wine, and you'll have a complete meal.

A slightly different version of Waldorf Salad might include two shredded raw carrots, some canned mandarin oranges, and watercress. Substitute Yoghurt Dressing (page 132) for the Mayonnaise.

Either recipe serves 3–4.

KIDNEY BEAN SALAD

This is a substantial salad and good on its own with dark bread and beer. It also goes with ham, beef, chicken, pork, and curries. Cooked string beans can be added, and white beans or chick peas can be substituted for the kidney beans.

1 cup cooked or canned kidney
   beans, heated through
Sauce Vinaigrette (page 131)
1 clove garlic, crushed
   Dash basil
   Dash oregano
3–4 stalks celery, chopped

3 small pickles, chopped, or 2
   tablespoons pickle relish
1 onion, chopped
1 head lettuce, washed and dried
1 tablespoon oil
3 hard-boiled eggs, sliced

Place beans in a large bowl. Combine Sauce Vinaigrette with garlic, basil, and oregano, and pour it on the beans. Add celery, pickles or relish, and onion.

In a salad bowl, toss the lettuce in oil until thoroughly coated. Line the edges of the bowl. Pour the kidney bean mixture into the middle. Garnish with sliced eggs. Serves 4–6.

SALADE NIÇOISE

This is a great French salad and traditionally contains tuna fish, anchovies, cold cooked string beans, olives, tomatoes, and hard-boiled eggs. Lettuce, peas, pimientos, peppers, and cucumber can also be included.

1 can tuna fish, with oil
2 tomatoes, sliced
2 hard-boiled eggs, sliced
½ cup cooked string beans

½ cup cooked potatoes, diced
¼ pound black olives, pitted
1 small can flat anchovies
   Sauce Vinaigrette (page 131)

Use a deep bowl and build up the ingredients in layers, using the oil from the canned fish. Strew the anchovies and olives over the top. Pour on dressing and toss well. Serves 4.

Eggs and Cheese

Eggs and cheese contain plenty of protein and are excellent meat substitutes, particularly for vegetarians, who should try to eat them every day.

This chapter contains egg dishes for lunch or dinner in addition to basic breakfast eggs, and a guide to the cheeses found most frequently in American markets. Most egg and cheese dishes are quick to make and inexpensive. They make good meals for people studying or in the midst of exams.

EGGS

BOILED EGGS

The joke about not knowing how to boil an egg isn't as silly as one might think. Boiling eggs is an art. Many people fail to produce eggs with soft yolks and tender creamy whites. Sometimes the yolk is hard, with an unpleasant greenish tinge around the yolk, or the white is runny and lumpy.

There are several methods for cooking a perfect egg.

1. Boil for 1 minute, remove from heat and let stand in the water for 5 minutes.
2. Plunge into boiling water, remove pan from heat immediately, and let stand, covered for 10 minutes.
3. Start in cold water. When the water comes to a boil, the eggs should be cooked.

High altitudes require longer cooking time. The best way to work out how much longer is by trial and error.

Eggs taken straight from the fridge and placed in boiling water may crack. Adding a little vinegar to the water isn't foolproof, but it may help. You should remove the water from the heat and gently add eggs with a spoon.

OEUFS MOLLET

These are really soft-boiled eggs. For people who do not have an egg poacher, they are an excellent substitute for poached eggs. Although the traditional way to poach eggs is to drop them into boiling water, I have never been able to find eggs fresh enough in the city. The whites become straggly and float away in the water.

Soft-boil the eggs. Run them under cold water for a few minutes to halt cooking and peel them. Now they are ready for one of the following combinations, which bring eggs out of the breakfast category into a full lunch or dinner dish. They are filling and you don't usually need much more than a salad with them.

Several suggestions for soft-boiled or poached eggs follow. Sauce Mornay can be refrigerated for a day or two, and it has infinite usefulness, so don't hesitate to make it for a one-person meal. Most of these suggestions are for serving 4, allowing one egg per person. They are quite economical.

OEUFS MOLLET SAUCE MORNAY

Make Sauce Mornay (cheese sauce, page 115). Serve the eggs on toast or on leftover heated mashed potatoes and cover with the sauce. Brown lightly under the broiler. Serves 4.

EGGS FLORENTINE

A recipe with the word "florentine" in it means that spinach is one of the ingredients. Serve the eggs on a bed of spinach, and cover with Sauce Mornay (page 115). Serves 4.

EGGS ON RICE

This is a good way to use up leftover rice. Put a cup of cooked rice into a baking dish. Heat it through, place the eggs on top and pour on a couple of tablespoons of melted butter seasoned with salt, pepper, and lemon juice. Serves 2.

EGGS ON CORN

Wash and drain a can of sweet corn. Put it in a dish with a couple of tablespoons of butter and seasonings. Heat through. Put the eggs on top and sprinkle with plenty of paprika. Serves 4.

EGGS BENEDICT

Toast and butter 2 English muffins. Put a slice of ham on each half, add the eggs, and cover with Sauce Hollandaise (page 87). Serves 4.

SCRAMBLED EGGS

Nothing simpler. The secret is to cook the eggs over *low* heat. They should be soft and very slightly runny, not solid and congealed. Allow 1–2 eggs per person.

Tarragon, chives, and fresh parsley are delicious with scrambled eggs.

For scrambled eggs with cheese, a good lunch or supper dish, add 2–3 tablespoons of grated cheese to the eggs before you cook them.

Crack the eggs into a bowl, beat with a fork, and season. Melt some butter in a saucepan and cook the eggs over low heat, stirring constantly. When the mixture starts to thicken, add a little extra butter cut into small pieces. Remove the eggs from the heat before they are completely cooked. The heat of the pan will complete the cooking process, without the eggs getting too hard.

OMELETTE

There is an art to making beautiful omelettes, but anyone can produce a passable and delicious omelette and serve it without embarrassment. Omelettes require little preparation or cooking time; they can use up small amounts of leftovers; and, if a few simple instructions are followed, there is no reason why they should fail.

If you're going in for omelettes seriously, make the lifetime investment in a special curved-edge omelette pan. The eggs will not stick so easily as they do in ordinary pans and they are easier to shape and remove. But don't neglect omelettes if you don't have an omelette pan. A good heavy skillet can also turn out a good omelette. To prevent sticking, soak the skillet in oil the night before. The next day, heat it and pour off the oil. Wipe it, and it's ready for your omelette.

Do not put too many eggs in the pan; 3–4 eggs are enough for a 10-inch pan. Allow 2 eggs per person.

1. Put the eggs in a bowl and stir them well (don't beat them). Season with salt and pepper.
2. Heat the skillet.
3. Put some butter in the skillet. When it is really hot, almost starting to brown, add the eggs.
4. Leave them for a few seconds.
5. With a fork or spatula, pull in the eggs from one side. Tip the pan and let more egg run into their place. Do this all around the pan.
6. When the omelette is slightly runny on the surface and set at the bottom, it is done.
7. Hold a warm plate near the skillet, slide half the unfolded omelette on it to the plate. Flip the other half of the omelette on top of the first half. Sigh with relief if it didn't hit the floor.

Another method is very gently to fold the omelette in half while it is still in the pan. Run spatula under one side to loosen it, then tilt that side of the pan up and flip loosened half onto other half. Gravity will help you. Before removing omelette from pan, loosen other half with spatula. Then just slip it onto your ready plate, or invert pan and flop it onto plate.

FILLED OMELETTES

Most fillings are added just as the eggs are beginning to set. Don't add too much; 1–2 tablespoons per omelette is enough.

Omelette Fines Herbes

Stir a tablespoon of chopped fresh parsley, tarragon, chives, or basil into the omelette *before* cooking.

Cheese Omelette

Stir a tablespoon of freshly grated cheese into the omelette *before* cooking.

Tomato Omelette

Sauté a chopped tomato in 1 tablespoon butter, and add to the eggs just as they are beginning to set.

Bacon Omelette

Add 2 strips cooked, chopped bacon (drained). Sprinkle on the eggs just as they are beginning to set.

Ham Omelette

Combine a slice of chopped ham and a tablespoon of chopped fresh parsley. Add to the eggs as they are beginning to set.

Mushroom Omelette

Sauté ½ cup of chopped mushrooms in a little butter and cream. Add to the eggs as they are beginning to set.

Leftovers Omelette

Heat in a little butter a couple of tablespoons chopped chicken, meat, vegetables, curry, casseroles, or seafood (whatever you like). Add to the eggs as they are beginning to set.

Potato Omelette

Sauté a cooked, diced potato in a little butter. Add as the eggs are beginning to set.

Spinach Omelette

Sauté a couple of tablespoons cooked, chopped spinach in a little butter; add sour cream if you like. Add as the eggs are beginning to set.

HUEVOS RANCHEROS

This Mexican egg dish is terrific on Sunday morning for a late breakfast. A marvelous smell wafts through the room (not the dish to make in a place where you're not supposed to cook).

The recipe which follows is the genuine Mexican thing, except that chili powder is used instead of chopped fresh chilis. If you can't get tortillas, it's all right to leave them out. The eggs can be cooked in the chili mixture instead of fried separately if you like. Make hollows for them, cover pan and cook over low heat until set.

5 tablespoons lard, bacon fat, or oil
1 onion, chopped
1 clove garlic, crushed
3 tomatoes, chopped
1 teaspoon chili powder, or more, to
    taste
  Coarse salt

Freshly ground black pepper
4 tortillas
4 eggs
4 tablespoons grated Cheddar cheese
1 avocado, sliced and sprinkled with
    lemon juice

Heat 2 tablespoons of the lard in a frying pan. Add the onion and garlic and cook until softened, then add the tomatoes and chilis or chili powder. Simmer until thick. Season.

In a separate pan, heat the rest of the lard and fry the tortillas. Remove and drain. Fry the eggs. Put an egg on each tortilla and spoon on the sauce, sprinkle with cheese, and garnish with a few slices of avocado. Serves 2–4.

PIPÉRADE

Delicious with ham, chicken, and cold meat, or by itself with fresh French or Italian bread. Be careful not to overcook the eggs—they will continue to cook even after they have left the stove.

4 onions, sliced
3 tablespoons olive oil
3 or 4 green and/or red peppers,
    chopped
3 tomatoes, chopped

Dash thyme, basil or marjoram
Coarse salt
Freshly ground black pepper
6 eggs, beaten

In a heavy skillet soften the onions in the oil and add the peppers. Cook for 2 minutes, then add the tomatoes and herbs. Stir in, cover, and let simmer for about 15 minutes, until the mixture is thick. Season, and add the eggs. Scramble them until they are just set. Serves 4.

EGGS WITH HOT SAUSAGE

If they sell *chorizos,* the Spanish hot sausage, in your neighborhood, use them instead of the hot Italian sausage. The Italian sausage is good, but the *chorizos* are more compact. Plenty of cold beer and a salad are needed with this hot dish.

1 onion, chopped
1 tablespoon oil
2 hot sausages, chopped
1 clove garlic, crushed
3 tomatoes, chopped

Coarse salt
Freshly ground black pepper
Dash sugar
4 eggs, beaten

Sauté onion in oil. Add sausage and garlic and cook for 5 minutes. Add tomatoes, salt, pepper, and a dash of sugar. Cook for 5 minutes. Stir eggs into the mixture. Cook over low heat until the eggs are set. Serves 2–3.

BAKED EGGS

Add leftover cooked vegetables to this dish if you like, and serve it as a lunch or supper dish with toast, French bread or muffins.

1 onion, chopped	Coarse salt
2 tablespoons butter	Freshly ground black pepper
6 eggs	Extra butter
1 cup grated cheese	

Soften the onion in the butter. Place in a fireproof casserole dish. Break the eggs in. Add the cheese and seasonings, and dot with a little extra butter. Bake until the eggs are set. Serves 4.

OEUFS A LA TRIPE

This very old French dish has nothing to do with tripe, but it is good with rice, toast, French or Italian bread, and a good tomato or mixed salad.

3 onions, chopped	Cayenne pepper
3 tablespoons butter	Sauce Mornay (cheese sauce, page
6 hard-boiled eggs, sliced	115)
Coarse salt	2 teaspoons dark mustard

Sauté onions in the butter. In a fireproof dish, layer the onions with the hard-boiled eggs, seasoning with salt and Cayenne as you go. Pour on the seasoned Sauce Mornay and brown in the broiler. Serves 4.

MONTANA EGGS

Use up boiled potatoes here. This is considered a breakfast dish, but unless you are going mountain climbing it is just as good for lunch or supper, served with a salad.

6 strips bacon	4 eggs
1 onion, chopped	Coarse salt
3–4 boiled potatoes, cubed	Freshly ground black pepper
1 green or red pepper, chopped	

Fry bacon, drain, and reserve. Drain off half the fat from the skillet. Add onion, potatoes, and pepper, and cook for 10 minutes, until the potatoes have browned. Break eggs into the pan and cook, covered, over low heat until set. Put bacon strips on top. Serves 4.

See also
EGGS MAYONNAISE, page 142

SMITH COLLEGE TOAST

Serve these unadorned or as sandwiches folded together with ham, bacon, or chicken inside. Salad, green beans, and beer are good accompaniments.

1 cup milk	3 tablespoons butter
4–6 eggs	1 tablespoon oil
Coarse salt	4–6 slices of bread, crusts removed
Freshly ground black pepper	Extra butter
Dash of nutmeg	

Beat milk with eggs. Season with salt, pepper, and nutmeg. Heat butter and oil in a heavy skillet. Dip the bread into the egg mixture and fry it until golden brown. Add extra butter, if necessary. Makes 4–6 pieces.

OBERLIN CURRY TOAST

A good meal for one. Cucumbers and beer are good with curry, which is also good served cold.

Buttered toast or muffin	(optional) per person
Chutney, relish, or chopped pickle	Small amount Mayonnaise (page
Hard-boiled egg	132)
1 teaspoon curry powder per person	1 teaspoon soft butter, per person
1 tablespoon leftover chopped ham,	Coarse salt
chicken, or other meat	Freshly ground black pepper

For each person spread a piece of buttered toast or muffin with chutney, relish, or chopped pickle. Mash a hard-boiled egg with curry powder, leftover meat, a little mayonnaise, and soft butter. Season and heat through under the grill.

EGGS BAKED IN CREAM

This goes with muffins, toast, and a green salad.

Preheat oven to 350 degrees. Line a buttered baking dish with slices of Swiss cheese. If you like, add some slices of cooked ham. Break in the eggs and add 3 tablespoons of heavy cream for every 2 eggs. Put some grated cheese on top, and dot with butter. Bake until the eggs are set. Sprinkle with chopped parsley and serve.

EGG AND MUSHROOM RAGOUT

Try this with fried zucchini and tomato or watercress salad.

Chop half a pound of mushrooms and sauté in 3 tablespoons of butter. Add about half a cup of light cream, a dash of thyme and nutmeg and season.

Put 6 chopped hard-boiled eggs on buttered toast or muffins. Pour the sauce over and serve. Enough for 4.

EGGS COLORADO STATE

This makes a good late-night snack or lunch dish and is great with beer.

6 hard-boiled eggs
1 tablespoon soft butter
1 teaspoon horseradish
3 tablespoons mayonnaise (bottled,
    if homemade is unavailable)
Dash of Tabasco

Coarse salt and freshly ground
    black pepper
4 slices buttered toast or English
    muffins
Grated Parmesan cheese
Extra butter

Preheat broiler to 400 degrees. Mash eggs with softened butter, horseradish, mayonnaise (the bought kind is all right here), a dash of Tabasco, and salt and pepper. Spread the mixture on toast or muffins, sprinkle with cheese, dot with butter, and brown under the broiler. Serves 4.

QUICHE LORRAINE

When my mother made her first quiche and brought the elegant little dish to the table, her children took one look at it and said, "Oh, good! Bacon and egg pie."

In fact, that is what a quiche really is. It is an attractive and very filling dish, and is best served with Green Salad (page 136), hot French or Italian bread, and red wine.

Nothing can compare with a homemade wholewheat pie crust, but if you do not have time to make your own, the frozen ones are quite good.

1 wholewheat pie crust (page 197)
    or 1 frozen pie shell, partially
    cooked
8 strips bacon, diced
1 small onion, chopped fine
4 eggs
½ cup heavy cream

½ cup milk
2 thin slices Gruyère cheese,
    chopped (optional)
Coarse salt and freshly ground
    black pepper
2 tablespoons butter, cut into bits

Preheat oven to 350 degrees. Cool the pie crust. Fry the bacon until soft. Drain on paper towels. Reserve. Cook onion in the fat until clear. Drain and reserve. Put the eggs, cream, milk, and cheese in a bowl and beat with a fork until light and blended. Do not whip. Season. Put the bacon and onion onto the bottom of the pie shell, add the egg mixture, and scatter bits of butter over the top. Bake for 25–30 minutes. Serves 4–6.

CHEESE

There are over a thousand cheeses in the world today, and five hundred of them are made in France alone. Nowadays everyone is trying to get into the act, with each country bringing out its own version of a Camembert or a blue cheese or a Cheddar, and everyone imitates everybody else. To top it off, manufacturers are now selling different kinds of processed cheeses and cheese spreads under misleading names.

Real cheese comes in five different categories: hard, blue-veined, semi-hard or semi-soft (whichever you want to call it), soft, and cream cheese. It is made from cow's, goat's, or ewe's milk, and is skimmed, partly skimmed, or enriched with cream.

No one knows how cheese first came into existence. There is a theory, and it sounds feasible, that cheese was first made in a hot country such as Persia, Turkey, Arabia, or Spain, where some unsuspecting traveler loaded his donkey with the day's supply of goat's milk in skin saddle bags and set off on his journey. When he arrived, the combination of the heat of the day and the movement of the donkey had caused the milk to curdle and separate. Thus the curds were formed and the first cheese came into being.

In France, cheese is usually served at the end of a meal, before the dessert. Dry red wine and French or Italian bread are good accompaniments. Beer is good with blue cheese; white wine with cream cheese.

Fruit goes well with blue cheese, soft, and semi-hard cheeses. Berries are particularly good with cream cheese.

All cheeses, except perhaps cream cheese, should be served at room temperature.

For cooking, Parmesan or Cheddar cheese is best for dishes requiring grated cheese. Gruyère is also good and is the classic cheese to use in fondue. Parmesan is excellent with pasta. For hot casseroles Mozzarella is good, because it doesn't get stringy. Cheddar is a good cooking cheese, but it occasionally gets stringy when heated.

Hard Cheese

Cheddar   In Great Britain and Canada, Cheddar is usually made from unpasteurized milk. It takes nearly two years to mature and, when it is old, has a full, sharp flavor and crumbly texture. Young Cheddar is buttery and less rich in flavor. American Cheddar is pasteurized and is rindless; it is produced in different varieties all over the United States.

Double Gloucester   A firm cheese with pale yellow or pale red flesh, it comes from Great Britain.

Gouda   A creamy firm cheese, strong but without bite, it is shaped like a wheel and has straw-colored rind and flesh. It comes from Holland.

Edam   Also from Holland, it is saltier than Gouda and has a mellow nutty flavor. It is a deep yellow cheese, shaped in a ball with a red wax skin.

Parmesan   The perfect grating cheese from Italy, it has no rival in any other country. It improves with maturity. It is pale straw in color with a black crust.

Swiss or Emmenthaler   A creamy, gold cheese from Switzerland, it has big holes in it. Widely imitated in the United States but with little success. Excellent for cooking, but it gets stringy if cooked too long.

Gruyère   Similar to Emmenthaler but with fewer holes. It is also from Switzerland and is a firm, almost hard cheese with a slightly sour taste.

Brick   An American cheese with a strong flavor and slightly sweet taste. It is cream colored and originates in Wisconsin.

Sage Cheese   An excellent American cheese made with herbs.

Blue Cheese

Danish Blue   An excellent blue-veined cheese made from rich milk. It is quite cheap in the United States and is often substituted for the more expensive Roquefort.

Gorgonzola   A strong, moist, blue-veined Italian cheese made by mixing morning and evening milk.

Roquefort   One of France's best and most famous cheeses, it is a creamy pungent cheese made from ewe's milk and veined with blue mould. It is matured in caves.

Stilton   Great Britain's most famous cheese. It is made from rich milk and is a blue-veined cheese with a brown rind. Often it is served with port poured into a hollow in the middle.

Semi-Hard Cheese

Bel Paese   A creamy, sweet Italian cheese, ivory colored, with a pleasant slightly rubbery texture.

Feta   A white, salty, and crumbly cheese from Greece, it is excellent in salads.

Limburger   A strong-smelling cheese flavored with tarragon, chives, and parsley. It is dried in the sun and has a salty crust.

Monterey Jack   A pale yellow cheese from the United States, it has a pleasant but sometimes quite strong flavor. Great for cooking, in place of Cheddar.

Mozzarella   An Italian cheese, eaten either fresh or mature. It is creamy white and excellent for cooking.

Muenster   A tan-colored cheese, powerful, made from whole cow's milk. It exists both in France and in Germany. Excellent for cooking.

Pont L'Evêque   A pungent, creamy French cheese somewhere between Brie and Camembert in taste, it is made from whole cow's milk.

Tilsit   Originally from Germany and also available in Denmark, it is a firm, pale yellow, creamy cheese with small holes.

Soft Cheese

Brie   The queen of cheeses, it is made from renneted cow's milk, slightly salted. It must be ripe when it is served; otherwise, it is chalky. If it is soft and bulges when it is pressed, it is ripe. A light creamy yellow inside with a reddish crust.

Camembert   The French classic, it comes in a round box and has a light orange-yellow crust with white streaks. Inside, it is soft and creamy. Like Brie, it should be eaten only when ripe.

Liederkranz   One of the best American cheeses, it should be runny and smelly; it should never be eaten when underripe. Similar in texture to Brie or Camembert.

Cream Cheese

Cottage Cheese   An American curd cheese. It is delicious plain or in salads or cooked dishes.

Cream Cheese   A creamy white American cheese, it is good in desserts and savory dishes and spread on dark breads.

Crema Danica   A delicious creamy Danish cheese, best served by itself.

Petit Suisse   Not Swiss, but a French cheese. It is an unsalted creamy cheese in a cylinder shape. It is delicious with fruit.

Ricotta   An Italian cheese also made in the United States. It is excellent for cooking.

WELSH RAREBIT

This is a good way to use up stale beer. Dark beer is the best kind to use. An excellent single-person dish, it makes a filling lunch or supper. A salad and beer are all you need with it.

Don't get the cheese mixture too hot or it will get very stringy.

Melt half a stick of butter (2 ounces) in a saucepan and add 6 ounces of cheese. When it has begun to melt, add a couple of glasses of beer, salt and pepper, a teaspoon of dark mustard, and a dash of Worcestershire sauce. Stir well and when heated through and beginning to get stringy, pour it on buttered toast. Enough for 4 people.

Note: A glass of dry sherry can be substituted for one glass of beer. You can also serve this over spinach instead of toast, or stuffed into tomatoes (their insides scooped out first) and grilled.

CROQUE MONSIEUR

Parisian students eat this in the little cafés which sprawl onto the streets of St. Germain and around the university. A glass of red wine or beer, and you have your lunch.

Toast 2 slices of white bread. Put some Gruyère or Swiss cheese and a slice of lean ham on the toast. Press the two sides together and fry in melted butter until heated through.

SWISS TOAST

Serve this with a green salad and a glass of white wine.

2 tablespoons butter
2 tablespoons flour
1 cup hot milk
½ cup, or less, of grated Gruyère
   or Swiss cheese
1 teaspoon dark mustard

1 clove garlic, crushed
Coarse salt and freshly ground
   black pepper
4 slices of buttered toast
Dash of nutmeg

Melt the butter in a saucepan and add flour gradually, stirring until smooth. Gradually add milk and cook until thickened, stirring constantly. Remove from heat. Add cheese, dark mustard, and garlic, if you wish. Season.

Spread mixture on the toast, sprinkle with nutmeg, and put under the broiler until hot and bubbly. Serves 4.

Note: As in Welsh Rarebit, this can also be stuffed into scooped-out tomatoes and grilled, or served over spinach instead of toast.

RADCLIFFE CHEESE TOAST

A good dish for one. Serve with ham or bacon and salad.

2 tablespoons Swiss or Cheddar
   cheese, grated
1 tablespoon milk
½ teaspoon mustard
Dash of nutmeg
Coarse salt and freshly ground

black pepper
Buttered toast, preferably
   wholewheat
Chutney, relish, or chopped
   pickles
Paprika

Mix cheese, milk, mustard, and nutmeg. Season. Spread a slice of buttered toast with chutney, relish, or chopped pickles. Add the cheese mixture. Sprinkle with paprika and brown under the broiler. Serves 1.

ROCHESTER BEER CHEESE

A delicious, gooey mess. Green vegetables, tomatoes, salad and a roll of paper towels are what you need here. Swiss cheese and white wine can be substituted for Cheddar cheese and beer.

2 tablespoons butter	1 egg yolk
2 tablespoons flour	Coarse salt and freshly ground
1 cup hot milk	black pepper
¼ pound Cheddar cheese or Swiss	Wholewheat bread in thick slices
cheese, diced	Stale beer or white wine

Preheat oven to 350 degrees. In a saucepan melt butter and add flour. Stir over low heat for 2–3 minutes and gradually add hot milk, stirring until smooth. Blend in cheese, an egg yolk, and seasonings. Do not let boil. Remove from heat. Dip bread into beer or wine. Then coat bread slices with the cheese mixture, put them in a baking dish, and bake for 15 minutes. Serves 1–2.

CURRIED CHEESE TOAST

This is good for single-person cooks. Serve it with cucumber or tomato salad.

For one piece of buttered rye toast, mix half a cup of grated cheese with half a teaspoon of curry powder and half a teaspoon of mustard. Add a tablespoon of milk to moisten it, and spread it on the bread. Brown under a grill and serve with chutney and, if you like, a little chopped raw onion.

CHEESE AND VEGETABLE PIE

Plenty of hot French or garlic bread, red wine or beer, and a green salad give you a complete and economical meal. You don't need potatoes, but if you want to serve them, sautéed potatoes would be good.

3 onions, sliced	Dash basil
3 tablespoons butter	½ pound Swiss or Cheddar cheese,
1 package frozen string beans,	grated
partially thawed and chopped	3 eggs, beaten
Coarse salt and freshly ground	1 cup hot milk
black pepper	Wholewheat breadcrumbs or
Dash sugar	wheatgerm
4 tomatoes, sliced	

Preheat oven to 350 degrees. Sauté the onions in butter without browning. Remove and drain. Add the string beans, with additional butter if necessary. Season and add the sugar. Stir the string beans in the skillet for 2–3 minutes. Set aside. In a buttered ovenproof casserole, layer the onions, beans, and tomatoes, seasoning them with basil. Combine the cheese with the eggs and hot milk and pour over the other ingredients. Top with breadcrumbs and bake for about 30 minutes. Serves 4–5.

BAKED BARLEY WITH CHEESE

Serve this dish with green beans, broccoli, Brussels Sprouts with Garlic and Ham (page 95), or Braised Leeks (page 114). Cucumbers Baked with Dill (page 105) also make a light vegetable accompaniment.

1 onion, chopped	black pepper
4 tablespoons butter	Dash basil
6 tomatoes, chopped	½ cup sharp Cheddar or Muenster
2 cups cooked barley	cheese, grated
Coarse salt and freshly ground	

Preheat oven to 350 degrees. Cook the onions in the butter until soft. Add the tomatoes and cook for 3 minutes. Set aside.

In an ovenproof casserole put a layer of the tomato mixture, season with basil, salt, and pepper, then put in a layer of barley, alternating until you get to the top, ending with the tomato mixture. Add grated cheese and bake for 30 minutes. Serves 4.

See also
CHEESE FONDUE, page 215

Pasta, Rice, Potatoes, and Beans

It goes without saying that all the dishes in this chapter are very cheap. Starchy vegetables are good for expanding meals, but some of these recipes can stand alone. When you want to entertain but feel you can't afford it, one of these dishes, properly cooked and served, will be appreciated far more than if you had tried to get away with a pound of steak for four people. A meal like this can be finished with a good green salad, real bread (French or Italian), good cheese, and beer or red wine to drink.

Few people, unless they are dieting, fail to appreciate fresh spaghetti, well cooked and served with plenty of butter, herbs, and cheese; a black bean casserole with ham and sour cream; or potatoes cooked in a casserole with tomatoes and anchovies.

What is not appreciated is a skimpy meal, or a meal that clearly comes out of a can.

Several of these dishes are also good for expanding meals. Starchy vegetables fill you up, and a good helping of noodles with your veal will make the veal go a long way. If the noodles are good, that is.

Fresh ingredients (with the exception, occasionally, of canned beans) are essential. Provided your sauces are freshly made, the pasta, beans or potatoes are not three years old, and you use good oils and butter, you can't go wrong (let's hope).

PASTA

In the 1930's, Italy was suddenly plunged into an uproar over its national food, pasta. The futurist painter Marinetti started the argument. Being very close to Mussolini, he said, "Spaghetti is no food for fighters." He contended that it induced "scepticism, sloth, and pessimism." "Heavy consumers of pastaciutta have slow and placid characters," he continued, and "meat eaters are quick and aggressive." Immediately the fight for and against pasta was taken up all over Italy, but, needless to say, the campaign did not work. The Italians continue to enjoy their pasta as before.

The kind of spaghetti often served in school cafeterias and some restaurants might indeed lead you to "scepticism, sloth, and pessimism." But properly prepared pasta is incredibly good. You can eat it a couple of times a week and be none the worse for it.

First of all, you need good pasta. Look in Italian neighborhoods for homemade pasta. If it isn't available, try health food stores. They often carry delicious wholewheat spaghetti and noodles. If all else fails, you'll have to make do with the supermarket.

You must use a *large* pot of rapidly boiling water (at least 2 quarts of water per ½ pound pasta), with a tablespoon of salt and a tablespoon of oil added. If there isn't enough water, the excess starch will make the strands stick together. To prevent its boiling over add a little fat or oil to the water. Add pasta to the water gradually, so that the water does not stop boiling. Cook for about 10 minutes. Stir occasionally while it is cooking. Lift out a strand and taste to see if it is done. It should be *al dente,* that is, slightly resistant to the bite, neither mushy nor hard.

If you have not been able to cook the spaghetti in a large pot, rinse it after it has been cooked to remove the starch.

When the pasta is done, drain it in a colander. Meanwhile, melt a good-sized lump of butter or some oil in the pan. Return the pasta to the pan and coat it thoroughly. Serve at once on hot plates with a hot sauce.

Grated Parmesan cheese can be served separately or sprinkled on top.

If the pasta is going to be cooked later in a casserole, take it out just before it is done.

Sauces for Pasta

These sauces can be used for spaghetti, macaroni, vermicelli, noodles, and fettucine, among the other countless kinds of pasta.

TOMATO SAUCE

This is especially good for lasagne, layered with Mozzarella, ricotta, and Parmesan cheese.

1 onion, chopped	Dash of sugar
6 tablespoons olive oil	Basil
3 stalks celery, chopped	Oregano
6 tomatoes, chopped	1 tablespoon chopped fresh parsley
2 tablespoons tomato purée	Coarse salt
2 cloves garlic, chopped	Freshly ground black pepper

Soften onion in olive oil. Add remaining ingredients and simmer over very low heat, covered, for about 1 hour.

Note: For a good 3-Minute Tomato Sauce, see page 229.

YOGHURT TOMATO SAUCE

1 onion, chopped	¾ cup yoghurt
2 cloves garlic, chopped	Dash of basil
3 tomatoes, chopped	Coarse salt
1 tablespoon tomato purée	Freshly ground black pepper

Soften onion and garlic in oil or butter. Add tomatoes, tomato purée, yoghurt, and basil, and season. Simmer for about 20 minutes.

MUSHROOMS AND PEAS SAUCE

1 onion, chopped	Small amount of water
2 strips bacon, chopped	¼ pound sliced mushrooms
1 pound peas or 1 package frozen peas	Grated Parmesan cheese
2 tablespoons butter	Coarse salt
	Freshly ground black pepper

Add onion, bacon, and peas to 2 tablespoons butter and a little water. Cook until the onion is soft. Add mushrooms and cook for about 15 minutes. Season and serve with cheese.

MUSHROOMS AND CHEESE SAUCE

2 tablespoons oil	½ cup grated Parmesan cheese
2 cloves garlic, chopped	Coarse salt
¼ pound sliced mushrooms	Freshly ground black pepper

Heat oil in a skillet and add garlic. Cook for 2–3 minutes. Add mushrooms and cook for 5 minutes. Add cheese and seasonings. Stir over low heat until the cheese melts.

MUSHROOM MARINARA SAUCE

1 onion, chopped	Dash paprika
1 clove garlic, chopped	Pinch of thyme
1 tablespoon olive oil	Coarse salt
4 tomatoes, chopped	½ pound sliced mushrooms

Sauté onion and garlic in oil until soft. Add tomatoes, paprika, thyme, and salt, to taste. Cook for 3 minutes, then add mushrooms. Cook 15 minutes.

TUNA FISH SAUCE

This sauce is also good on rice.

2 tablespoons butter or oil	Coarse salt
1 can tuna, drained	Freshly ground black pepper
1 clove garlic, crushed (optional)	2 tablespoons chopped fresh parsley
1 cup hot chicken or beef stock	

Melt butter or oil in a skillet. Add flaked tuna, garlic, if you like, and *hot* stock. Season well and cook for 5 minutes. Add chopped parsley.

VERY CHEAP AND EXCELLENT SPAGHETTI

Good spaghetti is one of the simplest things to cook, provided you do it correctly. Unfortunately, many people overcook spaghetti, then drown it in a canned tomato sauce. If you have an Italian shop near you, secure fresh homemade pasta. There is nothing like it. If you don't love garlic, skip this and read another spaghetti recipe.

1 pound spaghetti	1 tablespoon chopped fresh parsley
1 tablespoon melted butter	Freshly ground black pepper
2 garlic cloves, crushed in	Parmesan cheese (freshly grated)
2 tablespoons softened butter	

Cook the spaghetti (see page 166) for about 12 minutes in rapidly boiling water until it is tender but still firm. Drain. Put some melted butter in a large dish, add the spaghetti, and toss. Mix the parsley into the garlic-butter mixture and place on top of the mound of spaghetti. Crack some pepper over all and serve with freshly grated Parmesan cheese. Serves 4.

MACARONI CHEESE

Macaroni comes in long pencil-like tubes. You are most likely to come across it already cut into pieces about 1½ inches long.

Macaroni Cheese is no more Italian than chop suey is Chinese. It is an English dish as well known in that country as pumpkin pie is in the United

States. When properly made, it is delicious. It should be served very hot on hot plates. Green salad goes well with it.

½ pound macaroni	½ cup grated Parmesan, Cheddar,
1 tablespoon butter	or Swiss cheese
1 cup Béchamel Sauce (page 107)	1 tablespoon butter, in pieces
1 teaspoon mustard	Coarse salt and freshly ground
1 tablespoon breadcrumbs or	black pepper
wheatgerm	

Preheat oven to 450 degrees. Cook the macaroni in rapidly boiling salted water for 15 minutes. Drain. Toss it in butter in the saucepan.

Make the Béchamel Sauce. Mix with mustard and stir into the macaroni.

Put the mixture in a buttered baking dish, top with breadcrumbs, cheese, and butter and bake for about 10 minutes. To brown the top really well, put it under a hot grill for a few minutes. Serves 4.

MACARONI WITH HAM

A very quick and simple dish. Bacon can be used instead of ham, if you wish.

Serve the macaroni with green salad or tomato salad and red wine or beer.

3 tablespoons butter	Coarse salt and freshly ground
2 ham slices, diced	black pepper
¼ pound mushrooms, chopped	2 eggs, beaten
½ pound macaroni	Grated Parmesan cheese

In a skillet melt 2 tablespoons of the butter. Sauté the ham, remove, and drain. Add the mushrooms and sauté lightly.

Meanwhile, boil the macaroni for about 15 minutes, until tender. Drain and return to saucepan with a tablespoon of butter. Toss and put in a warm serving dish.

Return the ham to the mushrooms in the skillet. Add the beaten eggs, seasoned, and stir in over low heat until they begin to thicken, without scrambling them. Pour the mixture over the macaroni and sprinkle with Parmesan cheese. Serves 4.

BAKED GREEN LASAGNE BOLOGNESE

Lasagne noodles are flat square pasta, sometimes made with crimped edges. Green lasagne are made with spinach. Read through the package ingredients carefully though, because sometimes the green ones are artificially colored and it is pointless to buy them.

Most often lasagne is made with meat or tomato sauce and layers of Mozzarella, ricotta, or Parmesan cheese. It is a heavy dish, but this recipe is somewhat lighter, although still very filling.

You can make it in advance and refrigerate or freeze it.

Salad and red wine are the best companions for lasagne.

Ragù Sauce Bolognese

1 tablespoon butter	Dash basil
2 strips bacon, diced	Coarse salt and freshly ground
1 onion, chopped	black pepper
1 carrot, chopped	Dash nutmeg
1 celery stalk, chopped	3 glasses water
½ pound ground chuck	Sauce Béchamel, page 107
¼ pound chopped chicken livers or	1 pound lasagne noodles
minced pork	Parmesan cheese, grated
1 teaspoon tomato purée	

Preheat oven to 350 degrees. Melt the butter in a skillet with the bacon. Cook the bacon and remove, add the onion, carrot, and celery and cook until the onion has softened. Add the remaining ingredients, stir well, and simmer over low heat for about 40 minutes.

Meanwhile, make the Béchamel Sauce. Set aside.

Cook the lasagne in a large amount of boiling salted water for 10–15 minutes and drain. In a greased casserole, alternate layers of Sauce Bolognese, Sauce Béchamel, and lasagne and grated Parmesan cheese. Bake for 20–25 minutes, until lightly browned. Serves 4–6.

NOODLES BAKED WITH YOGHURT

If you can get wholewheat noodles, use them for this recipe. Serve with grilled or sautéed meat (it's especially good with liver or kidneys), green vegetables or tomatoes, and salad.

½ pound noodles	Dash sugar
Boiling water	Coarse salt and freshly ground
1 cup milk	black pepper
1 cup yoghurt	1 cup wheatgerm
4 eggs, beaten	Butter
Dash nutmeg	Grated Parmesan cheese, served
1 teaspoon mustard	separately

Preheat oven to 400 degrees. Cook the noodles for 8–10 minutes in plenty of rapidly boiling water. Drain.

In a mixing bowl put the milk, yoghurt, eggs, and seasonings. Mix well and combine with noodles. Pour into a greased baking dish and cover with wheatgerm. Dot with butter and bake for 15–20 minutes. Serves 4.

See also
NOODLES WITH THREE-MINUTE TOMATO SAUCE, page 229
NOODLES WITH MUSHROOMS, page 229

RICE

There are so many excellent rice dishes that it is hard to know which to choose. The advantage for college students is that rice is quick and cheap and usually requires only one pan. Risotti and pilafs are great for using up scraps and transforming them into delicious dishes.

Brown rice is the best of all from the health standpoint. It is generally available in supermarkets as well as in health food stores. Converted rice is also good for you, but white rice, like white flour, has most of its vitamins refined out of it. What you choose is up to you.

If you are using white rice, long grain is best for boiled rice and short grain for risotti.

BOILED RICE

Rice should never be overcooked. Soupy rice is usually rice that has been cooked too long, has been stirred with a spoon (which mashes the grains), and has not been run under cold water at the end to stop the cooking, separate the grains, and remove the starch. To top it all, if the rice has been made too early, it is then left to sit covered with a lid, which keeps it moist inside.

Method One

Allow ½ cup of rice per person. Half fill a large pot with water and salt it, bring to a boil and gradually add the rice, so that the water does not stop boiling. Stir with a fork and boil the rice rapidly. After 12 minutes, take a little out and taste it. If it is soft, it is done. It usually takes 15–20 minutes. Put the rice in a colander and run under cold water. In a dry saucepan, melt some butter over a low flame, add the rice, cover with a cloth, and leave for a few minutes.

Alternatively, melt some butter in a baking dish and put the rice in a slow oven until you are ready.

Half a lemon added to the boiling water keeps the rice white. To prevent its boiling over, add a little oil or fat to the pot.

Method Two

Allow 2½ cups of liquid and 1 teaspoon of salt for each cup of raw rice. Add 1 tablespoon butter to water and bring to a boil. Add rice gradually, cover and reduce to a very low flame. Simmer for about 20 minutes, or until done. Use a tight-fitting cover and do not remove it except to stir occasionally. The rice is done when it has absorbed all the water.

Brown Rice

Brown rice takes longer to cook, 30–40 minutes, and, if using Method Two, add an extra cup of water, or more as needed.

Serve with chopped parsley, yoghurt, or oil instead of butter, if you like.

RICE WITH BEANS

Use red, white, or black beans, and if you can't be bothered to soak them overnight and cook them for several hours, use canned ones. This dish is good with spicy foods, curries, chili dishes, chicken, or fish. It's also good with eggs. Chopped celery can be browned with the onion, and a bay leaf can also be added.

1 onion, chopped	1 can tomatoes, chopped, with
1 clove garlic, chopped	juice
(optional)	Coarse salt and freshly ground
2 tablespoons oil	black pepper
1 can or 1 cup cooked beans	1½–2 cups water
1 cup rice	

Brown onions and garlic in the oil in a large heavy skillet. Add beans, rice, tomatoes, salt and pepper, and water. Mix with a fork, bring to a boil, then cover and simmer for 20 minutes. Serves 4.

BANANAS WITH RICE

Delicious with curry, fried chicken, ham, or pork.

2 cups cooked rice, hot   ½ cup butter
  Butter   6 bananas
2 onions, chopped   Nutmeg or cinnamon

Dot hot rice with butter. Cut bananas in half, then split them length-wise. Keep warm.

Soften onions in butter in a heavy skillet. Add the bananas and sauté until lightly browned.

Top rice with banana mixture and sprinkle with nutmeg or cinnamon. Serves 4.

TOMATO PILAF

This simple pilaf is good with lamb, chicken, veal or fish, with a green vegetable dish, or with a cheese casserole.

2 tomatoes, chopped   1½ cups rice
¼ cup butter   Grated Parmesan cheese
2 cups beef or chicken stock   (optional)
1 teaspoon tomato purée

Cook tomatoes in a heavy skillet in the butter for 5 minutes. Add stock and tomato purée and simmer for 5 more minutes. Add rice, bring to a boil, then reduce heat and simmer for 20 minutes, or until done. If you like, sprinkle with a handful of grated Parmesan cheese. Serves 4 as a side dish.

MUSHROOM RISOTTO

This goes with ham, chicken, livers or kidneys, or fish. For a vegetarian meal, try it with green vegetables, Cucumbers in Yoghurt (page 106), Glazed Onions (page 118), Summer Squash with Cheese (page 124), or Tomatoes Provençales (page 179).

Chopped cooked chicken, chopped chicken livers, or ham can be added to the risotto to make it a meal by itself, with salad.

2 tablespoons butter
1 onion, chopped
1 clove garlic, chopped
2 cups rice
¼ pound mushrooms, chopped

2 pints chicken stock, boiling
Pinch saffron
Coarse salt and freshly ground
    black pepper
¼ cup grated Parmesan cheese

Melt the butter in a heavy skillet and soften the onion with the garlic. Add the rice and sauté in the butter until opaque. Add the mushrooms, cook for 1 minute, and add the hot stock and saffron. Simmer until the rice is tender, adding more liquid if necessary. Season, top with cheese, and dot with butter. Serves 4.

PERSIAN PILAF

A very pretty dish and great for parties. The orange strips of carrot and orange peel, the dark raisins, and the red of the tomatoes make a pleasing contrast. Green salad, Endive and Watercress Salad (page 136), and Spinach Salad (page 139) all go well with it, as do Peperoni (page 122) and Fried Eggplant (page 108).

If you are serving lots of people, salad and beer would be good accompaniments.

4 tablespoons peanut, olive, or
    sesame oil
2 onions, chopped
2 cloves garlic, chopped
2 cups rice
6 cups water
2 tablespoons raisins
2 tablespoons currants
2 teaspoons grated orange peel

2 carrots, shredded into thin strips
2 tomatoes, peeled, seeded, and
    chopped
1 tablespoon pine nuts (if
    available)
¾ cup cooked diced lamb, ham, or
    chicken
Coarse salt and freshly ground
    black pepper

Heat the oil in a heavy-bottomed saucepan. Add the onions and garlic and sauté for a few minutes. Add the rice and stir until it becomes opaque. Add the water, currants, and raisins, stir with a fork, and bring to a boil. Reduce heat to a low flame and simmer until the water has evaporated.

When the rice is cooked, add remaining ingredients and correct seasoning. Enough for 4–5.

See also
PAELLA, page 214
ARIZONA PILAF, page 215
RICE AND MEAT SALAD, page 147

POTATOES

Some people like to eat potatoes with every meal, while for others, out of necessity, the potato is the main part of their meal. In college one tends to fall between these categories, having neither the time nor the desire to cook them every day, and being just out of the poverty bracket where potatoes are served up day after day, thinly disguised with various sauces.

When you are feeling particularly poor, a potato casserole made with cheese, onions, or tomatoes provides a much better meal than a warmed-up can of baked beans or a greasy hot dog. And if you want to stretch a meal, potatoes usually do the trick.

In this chapter you will find some side dishes and main dishes made principally from potatoes.

NEW POTATOES

Put well-scrubbed, unpeeled potatoes into boiling water to cover. Cook until tender, about 15 minutes. Drain, salt and toss in butter. Sprinkle with parsley and add buttered peas, or add sour cream mixed with chopped fresh dill.

Small whole potatoes can also be sautéed in butter. Use a heavy pan and shake it often to prevent them from sticking. Cook over a low flame, covered, for about 25 minutes.

BOILED POTATOES

You may peel potatoes, if you like. They're better well scrubbed and unpeeled; most of the vitamins are in the skin.

Add quartered potatoes to boiling salted water to cover. Cook for 20–40 minutes. Test with a pointed knife to see if they're done; a fork will make them split. Drain potatoes and toss in butter. Chopped parsley, lemon juice, yoghurt, or cream cheese might be added.

Never cover boiled potatoes. This makes them mushy. To keep them warm, put a cloth over them.

MASHED POTATOES

Boil potatoes as above and mash them with a fork. Melt some butter in a saucepan, add milk or cream, salt, pepper, and nutmeg, and heat through. Never put cold milk into mashed potatoes; it will make them tacky.

Any of these additions are also good with mashed potatoes: two egg yolks; a couple of chopped onions browned in butter; chopped scallions; or cheese.

Leftover mashed potatoes can also be made into hashed browns. Mix them into a paste with a little flour and cook in butter or fat, turning often and mashing the brown bits in, until the potatoes are well browned.

BAKED POTATOES

Scrub well, dry, and bake in a hot oven for 1 hour. Serve with lots of butter, sour cream, and chives. Crumbled bacon bits are good, too.

ROAST POTATOES

Brown potatoes in fat either on top of the stove or inside the oven with roast drippings, for 30–40 minutes. They can be boiled for a few minutes first to hasten cooking time. Rosemary is good with roast potatoes.

FRENCH FRIES

Chop up the potatoes and dry them well. Heat plenty of fat or oil to smoking and increase the heat every time you add potatoes. Fry them for a few minutes, remove and drain, then put them back to fry again until done. This method makes delicious, crisp French fries.

GRATIN DAUPHINOIS

When potatoes are cooked this way, they come out creamy and browned on top. Serve them alone or with roasts, chicken, or cold meat and salad.

2 pounds potatoes, peeled and
 sliced
1 cup milk
1 egg, beaten
Nutmeg
Thyme

Coarse salt and freshly ground
 black pepper
¼ cup grated Gruyère or Parmesan
 cheese
Butter

Preheat oven to 350 degrees. Heat a cup of milk to boiling and re-move from heat. Beat in egg, nutmeg, thyme, salt, and pepper. In a but-tered baking dish, alternate layers of potatoes and milk mixture. Top with grated cheese and bits of chopped butter. Bake for about 45 min-utes, turning the oven up for the last 10 minutes of cooking to brown the top.

POMMES ANNA

A very simple dish which you can place in a slow oven and forget about. It is good with roasts and grilled meat or fish and green vegetables.

Preheat oven to 300 degrees. In a buttered baking dish, put layers of peeled and sliced potatoes (about 1½ pounds), distributing butter, salt, and pepper throughout. Cover and cook for about 1 hour.

EGG AND POTATO CASSEROLE

This goes with watercress, lettuce or tomato salad, Glazed Carrots (page 249), peas, peppers, or Stir-Fried Greens (page 112).

If you like, use up chopped leftover meat, adding it in a layer with the other layered ingredients.

1 pound potatoes, cooked and
 sliced
6 strips bacon, chopped
2 onions, sliced
 Coarse salt and freshly ground
 black pepper
6 hard-boiled eggs, sliced

½ cup chopped nuts (optional)
½ cup sour cream
¼ cup wholewheat breadcrumbs
 Paprika
1 tablespoon chopped fresh chives
 or parsley (optional)

Preheat oven to 400 degrees. Fry the bacon in a heavy skillet. Drain and reserve. Add the onions and fry until brown. Drain. In a buttered baking dish, alternate layers of sliced potatoes, onion, bacon and eggs, seasoning as you go, ending with onion and bacon. Add the nuts if you like, and the sour cream. Top with breadcrumbs sprinkled with paprika. Bake for 20 minutes. Garnish with chives or parsley. Serves 4–5.

POTATO CASSEROLE WITH CHEESE

You can use up slices of ham, tongue, or cooked sausage in this recipe. It goes with a green or tomato salad and green vegetables such as spinach or broccoli. Minus a meat filling, it is good with roasts and grilled meat.

2 pounds potatoes, cooked and
    sliced
2 onions, sliced
4 tablespoons butter
4 slices ham, tongue, or cooked
    sausage (optional)
1 tablespoon chopped chives or

parsley
Coarse salt and freshly ground
    black pepper
½ pound Cheddar cheese, grated
Extra butter
Paprika

Preheat oven to 425 degrees. Put the potatoes in a buttered casserole or baking dish. Cover with the onions. Add the butter, cut into small pieces, and the meat, if desired. Sprinkle with herbs, salt, and pepper. Top with cheese, dot with butter, and sprinkle with paprika. Bake for 30 minutes. Serves 4.

POTATO, BEEF, AND WALNUT PIE

This is a superb dish for a party. It is unusual, appeals to almost everyone, and stretches a long way. Serve with a salad and red wine or beer. You will need a large oven-to-table casserole.

2½ pounds boiled potatoes,
    mashed
½ stick butter (2 ounces)
¼ cup milk
¼ teaspoon turmeric (optional)
    Coarse salt and freshly ground
      black pepper
1 tablespoon olive oil
2 large onions, chopped
3 cloves garlic, chopped or put
    through squeezer
2 pounds ground chuck

Dash chili powder (optional)
Dash curry powder (optional)
1 teaspoon mixed herbs
1 tablespoon flour
¾ cup raisins
1–1½ cups chopped walnuts
    Coarse salt
    Freshly ground black pepper
½ cup grated Cheddar cheese
2 teaspoons butter
    Paprika

Preheat oven to 300 degrees. Mash potatoes with butter, milk, turmeric, and seasonings. Set aside.

Heat the oil in a large skillet and add the onions and garlic. Cook until clear. Remove from pan with the oil. Add the meat and spices and cook until brown. Sprinkle with flour and return the onions and garlic to the pan. Add the raisins and walnuts, and season. Put the mixture into a large casserole or pyrex dish. Spread the potatoes over the meat mixture and top with cheese, dot with small pieces of butter, and sprinkle with paprika. Bake for about 30 minutes. When ready to serve, run under the broiler to brown the top. Serves 8–10.

POTATOES PROVENÇALE

Serve this with salad or with roasted or grilled meat.

Anchovies taste quite different when they are cooked. Curiously, they develop an entirely new and really quite delicious flavor.

1½ pounds potatoes, peeled and sliced	black pepper
3 tablespoons olive oil	1 small can anchovies, with oil
3 onions, sliced	Dash thyme or basil
4 tomatoes, peeled and chopped	1 tablespoon chopped fresh parsley
1 clove garlic, chopped	¼ cup grated Parmesan cheese
Coarse salt and freshly ground	

Preheat oven to 350 degrees. Heat the oil and sauté the onions in a skillet. Add the tomatoes and garlic and cook for 3 minutes. Season and set aside. Mash the anchovies in their oil and add the herbs and parsley. In a buttered baking dish, alternate layers of potatoes, the tomato-onion mixture, and the anchovy sauce, ending with the tomato-onion mixture. Sprinkle with cheese, cover, and bake for about 1 hour, or until tender. Uncover for the last 10 minutes, to brown. Serves 4.

See also
POTATO SALAD, page 138

SOUTHERN SWEET POTATOES

3 sweet potatoes	sugar, or honey
2–3 tablespoons butter	Salt
Dash cinnamon	Freshly ground black pepper
Dash nutmeg	Brandy miniature (optional)
2 tablespoons molasses, brown	

Preheat oven to 350 degrees. Parboil sweet potatoes. Peel and slice them evenly. Put them in a shallow baking dish with butter, cinnamon, and nutmeg. Add molasses, brown sugar, or honey, and season well. If you're especially flush and want to impress *him* or *her,* add the brandy. Bake for 30–45 minutes. Serves 2–3.

BEANS

Beans are an excellent winter food and are particularly good at times when fresh vegetables are expensive. They have plenty of vitamins and make a good substitute for meat, especially when served with cheese or eggs.

Beans should not be too old. They get harder and harder, and if you leave them for months, they seem to fossilize. They should be soaked overnight, but not longer. They may ferment and lose their flavor.

If you have forgotten to soak them, slowly add them to rapidly boiling water, so that the water does not stop boiling. The starch grains burst and they can absorb the water more quickly. Then lower the heat and simmer them gently.

There are several kinds of beans, and they can all be cooked the following way. This includes lima beans (green), fava beans (green broad beans, dried), haricot or navy beans (white), pinto beans (pink), kidney beans (red), and black beans. They are delicious with lamb, pork, ham, sausages, and smoked meats.

Parsley Butter (page 50), lemon juice, raw onion, and hard-boiled egg slices are good garnishes for beans.

BASIC BEANS

1 pound beans, soaked overnight	1 tablespoon tomato purée
1 onion, chopped	Coarse salt and freshly ground
2 cloves garlic, chopped	black pepper
Bay leaf	5–6 cups water, plus more as needed
Dash thyme	

Combine all the ingredients except the salt and bring to a boil. Reduce heat and simmer for 2–3 hours, or until tender. Add extra liquid if necessary. Beans scorch easily. Season and serve. Enough for 4–6.

See also bean salads in SALAD chapter, pages 140–142

BAKED BEANS

Well, you could just open that can again. . . .

Or, heat through a can of white beans with the ingredients in this recipe.

Or, cook Basic Beans (opposite), and brown them in the broiler.

Or, cook beans until almost done, then bake for 1 hour in the oven.

Or go the whole way and bake them for 6–8 hours in the oven. If you're brave enough to try the latter, add liquid (stock, water, tomato juice) to cover and check occasionally to see if they need more.

Baked beans are delicious with eggs, meat, or sausage.

1 pound beans, cooked according to Basic Beans (above), almost done	1 teaspoon mustard
	3 tablespoons molasses
	Dash basil
2 strips bacon or 1 strip salt pork, chopped	Coarse salt and freshly ground black pepper
1 onion, chopped	Liquid to cover
4 tomatoes, peeled and chopped	

Preheat oven to 350 degrees. Sauté bacon or pork, remove and drain. Put in a fireproof dish. Soften the onion in the bacon fat and add the tomatoes. Cook for 2–3 minutes. Add the mustard, molasses, basil, and beans. Toss the beans thoroughly in the mixture and season to taste. Pour into an ovenproof casserole, add liquid, and bake for 45 minutes to 1 hour. Serves 4–6.

BEEF AND BEAN CASSEROLE

This dish is quite inexpensive. The beans must be soaked overnight in water. Use a chuck roast, shoulder, or round since these cuts of meat respond well to this type of cooking.

1 pound haricot or kidney beans, cooked	1 teaspoon thyme
	Coarse salt and freshly ground black pepper
2 pounds meat, in one piece	
1 medium-sized onion, chopped	Juice of half a lemon, mixed with 1 tablespoon dark mustard
1 teaspoon cornstarch	
1 tablespoon red wine vinegar	1 mild onion, chopped, to garnish
1 cup beef bouillon	1 tablespoon chopped fresh parsley, to garnish
1 bay leaf	

Soak the beans in water to cover overnight and cook according to Basic Beans (page above). Put the meat in a heavy casserole over very high heat and brown on all sides. Reduce heat and add the onion.

Sprinkle the cornstarch over the meat. Add the vinegar, bouillon, herbs, salt, and pepper. Bring to a boil. Mix the lemon juice and mustard and pour over the meat. Cover and cook over a low flame for at least 2 hours, or until the meat is almost tender. Add the beans to the beef casserole. Cook for another 30 minutes, so that the beans mix with the gravy. Chop the onion (soaked in water, if it is very strong) and scatter with the parsley over the top. Serve on heated plates immediately. Serves 6.

CHILI CON CARNE

This is a dish that frequently shows up at parties. And it can be very good. It tastes best when dried beans are used. They must be soaked overnight and cooked for about 4 hours in boiling, salted water. Canned kidney or pinto beans will do, however. An interesting variation can be made by using lima beans.

In Mexico the dish does not have tomatoes in it, but the border crossing and the trip through Texas somehow put them there.

With the chili, serve a green salad and plenty of beer or wine.

2 tablespoons butter	Dash oregano
2 tablespoons olive oil	1 large can tomatoes, with juice
2 onions, chopped	6 cups water or stock
3 garlic cloves, chopped	Coarse salt and freshly ground
2 pounds ground beef	black pepper
2 tablespoons chili powder	4–5 cups cooked kidney beans (see
Dash celery seed	page 180)
Dash cumin	

In a heavy saucepan or casserole heat the butter and the oil. Add the onion and garlic and cook until the onion is clear, without browning it. Add the beef and cook for 2 minutes. Add the chili powder and spices and cook for 2 more minutes. Add the tomatoes, pour in the water, and simmer gently for about 2 hours. Add the kidney beans, correct seasoning, and cook for 20 minutes. Serve on hot plates or in bowls. Serves 6–8.

See also
ROAST PORK WITH WHITE BEANS, page 70

RE-FRIED BEANS

Make this with cooked pinto or kidney beans. You can use up some of your leftover bacon fat for this recipe. The beans are good with grilled meat or chicken, as well as with Mexican dishes. If you like, sprinkle grated Cheddar cheese and chopped raw onion on the beans before serving.

Mash about 2 cups of beans. In a skillet, heat plenty of lard or bacon fat. Add the beans and mash them in, stirring continuously. Add some crushed garlic, cumin or oregano, if you like. More lard and more mashing, and when they are thoroughly hot and sizzling, turn them out and serve them. Enough for 4.

Chick Peas

Raw chick peas look like little yellow bullets and they're every bit as hard. Sometimes they are munched raw by the handful by hungry artists and students such as frequent Max's Kansas City restaurant in New York. To cook them, soak overnight, then boil for several hours.

They are delicious hot or cold.

Canned chick peas are very good and much less bother. They can be drained and used in salads or heated through and served as a vegetable instead of potatoes.

BOILED CHICK PEAS

Bring 6 cups of water to a rapid boil. Add 1 pound soaked peas little by little so as not to stop the boiling, turn down heat to simmer and cook, covered, for about 2–3 hours, until they are tender. Season and serve with oil, salt and pepper, or Parsley Butter (page 50). A little garlic squeezed into the oil or butter is very good.

CHICK PEAS WITH TOMATOES

This is good with lamb, chicken, or cold meat. For a pound or 2 large cans of chick peas soften 2 chopped onions and a clove of garlic chopped in 3 tablespoons butter. Add 3 tomatoes, dash of basil, and the chick peas and simmer for 20 minutes. Season with salt and Cayenne pepper. Serves 6.

See also
CHICK PEA SALAD, page 140

BLACK BEANS WITH HAM

These beans are excellent party food. They look attractive on the table and they cost next to nothing. Serve them with smoked meat, pork, chicken,

Mexican food, or with a cooked ham. A little sherry or rum is delicious added to the beans about 10 minutes before they are ready.

If you want to use canned beans, sauté the onion in the butter with the pepper and garlic, add the beans and heat through, then add remaining ingredients.

1 pound black beans, soaked overnight, with soaking water	¼ teaspoon mustard
1 onion, chopped	¼ teaspoon tomato purée (optional)
1 clove garlic, chopped	Coarse salt and freshly ground black pepper
1 pepper, chopped (optional)	Ham bone and diced leftover ham
2 stalks celery, with leaves, chopped	About 6 cups water, including the soaking water
Bay leaf	½ cup sour cream
Dash thyme	2 tablespoons butter
Dash Worcestershire sauce	

Combine all the ingredients except the sour cream and butter in a large pot. Bring to a boil, cover, then reduce heat and simmer gently for 2–3 hours, until the beans are tender. Dish up and put a dollop of sour cream and butter on top before serving. Serves 4.

See also
BLACK BEAN SOUP, page 13

Lentils and Split Peas

Lentils and split peas are good to have on hand for soup, to stretch stews and casseroles at the last minute, and to serve with leftovers. They are especially good with pork and sausages and as meat substitutes.

Split peas and lentils can be cooked the same way. If you have the time, soak them for an hour before you cook them, and cook them in the same water they have been soaked in.

BASIC LENTILS OR SPLIT PEAS

2 cups lentils	1 carrot, sliced
1 onion, chopped	1 stalk celery or celery leaves, chopped
2 cloves garlic, chopped (optional)	Coarse salt
Bay leaf	Freshly ground black pepper
Dash of thyme	Additional water, as needed
A few cloves	

In a large pot combine lentils with onion, garlic, if you wish, a bay leaf, dash of thyme, cloves, carrot, and celery. Season and simmer for about 1 hour, adding more water if necessary. Serves 4.

Lentils with Parsley Butter

Basic Lentils (above)
½ cup butter
3 tablespoons parsley, chopped very
    fine

Combine butter and parsley, and place on top of warm lentils, before serving.

Lentils with Bacon

½ pound bacon, in one piece
   Ingredients for Basic Lentils,
    above

Chop bacon into bits and brown in skillet. Sauté chopped onion and garlic (listed in Basic Lentils) until soft, then proceed as for basic recipe.

Alternatively, you may crumble cooked bacon into the lentils when they are cooked.

Lentils with Salt Pork

2 strips salt pork
  Basic Lentils, above
  Squeeze of lemon
  Chopped parsley

Cook salt pork with the lentils. Before serving, add a squeeze of lemon and sprinkle with parsley.

Lentils with Leftovers

Basic Lentils, above
Chopped leftover meat

Add chopped leftovers to lentils 10 minutes before they have finished cooking.

Split Peas with Sausage and Caraway Seeds

1 tablespoon caraway seeds
  Basic Split Peas, above
4 cooked sausages, chopped

Cook caraway seeds with Basic Split Peas. Add sausage about 10 minutes before peas have finished cooking.

Desserts and Baking

There are plenty of cookbooks packed with desserts. Anyone can find a recipe for raspberry rum cake, pumpkin pie, or apple strudel, but not many people in college want to take the afternoon off to make a dessert. None of the desserts in this chapter require much time or skill. None of them are particularly heavy. Unless the person you've lured up to your room is some dull cousin whom you'd prefer to fall asleep after dinner, heavy desserts are not what you want anyway. Only a football player of Italian-British origin might tackle a pasta meal followed by steamed pudding. Having been impressed with your excellent meal ("Oh, it's nothing"), your guest will still be fit for chess or looking at etchings after Georgetown Baked Peaches or Bananas in Sour Cream.

In this chapter you will also find simple breads and cookies. Some of the breads do take time, but perhaps you will want to try them over the weekend or some afternoon when you're working in your room. Others, however, take no more than a few minutes to make.

POIRES BELLE HÉLÈNE

For one can of pears melt four ounces of bitter chocolate with a little of the pear juice over a low flame. Pour it over the pears and serve. Enough for four.

CHOCOLATE MOUSSE

For each person you need one egg, a teaspoon of butter, a teaspoon of water and an ounce of chocolate. Heat the chocolate with the butter and water over low heat until it has melted. Separate the egg and add the yolk to the mixture. Beat the white until stiff, fold it into the warm mixture and refrigerate overnight.

FRUIT SALAD

Apples, pears, bananas, and strawberries are all good in fruit salad. Cut them up over the bowl so that all the juice is saved. Add a little

187

sugar and some lemon and orange peel. The fruit must be carefully chopped, all the seeds and skin removed. Don't add cherries, prunes or blueberries; they are not good in fruit salad. A little melon is good, but don't add too much.

Fresh cream is delicious with fruit salad, and if you're trying to impress someone, a little kirsch, bought in a miniature, makes a big difference.

RASPBERRIES WITH CREAM CHEESE

If you have a blender, this dessert will take only about 10 minutes to make. Otherwise, you have a bit of mashing to do.

Thaw a package of frozen raspberries and mix, either in the blender or with a fork, with an 8-ounce package of cream cheese. Reserve a few raspberries for decoration. The mixture will turn pink and should be fairly smooth. Decorate with raspberries and refrigerate until needed. This is a superb dessert and most people don't even know what it is when they taste it for the first time. This amount *may* be enough for 3. Serves 2–3.

PRUNES WITH CREAM CHEESE

This dessert is similar to Raspberries with Cream Cheese (above), except that you add nuts and it can be baked.

Soak a cup of prunes overnight, cook them, pit and chop them up. Mash them with a large package of cream cheese and a little sour cream. If you have a blender this can be done in a second.

Chop finely half a cup of almonds (or pulverize them in the blender before you put in the prunes and cheese) and mix with the prunes and cheese. Enough for 3.

If you like, increase the amounts slightly and bake it in a cooked pie shell (either frozen or homemade, see page 197) for 30 minutes in a 350-degree oven. It is one of the most delicious desserts there is.

BANANAS OR GRAPES WITH SOUR CREAM
AND BROWN SUGAR

This is an excellent dessert to follow a heavy meal, or for those who have only a hot plate or electric skillet, since it requires no cooking.

Seedless green grapes are delicious in this combination. Now that the grape strike has been won, we can all eat grapes again—and enjoy them.

If using grapes, about ¾ pound is sufficient.

Slice 4 bananas and cover immediately with sour cream and brown sugar. Add a squeeze of lemon juice and toss well. Serves 3–4.

GUAVA SHELLS WITH CREAM CHEESE

An incredibly simple Latin American dessert, this requires no cooking at all. It is often served with salted crackers. The guava shells are very sweet and make an interesting contrast with the cream cheese.

For each person, allow 2 guava shells. Serve them on a plate with about 2 tablespoons cream cheese. A can of guavas is enough for 3–4 people.

MANJAR BLANCO

This is a Chilean dish that can be made simply by boiling an un-opened can of condensed milk in a pan of water for 3–4 hours. Keep adding water as it evaporates. Then refrigerate until cold.

Use sweetened condensed milk. The result is a thick caramel absolutely delicious on its own, with fruit (great with bananas), or as a filling for cakes. This is a good thing to keep on hand for emergencies. Boil several cans at once in a big pot and don't open them until you need them.

Caution: Do *not* open the can while it is still hot or the contents will shoot all over the room. It's a dead giveaway that you've been cooking in your room, and, what's more, you could be badly burned.

BUTTERED APPLES

Apples are a good cheap dessert and, when cooked properly, are delicious. They can be served hot or cold, but they should not be overcooked.

This dish can be cooked on top of the stove, but it's better in the oven. Carefully peel and slice a couple of pounds of good tart apples. Put them in a baking dish with a couple of tablespoons butter, lemon juice, about 4 tablespoons brown sugar and some grated lemon peel. Cook for about half an hour in a moderate (350-degree) oven.

GOUCHER COLLEGE APPLE CRISP

This is incredibly simple. Using foil makes cleaning up easier.

Cook 2 pounds of apples, peeled and chopped, in a pan with cinnamon and a little butter.

On a piece of foil, mix ½ cup uncooked oats, 4 tablespoons butter, and 3 tablespoons brown sugar. Cook in a moderate oven (350 degrees) or under the broiler until crisp. Don't let it burn.

Top apples with the oat mixture and serve hot or cold. Serves 4.

APPLE CHARLOTTE

Slice 2 pounds of tart apples and cook them with 3 tablespoons butter, grated lemon rind, and sugar to taste. Stir often and remove from heat when thick.

Trim the crusts off about 8 pieces of stale bread. Dip them in melted butter (or fry them on one side only in butter) and, buttered side out, carefully line a baking dish with the bread, so that the apple won't leak out. Pour in the apples and top with more bread, buttered side up. Bake in a hot oven for about 30 minutes. Serve with melted apricot jam, if you like. Enough for 4–6.

BAKED BANANAS UNIVERSITY OF PUERTO RICO

In Puerto Rico, where they practically give bananas away, this dessert costs next to nothing, and you can be lavish with the rum. Bananas are cheap elsewhere in the States, too, and if you're anxious to impress someone, buy a miniature of rum (it costs about 50 cents) and pour it on the bananas before you bake them. To be really impressive, heat the rum after the bananas have cooked, pour it on, taking care that you're not standing under the curtains or that your hair isn't falling into it, light the rum and run to the table before the flames die out. If that doesn't work, nothing will.

Peel and cut about 6 to 8 bananas in half lengthwise. Put them in a baking dish and dot with butter, brown sugar, one tablespoon of honey, the juice of an orange and half a lemon, some nutmeg and cinnamon, and bake for half an hour in a moderate oven.

You can also put in some bitter marmalade (instead of the orange juice). If you like, serve the bananas with heavy cream.

GEORGETOWN BAKED PEACHES

This is another instant seduction dessert. Make it when peaches are cheap.

Drop about 6 peaches into boiling water, remove, and peel them. Cut them in half and remove their stones. Place in a buttered baking dish and dot with butter and a little brown sugar and bake for half an hour in a moderate oven.

Take a miniature bottle of brandy (costs about 50 cents) and warm it slightly over a low flame. Make sure all inflammable things are out of the way (or the whole evening will be ruined) and pour it over the peaches. Set it alight and run to the table. If you're greedy, serve the peaches with heavy cream. Enough for 4.

ORANGE CUSTARD

This is an easy custard which is cooked on top of the stove and can be served hot or cold.

Squeeze the juice from about five oranges, strain and combine in a saucepan with 3 beaten eggs, a tablespoon of sugar and a dash of cinnamon. Stir over low heat until it thickens, without letting it boil—or you will get scrambled eggs. Served in individual bowls, it is enough for 4.

BAKED CUSTARD

A simple and very healthy custard which is good with fruit.

Heat a pint of milk nearly to boiling and add 2 eggs and 2 egg yolks beaten together, and 2½ tablespoons of sugar. Mix well and pour into a buttered baking dish. Grate some nutmeg on top. Cook in a pan of water for about an hour in a moderate (350-degree) oven. Enough for 4.

WINTER FRUIT COMPOTE

Preheat oven to 350 degrees. Soak 1 cup of dried prunes and 1 cup of dried apricots overnight. Put them in a baking dish with 1 cup of the liquid, and add a squeeze of lemon and 2 tablespoons of honey. Bake for 30 minutes. Serves 4.

EMERGENCY DESSERTS

Almost everyone, some more than others, knows that desperate feeling that comes upon you late at night when for one reason or another you become *very* hungry, and hungry for something sweet. When you look in the refrigerator, cold greasy hamburger, a green-rimmed three-week-old sauce that you said you were going to use up, a jar of pickles and some frozen chicken stock stare you in the eye.

Well, if you have some eggs, some sugar, honey or molasses, some stale bread, some kind of cereal, or some cooking chocolate, you're in business for one of these emergency desserts.

BILL'S BAKLAVA

Crunchy Granola is a delicious cereal available in all health food stores, and worth getting acquainted with.

Add to a bowl of crunchy Granola a dollop of honey or molasses, or both. Stir together until it's like baklava. Add some pistachio nuts, if you're lucky enough to have some on hand. Tell everyone it's *baklava*.

CHOCOLATE CRISPIES

Use Rice Krispies or corn flakes. Rice Krispies are better.

To one cup of cereal melt 4 ounces bitter chocolate over low heat with a little water, sugar to taste, and a teaspoon of butter. Coat the cereal with the chocolate and form it into balls. Let the chocolate set (if you can control yourself for a few minutes) and eat.

Milk chocolate can also be used for these. Omit the sugar.

KENYON COLLEGE FRITTERS

Use up stale bread for this recipe.

8 slices bread, with crusts removed

Syrup

½ cup honey and/or brown sugar
  Small amount of water
  Dash cinnamon
  Grated lemon peel
2 cups milk

1 tablespoon honey
  Dash mace (optional)
2 eggs, beaten
2 tablespoons oil and/or butter

Combine honey or brown sugar (or a mixture of the two), cinnamon, and lemon peel with a little water. Cook for about 10 minutes.

Combine milk, honey, and mace, if you like. Warm a little to melt the honey. Soak the bread slices, halved, if you like, in the milk mixture. Drain. Now soak the bread in the beaten egg. Drain.

Heat oil, or oil and butter mixed, in a skillet. Add bread and fry until golden. Serve with the syrup. Serves 4.

MINUTE RICE PUDDING

1 cup Minute Rice, cooked
2 cups milk
2 eggs
¼ cup sugar

½ teaspoon vanilla
  Nutmeg
  Chopped nuts, raisins, or dates
    (if available)

Scald milk and add cooked rice. Beat together eggs, vanilla, and nutmeg. Pour a little of the hot milk mixture into eggs, stirring constantly. Return the mixture to the rice and milk, and cook over very low heat (use a double boiler, if you have one) until thick but not scrambled. Add chopped nuts, raisins, or dates (whatever is on hand). Serve hot or cold. Serves 2–3.

BREAD

In many parts of the country it is impossible to get any other kind of bread except the dreadful plastic-packaged kind, cut into even slices and made from a concoction of chemicals that would warm the heart of any chemistry student—except that these chemicals are supposed to be *eaten.* Even wholewheat bread, supposedly such a healthy food, is more often than not made to look "wholewheat" by adding caramel coloring to white flour, rather than by using wholewheat grains.

Few people understand what the additives in breads are and why so many breads are called "vitamin enriched." Adelle Davis says in her book *Let's Cook It Right* that "it is as logical to say you were enriched by a burglar who robs you of 25 or more articles but drops three small ones during his getaway as to claim that flour is enriched by being robbed of 22 or more nutrients."

Obviously, if you eat bread, and if there isn't a health food store or a decent bakery near you, you have only one way out: bake your own.

WHOLEWHEAT BREAD

Yeast is a living organism and grows at a temperature of 80–85 degrees. If it is allowed to grow too much or not kept warm enough it becomes sour. It is killed when put into a hot oven.

The more you beat and knead the dough, the better your bread will be. And it's a great way to work off frustrations.

3 cups warm, not hot, milk	6 cups wholewheat flour
¾ cup molasses or honey	2 teaspoons salt
½ cup (4 ounces) butter, oil, or	Sesame or poppy seeds (optional)
margarine	Melted butter (optional)
2 tablespoons yeast	

Mix milk with the molasses, butter, and yeast. Leave for 5 minutes.

In a mixing bowl, make a well in 4 cups of flour. Beat the yeast mixture with the salt into the flour for about 10 minutes. Add the rest of the flour and beat in. Knead the dough on a floured board by folding it over toward you, then pushing it away with the heel of your palm. Do this for about 8 minutes, until the dough is smooth and elastic. Put it in a large bowl in a warm place (the sun on a summer day, the top of a warm stove, in a warm turned-off oven, or in a bowl of warm water) and cover with a cloth. Allow to rise until double in bulk (about 1½ hours). Punch down, divide into 3 loaves, and put into three 1-pound bread tins. Preheat the oven to 350 degrees. Allow to rise again for another 30 minutes. Bake for about 1 hour. One test for doneness is to invert loaf (protect your hands) and tap bottom of loaf with a pencil. If it sounds hollow, it is done. Brush crust with melted butter, if desired.

OATMEAL BREAD

This is made by the same method as Wholewheat Bread (above). A mixture of wholewheat and plain flour will lighten the bread, although it won't be as good for you.

3 cups warm milk	2 teaspoons salt
¾ cup honey or molasses	2 cups regular oats (not instant)
½ cup butter or margarine	4–5 cups flour
2 tablespoons yeast	

Mix the milk with the molasses, butter, and yeast. Leave for 5 minutes.

In a large mixing bowl, make a well in the oats and 2 cups of flour. Beat the yeast mixture with the salt into the flour and oats. Beat for about 10 minutes. Add the remaining flour and knead. (See recipe for Wholewheat Bread for kneading and rising of the dough.) Let rise. Beat down. Let rise again. Bake in a preheated 400-degree oven for about 45 minutes. Makes 3 loaves.

BANANA BREAD

A delicious bread for breakfast, with meals or for sandwiches. It takes only a short time to prepare and cook.

½ cup butter or margarine
½ cup honey or molasses
3 eggs, beaten
⅔ cup milk
4 ripe bananas, mashed

1¾ cups wholewheat flour
2 teaspoons baking powder
½ teaspoon salt
⅓ cup raisins or chopped nuts or both (optional)

Preheat oven to 350 degrees.

Cream the butter and add the molasses. Beat together until light, and add the eggs and milk.

Sift together the flour, baking powder, and salt. Add raisins and coat in the flour. Alternately add the flour mixture and the mashed bananas to the butter-egg mixture, a little at a time, beating well after each addition. Turn the mixture into a greased baking tin and bake for about 1 hour. Makes 1 loaf.

IRISH SODA BREAD

This is a great last-minute bread. It is incredibly simple to make and takes only 45 minutes to bake. Serve it for breakfast, or anytime.

3 cups wholewheat flour (or two cups wholewheat, one cup white)
1 teaspoon salt
1 teaspoon sugar (optional)

2 teaspoons baking powder
½ cup sour milk, buttermilk, or plain milk
Additional milk, as needed

Preheat oven to 350 degrees. Put the flour in a large mixing bowl and add the salt, sugar (if you like), and baking powder. Mix well, make a hole, or well, in the middle, and add about half a cup of milk.

Mix. Add more milk as necessary to make a stiff dough. Shape into a round loaf and bake for about 45 minutes.

SCONES

Make these at the last minute for breakfast, or to serve with meals. They can be made with white flour, but wholewheat is better.

2 cups wholewheat flour
2 teaspoons baking powder
½ teaspoon salt

¼ cup (2 ounces) butter or
    margarine, cut into pieces
½ cup or more of milk or sour milk

Preheat oven to 375 degrees.

Mix the flour with baking powder and salt. Add the butter, cut into little pieces, and work it into the flour with your fingers until it is like fine breadcrumbs (as you do for making pastry). Make a well in the middle and add the milk. With a fork, gather the mixture into a dough, adding more milk if necessary. Roll out on a floured board and cut rounds with a glass or biscuit cutter. Put the scones on a floured pan and cook for 15–20 minutes, until lightly browned.

OATMEAL BISCUITS

No better directions are needed than Oscar Tschirky's own, from this 1896 recipe in his cookbook from the Waldorf:

"Mix with one pound of oatmeal half a pound of flour and one tablespoonful of baking powder, rub in half a pound of butter, and, when it is smooth, stir in enough warm water to knead the whole into a paste, turn onto a table and roll out very thin. Cut the paste into rounds, lay them on a baking sheet, and bake in the oven. When they are cooked, leave the biscuits until they are cold, then pack them in biscuit tins, and keep them in a dry cupboard. They are served at luncheon very often."

WHEATGERM MUFFINS

These are great anytime.

1 cup warm milk
4 tablespoons honey or molasses
1 egg, beaten
1 cup wheatgerm

1 cup wholewheat flour
1 teaspoon salt
2 teaspoons baking powder

Preheat oven to 400 degrees. Melt the honey or molasses in the warm milk and cool. Beat in the egg, then the wheatgerm. Mix the flour, salt, and baking powder, and add. Mix well into a stiff dough. Turn out on a floured board and cut into rounds with a biscuit cutter or a glass. Bake on a floured pan for about 20 minutes.

WHOLEWHEAT PIE CRUST

This is very easy to make. Many of the recipes in this book call for a cooked pie crust, and this is so very much better than the frozen ones that it is worth taking the trouble to make it.

This can, of course, be made with white flour, but wholewheat is better.

2 cups wholewheat flour	¾ cup butter or margarine
½ teaspoon salt	6 tablespoons cold water, or more
½ teaspoon sugar	if necessary

Mix the flour, salt, and sugar in a bowl. Chop up the butter and add. Blend it in with the tips of your fingers or a pastry blender until it is like breadcrumbs. Add the water gradually and stir, working into a dough. Add more water, if necessary. Put the dough on a floured board and knead it away with the heel of your palm, once or twice. Shape into a ball and roll out very thin on a floured board. Enough for two 8-inch pans.

Partially Cooked Pie Crust for Fillings

When you have rolled out the crust, gently ease it onto the pie tin. Move it as near the center as possible. Ease the sides down and gently press the pastry flat at the bottom. Then press the sides to the tin. Trim off all but an inch of the pastry hanging over the top. Pinch it together to make a fat rim around the top of the tin. With the prongs of a fork, press down on the rim all the way around, to make it look pretty and even. Then prick the pastry all over with the fork to prevent bubbles from forming as it cooks.

Cut aluminum foil into strips about four inches wide. Arrange them around the sides of the pastry shell. Fill shell with dried beans and bake in a preheated 400-degree oven for about 10 minutes. Take it out of the oven and remove the foil and the beans. Return it to the oven and cook it for 8 minutes more. Remove. It is now ready to be used for whatever filling you have chosen.

All this may sound very complicated, but it isn't. When you have done it once or twice, it will become so easy that you won't even have to look at the instructions.

CREPES

Crêpes are nothing more than glorified pancakes. They are cheap and are easy to make. They can be refrigerated for a week, or frozen.

They are great for using up leftovers. You can fill them with chopped meat, chicken, fish, mushrooms, and spinach or other vegetables, cooked and mixed with a little Sauce Béchamel (page 107) or Sauce Mornay (page 115). Pour the rest of the sauce on top, sprinkle with a little grated cheese, and brown under the broiler.

Crêpes are also good for desserts, filled with various kinds of jam or honey, chopped fruits, or even ice cream.

There are two very important points to remember:
1. The crêpes must be extremely thin.
2. They must be cooked with almost no fat.

Batter

½ teaspoon salt	2 cups milk
2 cups flour (preferably wholewheat)	4 eggs
	4 tablespoons melted butter

If you have a blender, the job is practically done for you. Simply blend all ingredients at top speed for a few seconds. Stop, scrape down any flour which has stuck to the sides, and blend for a couple of seconds more.

If making by hand, combine the flour and salt. Mix the eggs with the milk and butter, and stir into the flour. Stir together (don't beat) until thoroughly mixed.

Let the batter stand for a few hours or overnight before you use it.

Take a small frying pan about 8–10 inches in diameter. If you have only a large pan, you'll have to make huge crêpes and cut them in half. Put the batter and a ladle or large spoon next to the stove. Dip a paper towel into oil. Heat the pan and wipe it round with the oiled towel. When it starts to smoke, spoon in about 1 tablespoon of batter and tilt the pan so that it runs all over it and covers the bottom with a thin layer. This is the hard part, but with practice you'll be able to tilt the pan in all directions at once. Pour off any excess batter; otherwise, the crêpes will be too thick.

Leave the pancake in the pan until it starts to curl very slightly around the edges. Either with a fork or with your fingers, lift it out and turn it over. Cook for a couple of minutes and remove. Repeat the process with the next crêpe, but don't add any more butter until it's really necessary.

The first crêpe always tastes awful. By the time you're to your third or fourth, they'll be delicious. The last ones are usually perfect.

Pile the crêpes up on a plate and, if you are going to use them right away, cover them with a cloth and keep them warm in the oven. The cloth prevents their drying out.

Add a little filling to each crêpe, and fold its edges over filling. Arrange filled crêpes in a shallow baking dish, and pour on the sauce you have chosen. Sprinkle with cheese, if you like, and run under the broiler until browned.

BREAKFAST PANCAKES

Everyone loves pancakes served with molasses and strips of bacon. Make the batter before you go to bed the night before.

1½ cups flour (preferably
    wholewheat)
1 teaspoon baking powder
½ teaspoon salt
1 egg, beaten

1½ cups milk
2 tablespoons oil, melted butter
    or margarine
Melted bacon fat or oil

Mix the flour, baking powder, and salt. Combine the egg with the milk and fat. Mix into the flour to form a thick batter. If possible, leave for a few hours or overnight.

Wipe a small skillet round with a paper towel dipped in a little melted bacon fat or oil. Have the batter next to the stove, with a ladle or large spoon handy. Pour some batter into the pan and leave for a few minutes. When the pancake begins to curl slightly at the rim edge and bubbles form on top, turn it over with a spatula. Cook until done on the other side and transfer to a heated plate. Keep warm in the oven.

Unlike crêpes, pancakes should be fairly thick. They should not be greasy, but the first one almost always is. This recipe makes about 10 pancakes.

SOUTHERN CALIFORNIA
REFRIGERATOR DATE ROLL

This will keep for two weeks in the refrigerator. It is delicious with ice cream or whipped cream. It needs *no cooking.*

2 cups bran flakes, rolled fine
2 cups corn flakes, rolled fine
1 cup California dates, chopped fine
¾ cup milk

¼ cup dry sherry or rum (optional)
1 cup chopped white marshmallows
1 cup chopped Brazil nuts
¼ pound powdered sugar

Reserve ½ cup of the combined rolled flakes for the top. Mix all the remaining ingredients together thoroughly and shape into a long roll. Toss in the reserved flakes, wrap, and keep overnight in the refrigerator. Serve sliced, with cream or ice cream.

BRANDY SNAPS

There isn't any brandy in these traditional English cookies. Where did the name come from? These are easy to make and take only 12 minutes to bake. They are soft when they come out of the oven and should be quickly curled round the handle of a wooden spoon. Then, if you like, you can fill them with whipped cream.

1 cup molasses
1 pound flour
2 teaspoons ground ginger
1½ cups sugar
¼ cup butter (2 ounces) melted

Preheat oven to 400 degrees. Mix everything together and drop, a tablespoon at a time, on a greased baking sheet. Bake for about 12 minutes.

HASHISH FUDGE

This recipe was inspired by the famous Alice B. Toklas "haschich fudge" and is excellent even without the "haschich," although it does not produce quite the same aftereffects. But no one is urging you to risk five days to ten years in jail (depending on which state you are lucky or unlucky enough to be in) over a piece of fudge, so please yourself.

½ cup milk
1½ cups brown sugar
¾ cup granulated sugar
Pinch salt
2 tablespoons butter

½ cup chopped walnuts
½ cup chopped almonds
½ cup dried apricots
½ cup dried figs
Powdered hashish (if desired)

In a saucepan combine the milk, brown sugar, granulated sugar and salt and bring to a boil, stirring constantly. When a spoonful of the syrup forms a soft ball when put into cold water, the mixture is done.

Remove from heat and add 2 tablespoons butter. Add a cup each of chopped nuts and dried fruit. At this point you may add your powdered hashish.

Mix well, shape into a cake, cool and slice. For heaven's sake don't eat the whole thing.

BROWNIES

Brownies have become very popular recently in colleges all over the country. Here is a simple little recipe which can be improved upon, according to your discretion.

2 ounces melted chocolate	2 eggs
⅓ cup butter, melted with the chocolate	1 teaspoon vanilla
	Dash salt
½ cup molasses	½ cup milk
½ cup brown sugar	½ teaspoon baking powder
⅓ cup chopped walnuts or pecans	

Preheat oven to 350 degrees. Melt butter and chocolate together over very low heat. Mix everything together. Put in a greased 8-inch pie pan. Bake for about 30 minutes. They are done when a knife inserted in the middle comes out clean.

Electric Skillet
and Hot Plate Dishes

If you are living in a kitchenless one-room apartment and have been lucky enough to secure an electric skillet, you are in business. On the other hand, if you can afford only a hot plate, although you won't be able to cook the variety of things you could in the skillet, you will still be able to make plenty of good meals, and even have people to dinner.

Although the recipes given in this chapter are specifically for kitchenless cooks, you will find a great many recipes elsewhere in the book that can also be done easily in the skillet or on the hot plate—most of them in fact.

If you are used to eating a green vegetable with every meal, you may have to substitute a salad. Instead of potatoes, rice, or pasta, unless they are to be cooked in the same pot, you can substitute good bread such as French, Italian, dark, or rye. Many recipes are suitable for being cooked together at the same time in the skillet, and sometimes this is possible on a hot plate, with the use of aluminum foil. But this can sometimes get complicated if you are serving a lot of people. A casserole, served with fruit, cheese, salad, and bread, will feed quite a few people. As long as the ingredients are *real* and fresh, no one could ask for more.

Cooking in the Skillet

The electric skillet is one of the most versatile cooking tools there is. In it you can deep-fry, stir-fry, pot-roast, poach, stew, boil, even bake. By using foil separators, you can cook several foods in the skillet at the same time. Either use foil paper and wrap the food tightly, so that the juices won't escape, or buy several small aluminum containers to be used for cooking vegetables, sauces, or whatever you like at the same time you are frying or stewing something else in the skillet.

The recipes in this chapter are intended to show you what kinds of recipes and complete meals can be cooked in one pan. When you get the hang of it, you will see other recipes that can be successfully prepared in the skillet.

Electric skillets take longer to heat up than gas, but they cool off slower. When you put your food in, the temperature falls, so turn it up to maintain the right heat, then turn it down again.

Stews, soups, and casseroles are excellent cooked in the skillet. They can also be kept hot for a long time. If you wrap food in foil, you can keep it hot for a long time at 150–180 degrees. Food can also be steamed in a small amount of liquid in aluminum foil or in a container. For parties, casseroles can be kept hot all evening. French or garlic bread can be wrapped in foil and heated through in the skillet. As a chafing dish for fondue, the skillet is excellent, and you can keep it warm for as long as you like, adding more liquid if it gets dry.

Stir-fried Chinese food is great cooked in the skillet; the flat surface and the even heat are perfect for stir-fried foods. Pancakes take well to the skillet for this reason.

To clean the skillet, wipe it around with soapy water. If anything is sticking, soak it overnight and scrape it off the next day with a wooden spoon. Never put the temperature control in water.

Cooking on a Hot Plate

A frying pan, a small saucepan, and a large casserole are the basic utensils you need. The best kind of hot plate to buy is the one with two controls, so that you can turn it down. You must also have an asbestos mat, so that food can be kept hot without burning.

You can cook several dishes on the hot plate at once, in a large frying pan with a lid. It must be a heavy frying pan; otherwise, the food will stick and burn. If you are cooking for more than two or three people, unless your pan is a very good one, you might be safer with a casserole. All the food goes into one pot, cooks slowly, and gives off a delicious smell. There's no chance of its burning while you answer the telephone. If you are cooking for yourself, you can reheat a casserole the next day, and it will have improved on sitting overnight.

A bucket of water next to you, into which you can dip spoons, etc., will be a great help if you have no water in your room; a sheet of newspaper will protect your landlady's carpet.

BOSTON SHRIMP CHILI

A very simple last-minute skillet dish. Serve it with Green Salad (page 136) and Italian or French bread. Have beer to drink with it, and cheese for dessert.

1 pound small shrimp	parsley
Juice of ½ lemon	About ¾ cup water or white
2 tablespoons chopped dill or	wine

2 cans chili, with beans   Coarse salt and freshly ground
1 clove garlic, chopped   black pepper
Dash Tabasco   ¼ cup grated Parmesan cheese
Extra chili powder, to taste

Wash the shrimp. Put the lemon and dill in the skillet with enough water to cover the bottom. When it is boiling, add the shrimp and cook for 2 minutes. Remove and peel.

Empty out the shrimp water (save it for stock, if you like) and add the chili with beans. Season with garlic, Tabasco, and chili powder (if you want it hotter), salt and pepper. Return the shrimp to the chili when it is bubbling, sprinkle with cheese, and cook for a couple of minutes. Serve very hot. Serves 3–4.

See also
SHRIMP WITH MAYONNAISE, page 28
FRIED, GRILLED, AND POACHED FISH, see fish chapter, page 20

FISH WITH CAPERS, OLIVES, AND LEMON JUICE WITH FRIED ZUCCHINI

Serve French bread with this dish for a filling meal. By using aluminum foil, you can cook both the fish and the zucchini at the same time. Put the foil across half the skillet, turning the edges up so that the liquid will not spill over. Make sure you have a large enough piece of foil, so that you can turn the edges over and cover the fish. While the fish is cooking in the foil, the zucchini is frying in the other half of the skillet. If you peel zucchini, it cooks faster.

2 fish fillets, washed and dried   Coarse salt and freshly ground
1 tablespoon butter   black pepper
1 tablespoon olive oil   2 medium-sized zucchini, peeled and
Juice of a lemon   sliced
2 tablespoons capers   1 tablespoon olive oil
2 tablespoons chopped olives   1 garlic clove, crushed

Arrange the foil and turn skillet to medium-high heat (about 350 degrees). Put the butter and oil in the foil part, and the oil in the other part of the skillet. Add the garlic to the zucchini part of the skillet. When the oil and butter are hot, add the fish and fry lightly on both sides. Add zucchini to the skillet and fry it until brown on all sides. While the zucchini is cooking, add the lemon juice, capers, and olives to the fish, season, and seal the foil over it, so that it will bake inside and retain its juices. By the time the zucchini is done, the fish should be ready. Fish is done when the flesh is white and flakes with a fork. Serves 2.

CHICKEN SAUTÉ WITH CUCUMBERS

Before sautéing the chicken, read instructions on page 37.

French bread, white wine, and a tomato salad would go very well with this dish.

1 frying chicken, cut up	1 cup white wine
3 tablespoons butter	Squeeze of lemon juice, to taste
1 tablespoon olive oil	Coarse salt and freshly ground
3 medium-sized cucumbers, peeled	black pepper
and seeded	1 tablespoon butter, to enrich sauce
2 tablespoons chopped fresh dill	

Dry the chicken pieces with paper towels. In the skillet heat the butter and oil to 360 degrees. Brown the chicken lightly on all sides. Remove. Cut the cucumber into half-inch pieces and add to pan with the dill. Cook, stirring, for 2 minutes. Return the dark meat to the pan. Cover and cook 7–8 minutes. Add the white meat and cook 15 minutes more. Remove the chicken and cucumber from the pan to a warm side dish. Add the wine and scrape up the cooking juices. Boil until reduced to one-third of its volume. Add the lemon juice, seasonings, and butter. Return the other ingredients to the pan. Heat through. Serves 4.

SAUTÉED CHICKEN WITH CHEESE POTATOES

Serve this meal with salad and, if you like, red wine.

1 frying chicken, cut up	sliced
3 tablespoons butter	2–3 tablespoons grated Cheddar
1 tablespoon olive oil	cheese
3 strips bacon, chopped	Coarse salt
1 clove garlic, crushed	Freshly ground black pepper
1 pound potatoes, peeled and	

Dry the chicken thoroughly with paper towels. Heat the butter and oil and when hot, sauté the chicken until brown. Remove. Return the dark meat and cook 7–8 minutes, covered. Then add the light meat and cook for about 15 minutes. When the juices run clear when pricked by a fork, the chicken is done. Remove, drain, season, and wrap in foil. Put the foil in a corner of the skillet.

Add bacon and garlic to the skillet. When crisp, remove it and add the potatoes. Fry until golden brown. Add the cheese, toss the potatoes in it, add the bacon, and turn the skillet off. Wait a few minutes until the cheese melts through. Season. Serves 4.

For other sautéed chicken recipes, see
POULTRY chapter, page 31

CHICKEN BONNE FEMME

Bonne femme means "good woman." With the good woman's dish you need serve nothing but salad, since everything else is in the pot.

1 frying chicken, cut up	2 cups chicken stock or bouillon
2 strips bacon, chopped	Dash thyme
1 tablespoon butter	Bay leaf
¼ pound mushrooms, sliced	1 pound potatoes, peeled and diced
6 small white onions	1 tablespoon chopped fresh parsley,
1 tablespoon flour	to garnish

Dry the chicken pieces thoroughly. Heat the skillet and fry the bacon with the butter. Remove and add the chicken. Brown on all sides. Remove and drain. Add the mushrooms and onions and brown. Return the bacon and chicken to the skillet and add all remaining ingredients except the potatoes. Cook for 40 minutes, or until the chicken is done.

Fifteen minutes before the end, add the potatoes. Garnish with parsley. Serves 4.

CREAMED CHICKEN LIVERS
WITH POTATO CAKES

Fried chicken, liver, kidneys, or brains can also be cooked with these cakes. Don't overcook the meat because it will continue cooking while wrapped in foil in the corner.

Tomato Salad (page 139) or Green Salad (page 136) and red wine go well with this.

1 pound chicken livers	Dash thyme or rosemary
3 tablespoons butter	Coarse salt and freshly ground
¼ cup heavy cream	black pepper

Potato Cakes

2 cups mashed potatoes	2 tablespoons butter (softened)
1 egg, beaten	2 tablespoons flour

Coarse salt and freshly ground	Cheddar cheese, grated
black pepper	(optional)
Oil or bacon fat	Butter (optional)

Mash the potatoes with the egg, butter, and flour. Season. Roll out and cut into squares.

Remove the membranes from the chicken livers. Wash and dry livers. Heat the butter in the skillet and fry the chicken livers until they are almost done. Put them in foil or in an aluminum container. Scrape up the cooking juices with the cream, add herbs, and season. Pour the sauce into the container with the chicken livers, wrap, and place in a corner of the skillet.

Heat oil or fat to cover the bottom of the skillet well, and fry potato cakes until brown. Serve them split open with cheese and butter inside, if you like. Serves 4.

STEAK AU POIVRE

Prepare the steaks in advance and cook them just before you are ready to eat. Serve them with a mixed salad and a good bread with butter.

To crush the peppercorns, wrap them in a cloth and crush them with the thick handle of a large knife or some other suitable blunt instrument.

4 small steaks	2 tablespoons olive oil
1½ teaspoons whole black	1 jigger brandy (optional)
peppercorns	Coarse salt

Trim the steaks and dry them with paper towels. Crush the peppercorns and press them into the steak. Smack them in with the flat of the blade of a large knife. Heat the oil in the skillet. When hot, add the steaks. Cook them according to taste, season, and remove. Add the brandy if you like, swirl it around the skillet, light it with a long match, and pour it flaming over the steaks before serving. (If you try to pour it for individual servings, the last person will end up without sauce.) Serves 4.

See
HAMBURGERS, page 50 and STEAKS, page 49

Also see
Beef stews under BEEF, page 54

LAMB AND RICE PILAF

You can make this in advance and reheat with the tomato sauce. All you need to serve with it is a salad. Since you need only ½ pound of meat to serve four people, this is an extremely economical dish.

4 tomatoes, chopped	1 clove garlic, chopped
Coarse salt and freshly ground	1 cup rice
black pepper	2 tablespoons raisins
½ cup sour cream or yoghurt	1 green pepper, diced
2 tablespoons olive oil	Dash rosemary or thyme
½ pound lamb, cut into ½-inch	1 can chicken bouillon
cubes	1 can water
2 onions, chopped	Chopped parsley (optional)

Heat the skillet and add the tomatoes. Season, and cook until they become a thick purée. Add the cream or yoghurt and remove.

Wipe out the pan. Heat the oil and brown the lamb. Remove. Add the onion and garlic. Cook for about 7 minutes, without burning. Add the rice and cook, stirring frequently, until it becomes opaque. Add the lamb, raisins, pepper, and herbs with chicken bouillon and water. Bring to a boil, then turn down heat and simmer gently until the rice is cooked (about 20 minutes). Put the tomato mixture on top, heat through, and sprinkle with chopped parsley, if desired, before serving. Serves 4.

See
LAMB PATTIES page 62, and lamb casseroles under LAMB, page 65

HUNGARIAN POTATOES AND PORK

This might be called a very inexpensive goulash. A green salad, with wine or beer, is all you need for dinner. This recipe is easily doubled.

1 pound stewing pork, cut into small	1 cup stock or bouillon
pieces	Coarse salt and freshly ground
1 pound potatoes, sliced and dried	black pepper
1 onion, sliced	1 cup sour cream
3 tablespoons butter	1 tablespoon chopped chives or
1 tablespoon oil	parsley (optional)
1 teaspoon Hungarian paprika	

Dry the pork thoroughly. In the skillet, heat the oil and butter. Fry the pork and remove. Fry the onion and the potatoes until brown, return the pork to the pan, and add the paprika and stock. Stir well, season, and cover. Cook for 1 hour. Stir in sour cream and herbs just before serving. Serves 4.

SWEET AND SOUR PORK WITH CABBAGE

When it is cooked by the Chinese method, a little meat goes a long way. When shredded and quickly stir-fried in oil, it is very tender and juicy.

1 onion, chopped
1 clove garlic, chopped
4 tablespoons peanut or vegetable
  oil
½ pound pork, shredded
1 cabbage, shredded (Chinese
  cabbage, if possible)

3 tomatoes, chopped
2 tablespoons red wine vinegar
1 teaspoon cornstarch mixed with
  1 teaspoon water
2 tablespoons sugar
  Dash soy sauce
  Freshly ground black pepper

In a skillet, heat the oil to 375 degrees and stir-fry the onion and garlic for 2 minutes without burning. Make sure that the pork is thoroughly dry before you fry it. Add the pork and stir-fry for 3 minutes. Add the cabbage and stir-fry. When it is considerably reduced in bulk, add the tomatoes and cook until the mixture thickens. Add the vinegar and the cornstarch mixture and cook for about 5 minutes more. Just before serving add sugar, soy sauce, and pepper. Correct seasoning. Serves 4–6.

See

PORK WITH SAUERKRAUT, page 224
CHINESE PORK WITH WATERCRESS, page 224

CHOPS WITH STIR-FRIED SPINACH

Pork chops are the cheapest chops, but they take the longest to cook (about 30 minutes). You should cover pork chops while they cook; veal and lamb chops do not need to be covered. When the chops are ready, remove them from the pan and scrape up the cooking juices with a little wine or stock. Remove them to a side dish with the sauce, wipe out the pan with paper towels, and add the oil for the spinach. The spinach is done in about two minutes so there's no need to keep the chops warm. Naturally, you should serve this at once.

1 onion, sliced
2 tablespoons olive oil
4 chops, dried
  Flour or cornstarch, as needed
¼ cup wine or stock for sauce
¼ teaspoon mixed herbs
  Coarse salt and freshly ground
  black pepper

1 tablespoon peanut or vegetable
  oil
1 clove garlic, crushed
1 tablespoon chopped fresh ginger,
  if available
1 pound spinach, washed and dried
  Coarse salt
  Freshly ground black pepper

Dry the chops and slice the onion. Heat the skillet to 375 degrees, add the onion and fry lightly. Add the chops and brown on both sides. Cook until done, remove from pan, and pour out as much fat as you can without losing the good brown juices. If very greasy, add a little flour or cornstarch. Scrape up the cooking juices with the wine, add the herbs, season, bring to a boil and pour over the chops. Wipe the pan and add the oil. When hot, add garlic and ginger. Cook for 2 minutes. Add the spinach and fry, stirring constantly, for about 2 minutes. Season. Serves 4.

BRAISED PORK CHOPS
WITH APPLE-HORSERADISH SAUCE

Cook frozen spinach, broccoli, or asparagus at the same time, in foil paper or in an aluminum container placed at the back of the skillet.

Serve with Tomato Salad (page 139), rye bread, and beer or cider. End with cheese.

4 pork chops, dried	Bay leaf
1 tablespoon butter	Dash thyme
1 tablespoon oil	Coarse salt and freshly ground
1 cup beef or chicken stock or	black pepper
bouillon	

Apple-Horseradish Sauce

1 cup applesauce or purée	1 teaspoon mustard (dark)
½ cup sour cream	Coarse salt
¼ cup horseradish	Freshly ground black pepper

Heat the butter and oil in the skillet and brown the chops on both sides. Add the stock and herbs. Simmer gently for 30 minutes. Season.

Meanwhile, make the sauce. Mix together all the ingredients and serve either hot or cold. To serve hot, pour it into the skillet with the chops and use to scrape up the cooking juices. Sprinkle some chopped parsley on top, if you like. Serves 4.

For other pork chop recipes, see
PORK, page 67

LIVER AND ONIONS

If you want to serve this over mashed potatoes, boil the potatoes in the skillet first. Mash them in a corner of the skillet, checking occasionally to see that they don't burn.

Nothing more is needed with this meal except perhaps a salad. Double the ingredients to serve 8.

4 strips bacon
4 large onions, sliced
4 pieces of liver
    Flour, for dredging
    Coarse salt and freshly ground

black pepper
1 tablespoon chopped fresh parsley,
    to garnish
Mustard

Heat the skillet to 350 degrees. Cook the bacon, remove, and drain. Add the onions and fry until brown. Remove and drain. Scrape up any bits that have stuck to the skillet. Roll the liver in flour and fry lightly on each side, so that it stays rosy in the middle. Season. Put the mashed potatoes on a large plate. Arrange the liver, bacon, and onions around them and sprinkle parsley over the top. Serve with mustard. Serves 4.

For other liver recipes, see
FOODS FOR THE BRAIN, page 230

SAUSAGES WITH CORN AND TOMATOES

Use either a large can of corn or about 2 cups of corn scraped from the cob. You can simmer the fresh corn first, empty out the water, and cook the sausages while you are scraping off the kernels.

You need a foil container in which to keep the sausages warm in a corner of the skillet while the corn-tomato mixture is cooking.

8 pork sausages or hot Italian
    sausages
2 cups cooked corn or canned corn
3 tomatoes, chopped
    Dash basil

Dash thyme
Bay leaf
Coarse salt and freshly ground
    black pepper

Prick the sausages and cook them, using a little water. The water will evaporate. Remove sausages and drain out the fat. Put the sausages in the foil container and place it to one side of the skillet. Heat the butter and add the corn and tomatoes. Add the spices and seasonings and simmer for 15 minutes. Serves 4.

See also
SAUSAGES WITH SAUERKRAUT, page 76
BANGERS AND MASH, page 77

SPINACH CROQUETTES
WITH FRIED HAM OR CHICKEN

Eggs are also good with these croquettes, and dark mustard goes well with this combination.

First, the rice can be cooked in the skillet and drained. Then you can stir-fry the spinach in a couple of tablespoons of oil. Now the pan is ready for the meat. Meanwhile, you can make the croquettes. Finally, the meat remains hot in a foil container while the croquettes are fried.

4 thick ham slices or 4 chicken legs
3 tablespoons oil
1 tablespoon butter

Spinach Croquettes

2 pounds cooked, chopped spinach   **Coarse salt and freshly ground**
1 cup cooked rice   **black pepper**
2 eggs, beaten   **Flour, for dredging**
2 tablespoons grated cheese   **Oil**
3 tablespoons melted butter

Cook the meat in the oil and butter.

Meanwhile, mix the spinach and rice with the eggs, cheese, butter, and seasonings. Shape into patties. Dredge with flour.

When the meat has finished cooking, remove to a foil container. Heat more oil in the skillet, scraping up any cooking juices. Fry the croquettes on high heat and drain on paper towels. Serve with the meat. Serves 4.

VEAL ESCALOPES WITH ASPARAGUS

For   complete information on cooking asparagus, see page 89.

After the asparagus is cooked, the scallops, which take only a few min-utes, are sautéed and their juices swirled into a cream sauce. This is the sort of meal to prepare when you want to impress someone. Since veal scallops aren't the cheapest cuts of meat, it had better be someone who is worth it. It's handy because it is quick and requires little attention. Double the quan-tities for 4.

1 pound asparagus, prepared for   **2 good-sized veal escalopes**
cooking (page 89)   **¼ cup asparagus water**
1 cup water   **Squeeze of lemon juice**
1 tablespoon oil   **2 tablespoons grated cheese**
2 tablespoons butter   **Coarse salt and freshly ground**
¼ pound mushrooms, chopped   **black pepper**

Turn the skillet to 350 degrees and bring the water to a boil. Add the asparagus, allowing the tips to stick out under the lid, over the side of the casserole. After 15–20 minutes (depending on how fat the asparagus is), stick the heads in the water. When cooked, remove to a side dish. Pour out the asparagus water and reserve it.

Heat the butter and oil in the skillet and add the mushrooms. After 5 minutes, add the scallops and fry quickly on both sides. Add cream, asparagus water, and lemon juice. Scrape up the cooking juices. Return the asparagus to the pan, scatter cheese over the top and heat through. Serves 2.

For other veal escalope recipes, see
TEN-MINUTE MEALS, page 217

TOMATO AND EGG CASSEROLE

Serve this with fresh French or Italian bread, red wine, and a green salad. A little good cheese to follow and you have an excellent dinner.

Don't put on the eggs until you're ready to eat.

6 medium-sized onions, sliced	1 clove garlic, chopped
4 tablespoons olive oil	Coarse salt and freshly ground
6 tomatoes, sliced	black pepper
3 peppers, chopped	4 eggs
1 small jar pimientos, chopped	Grated cheese (optional)
Dash thyme or basil	

Heat the oil in the skillet and brown the onions lightly. Add all remaining ingredients, except eggs, and cook together until soft and stewed. Make four indentations in the sauce, so that the eggs won't spread. Break each egg into a cup, one at a time, and slip it into its "nest." By breaking the eggs first into a cup you save yourself the tragedy of damaging a yolk in the skillet. If you break a yolk, save it for scrambled eggs tomorrow.

Cover the skillet and bake until the eggs are set. Sprinkle with cheese, if desired. Serves 4.

STUFFED ZUCCHINI

Serve this dish with a mixed salad, wholewheat bread, and red wine or beer. It is very filling.

Leftovers can also be used for stuffing.

12 medium-sized zucchini	1 onion, chopped
4 tablespoons olive oil	1 clove garlic, chopped

1 cup rice
1 cup minced beef or lamb
1 can tomatoes (reserve juice)
1 tablespoon chopped fresh parsley

Dash basil or tarragon
Coarse salt and freshly ground
    black pepper

Cut the zucchini in half, scoop out their insides, and put the pulp in a bowl. In the skillet, heat the oil and cook the onion until soft. Add the garlic and the rice and cook, stirring, until the rice becomes opaque. Add the beef or lamb and cook for a few minutes more. Add tomatoes with their juice, herbs, and seasonings. Mix well and turn out into a bowl. Stuff the mixture carefully into the zucchini halves. Put them back into the skillet, adding the juice from the canned tomatoes and water as needed, to come about halfway up the sides of the zucchini. Cover and simmer for about 1 hour, or until the rice is cooked. Serves 4 (3 each).

PAELLA

Most people love this dish and it is always attractive to look at, with the yellow rice contrasting with the green of the peppers and the red of the tomatoes. It is an excellent dish for entertaining, since it is cheap, pretty, and needs only a salad and red wine with it.

There are endless variations. The main ingredients are rice, saffron (which colors the rice yellow), chicken, tomatoes, and peppers. Shrimp are usually added, but since they are often expensive, they are listed at the end of the recipe as an alternative. Saffron is expensive, too, but you need only a tiny bit.

You can make this easily in an electric skillet (it is the perfect pan for it) or in a *large* pot on your hot plate.

3 tablespoons olive oil
1 frying chicken, cut up small
1 onion, chopped
1 clove garlic, crushed
4 tomatoes, chopped
5–6 cups of water
3 cups of rice

1 cup diced ham
Dash oregano
2 peppers, chopped
Pinch of saffron
Coarse salt and freshly ground
    black pepper

Heat the oil in the pan or skillet. Add the chicken, well dried, and fry until golden. Remove from pan. Add the onion and garlic and cook until soft. Add the tomatoes and cook for a couple of minutes. Then add the water and return the chicken to the pan. Simmer for 10 minutes. Add the rice, ham, oregano, and peppers, a little at a time so as not to lower the heat too much. Cook for 10 minutes. Add the saffron and seasoning. Cook for a further 10–12 minutes, adding more water, if needed. *Do not stir.* In an emergency, stir only with a fork. Enough for 6.

Variations

Chopped pork
Peas or string beans
Clams
Mussels
Hot sausage, diced
Chopped bacon
Chopped pimientos
Shrimps

ARIZONA PILAF

Another good party dish. As in the Paella, vary the ingredients as you please. This is a hot dish (add more or less chili as you like) and goes best with beer and a green salad.

If you're not cooking this in an electric skillet (which is the best thing for it), use a large pot.

3 tablespoons oil	3 hot sausages, chopped
2 onions, chopped	1 tablespoon chili powder
2 cloves garlic, chopped	Dash thyme
3 cups rice	Bay leaf
¼ pound mushrooms, diced	1 can tomatoes, with juice
1 cup cooked ham or tongue, chopped	5–6 cups beef or chicken stock
4 chicken livers, chopped	Coarse salt and freshly ground black pepper

Heat the oil in the pan and gently fry the onions with the garlic. Add the rice and cook until transparent. Add the mushrooms, ham, livers, sausages, spices and herbs, and the tomatoes, chopped, with their juice. Cook for 2 minutes, then add the stock. Cook for about 15–20 minutes, until most of the liquid has evaporated. Correct seasoning. Serves 6.

CHEESE FONDUE IN AN ELECTRIC SKILLET

A fondue is usually kept hot in a chafing dish over a slow flame. To keep it hot in the skillet, turn control down to "warm" and add more wine if it gets too thick. This dish is excellent for parties and goes well with wine or beer. You can also serve it with a salad as a main course, either for lunch or for dinner. This recipe serves about 8 people. To serve 16, you can double the amount; the skillet will hold it.

1 garlic clove, split
2 cups dry white wine
1 pound grated Gruyère cheese
  (don't use processed cheese)
1 tablespoon cornstarch
½ cup kirsch (you can buy it in
small bottles)
Freshly ground black pepper or
  white pepper
3–4 loaves hot French or Italian
  bread

Rub the garlic clove around the skillet, so that its flavor will be imparted to the fondue. Add the wine and heat almost to the boiling point. Add the cheese, stirring constantly, and bring to a simmer. Mix the cornstarch with the kirsch until smooth, then add to the cheese. Heat until the mixture bubbles. Season with pepper to taste and turn down to "warm." Serve with hot French bread. Serves about 8.

Ten-Minute Meals

When you've been working all day and come home late, the last thing you feel like doing is a lot of cooking. And when you're tired and hungry you want to eat right away, not three hours later. This usually results in a monotony of canned baked beans and frankfurters.

If you are having someone to dinner at the last minute and you're both starving, you certainly don't want to leave your guest hanging around while you toil in the kitchen for hours. Simple dishes, prepared with fresh ingredients and attractively served, will be far more impressive than a series of complicated dishes requiring the use of every pan in the kitchen. There are many simple meals that can be prepared in ten minutes. What's more, they don't all have to come out of the freezer or a tin can.

None of the dishes in this chapter takes longer than ten minutes. Steaks, fish, organ meat, hamburgers, chops, and eggs take a very short time to cook.

While you are preparing your ten-minute meal, your friend can be sitting happily with some hors d'oeuvres. These always impress and you don't have to get mixed up and complicated about them. On your way home get a loaf of good French or Italian bread (or dark bread), some butter (unsalted is best for eating with bread), and perhaps a can of tuna, some salami, a small jar of pimientos or artichoke hearts, some good black or green olives, a tomato, and a hunk of good simple cheese. Arrange them attractively on a plate. You don't have to be lavish with them; just make them look good, and eat any leftovers the next day.

Alternatively, sliced ripe melon served with ginger and a slice of lemon makes an excellent first course. Or try an avocado halved and served with oil and lemon juice, or just plain lemon juice if it's a good one. A can of pâté served with toast is also a good beginning, as is lox with sour cream or smoked fish.

If you want soup, heat a can of bouillon with some vermicelli, chopped ham, or grated Parmesan cheese. Serve with a piece of toast.

For dessert, fresh fruit, fruit salad, bananas with cream or bananas fried in butter and served with sugar and cinnamon, and Guava Shells with Cream Cheese (page 189) take virtually no time at all.

If you're cooking a ten-minute meal for yourself, you could make enough to reheat and eat the next day. Although many of these dishes can stand reheating, each dish takes only ten minutes to prepare fresh, so you might just as well make a fresh one each night.

SARDINES WITH TOMATOES

The sardines may be out of a can, but they are excellent cooked this way. Serve them with buttered wholewheat toast and buttered string beans (frozen ones).

1 can sardines, with oil	Coarse salt and freshly ground
1 onion, chopped	black pepper
1 clove garlic, chopped (optional)	Grated Parmesan cheese
1 small jar pimientos, chopped	Chopped parsley, to garnish
2 tomatoes, chopped	

Empty the oil from the sardine can into a skillet. Sauté the onion with the garlic. Add the pimientos and the tomatoes. Cook for 2 minutes. Add the sardines and season. Simmer for 5 minutes and sprinkle with cheese. Cook another minute to melt the cheese and serve hot. If you like, sprinkle a little chopped fresh parsley on top. Serves 2.

SARDINES ON TOAST

This is so simple to make that it's hard to believe it tastes so good. Tomatoes grilled in the broiler for ten minutes and a can of sweet corn drained and heated with grated Cheddar cheese make a meal.

1 can sardines	Coarse salt and freshly ground
1 tablespoon dark mustard	black pepper
Lemon juice	2 pieces toast, buttered
Dash nutmeg	Dash cayenne pepper
Dash curry powder	

Mash the sardines in a bowl with mustard, plenty of lemon juice, spices, and seasonings. Spread thickly on toast, sprinkle with Cayenne, and put under a hot grill until sizzling. Serve at once. Serves 2.

See also
BRANDEIS SARDINE PATTIES, page 27
SARDINE-STUFFED TOMATOES, page 145

SAUTÉED FISH ROE WITH CREAMED SPINACH

Fish roe is very cheap; many fishmongers almost give it away. It is delicious for a quick meal, cooked in plenty of butter and served with a vegetable to soak up the sauce. Fish roe is also good on buttered toast.

Frozen creamed spinach will save you the bother of chopping and washing fresh spinach (which *will* take you more than 10 minutes).

1 package creamed spinach or	needed
1 package frozen spinach	Juice of half a lemon
1 pound fish roe	Coarse salt and freshly ground
4 tablespoons butter, or more as	black pepper

Wash the fish roe. Bring some water to a boil for the spinach if it is the kind that comes in a plastic bag. Otherwise, put the frozen spinach in a pan over very low heat until it has thawed out. Cook the spinach while you are doing the roe. Melt the butter in a small pan and toss the roes in it until they are cooked. Squeeze lemon on them, season, and serve hot. Season spinach. Serves 2.

See also
Grilled fish with GREEN SAUCE, page 21
Fried fish with SAUCE TARTARE, page 23
GRILLED MACKEREL, page 22
HERRING SALAD, page 144
SHRIMP WITH MAYONNAISE, page 28
BOSTON SHRIMP CHILI, page 203

DEVILED CHICKEN
WITH FRIED POTATOES AND PEPPERS

Last-minute cooks sometimes have to make do with precooked chicken. However, if you try it this way, it will have a completely different flavor. If possible, buy the chicken the day before and leave it to marinate in the sauce overnight.

1 cooked chicken (barbecued, or	1 green pepper per person, sliced
whatever), cut up	Oil or bacon fat for frying
1 potato (large) per person, sliced	

Sauce for Deviled Chicken

1 tablespoon mustard
Juice of half a lemon
1 teaspoon Worcestershire sauce
Dash Tabasco
¼ teaspoon Cayenne pepper

1 teaspoon grated lemon peel
¼ cup sherry (optional)
Coarse salt and freshly ground
    black pepper

Put the fat in a frying pan and heat until smoking. Meanwhile slice the potatoes and peppers. Fry the peppers for a couple of minutes and remove. Fry the potatoes for 5 minutes. Remove and drain.

Meanwhile, put the sauce ingredients in a small saucepan with the chicken and heat through, but do not boil.

Return potatoes and peppers to smoking fat for 2 more minutes. Drain and season.

Serve the chicken hot with the fried potatoes and peppers. Serves 4.

SPINACH PANCAKES WITH COLD CHICKEN

The pancakes take a couple of minutes to make. Don't cook them until you are ready to eat.

To make a complete dinner, serve a quick soup (see soup chapter), the pancakes, and, for dessert, fruit and cheese or some good homemade-type bought pastries or cake.

Barbecued chicken
Sliced fresh tomatoes
Chopped parsley

Spinach Pancakes

2 eggs
2 cups milk
2 tablespoons flour
Coarse salt and freshly ground
    black pepper

Oil for frying
2 pounds spinach or beet greens or
    Swiss chard, washed thoroughly
    and chopped fine

Put the barbecued chicken on a large plate. Arrange sliced fresh tomatoes and chopped parsley around it, and forget about it.

Mix together the eggs, milk, flour, and seasonings. Add the spinach to the batter. Heat the oil. Pour in the batter to make either 4 small pancakes or 2 large ones. Turn them once. Serve them right away. Serves 4.

CHICKEN LIVERS WITH MUSHROOMS

Chicken livers are excellent for last-minute meals. Do not overcook, or they will become gray and rubbery.

1 package frozen peas
Butter for the peas
1 pound chicken livers, washed and dried
½ pound mushrooms, sliced

½ cup (4 ounces) butter
Coarse salt and freshly ground black pepper
½ cup red or white wine
4 slices toast

Cut chicken livers in half where the membrane holds the two sides together.

Put the frozen peas in a saucepan with a little butter (no water) on low heat. Check occasionally, and stir.

Start the toast.

Melt the butter in the skillet. Add the mushrooms and livers and fry until golden. Add the wine and season. Simmer for about 3 minutes; meanwhile, butter the toast.

Serve the livers on toast, with peas on the side. Serves 4.

PINEAPPLE AND CHICKEN LIVERS

This is a quick meal and doesn't require the chopping that most oriental meals need beforehand. Serve it with Minute Rice, if you like, or frozen snow peas stir-fried at the last minute in peanut or vegetable oil with a can of drained bamboo shoots or bean sprouts added.

¼ cup peanut or vegetable oil
2 scallions, chopped
1 clove garlic, crushed (optional)
1 pound chicken livers, washed and dried
1 can pineapple chunks

¼ cup vinegar
¼ cup sugar
1 tablespoon cornstarch mixed with 2 tablespoons soy sauce
Freshly ground black pepper

Cut the chicken livers in half where the membrane joins them. Heat the oil in the skillet and sauté the scallions and garlic for a minute. Add the chicken livers and fry for 2 minutes. Drain the pineapple chunks, reserving the liquid, and add them. Cook 1 more minute. Add the vinegar, sugar, and 1 cup of the pineapple juice, adding water if needed to make a full cup. Mix the cornstarch and soy sauce and add it. Season. Simmer until the sauce is thick and the livers are cooked. Serves 4.

If you have only one pan and want to stir-fry the Chinese vegetables, remove the livers and keep them warm. Clean the pan. Heat the oil and fry vegetables for not more than 3 minutes on high heat.

See also
CREAMED CHICKEN LIVERS, page 206
GRILLED KIDNEYS, page 241
BROILED LIVER WITH BREADCRUMBS, page 241
STIR-FRIED HEART, page 242
BRAINS IN BLACK BUTTER, page 245
SAUTÉED SWEETBREADS OR BRAINS, page 245
SCRAMBLED BRAINS OR SWEETBREADS, page 246

STEAK TARTARE

For people with no cooking facilities at all, this dish is a lifesaver. Buy good lean meat and ask the butcher to grind it in front of you.

Steak Tartare is delicious with a salad; French, Italian, or black bread; and beer.

2 pounds ground lean meat	Dash Tabasco
Dash cumin	Dash Worcestershire sauce
Dash cayenne pepper	Dash soy sauce (optional)
Dash curry powder	Coarse salt and freshly ground
½ teaspoon powdered mustard	black pepper
Dash thyme	

Garnish

4 egg yolks
2 tablespoons drained capers
4 teaspoons chopped parsley
2 tablespoons chopped onion

Combine all the ingredients in a mixing bowl, tasting as you go (try not to eat too much before it arrives at the table), until you are satisfied that the seasoning is correct. Divide the mixture into four patties, make a hole or depression in each for the egg yolks, and garnish with the capers, parsley, and onions. Each person mixes his own meat with the egg yolk and garnish. Serves 4.

See also
STEAK AU POIVRE, page 207
HAMBURGERS, page 50

LAMB CHOPS WITH WATERCRESS

Here's a delicious meal for four—lamb chops, fried potatoes, fried or grilled tomato halves, and watercress salad. When you come in, light the grill or turn on the gas flame (depending on how you intend to cook your chops). If you have both a grill and a frying pan, the chops and tomatoes can be cooking under the grill while the potatoes are frying on top of the stove. If you have two burners and no grill, fry the potatoes in one pan, the chops in another, with tomatoes. If you are a one-burner owner, do potatoes first, in a *large* frying pan or electric skillet, and when they are cooking, add the chops and the tomatoes.

The chops will be even better if you marinate them in a mixture of yoghurt and oil overnight. Do not salt them until just before serving.

4 lamb chops
  Melted butter or 1 tablespoon olive
    oil brushed on the chops
1 package frozen French fries (or
  fresh sliced potatoes)

Vegetable or peanut oil for frying
  potatoes
2 tomatoes, halved
1 bunch watercress, washed and
  dried

Dressing for Watercress

3 tablespoons olive oil
1 tablespoon lemon juice
1 garlic clove, squeezed
  Coarse salt and freshly ground
    black pepper

When the oil is smoking, add the potatoes. Turn often, so that they brown on all sides. Reduce heat before you add the chops to prevent shrinking. When done, drain on paper towels.

Grill tomato halves for 15 minutes, coating tops with oil and seasonings.

The chops are done when they are pinkish inside and juicy. If you prefer them well done, allow an extra 10–15 minutes. Season.

While potatoes and chops are cooking, make the salad dressing. Coat watercress with the dressing. Serve on the side.

Arrange the cooked chops on a plate with the potatoes and halved tomatoes. Decorate with extra watercress, chopped. Serves 4.

See also
LAMB PATTIES, page 62

PORK WITH SAUERKRAUT

This is good with beer and black bread. Since the pork is chopped small, it takes only a few minutes to cook. This can be stretched with kosher frankfurters, sliced and added with the sauerkraut.

½ pound pork, chopped small	1 tablespoon caraway seeds
1 tablespoon butter	¼ cup sour cream
1 tablespoon oil	Coarse salt and freshly ground
1 can sauerkraut, drained	black pepper

Chop the pork into small cubes. Heat the butter and oil in a frying pan and brown the pork. When it is almost done, add the sauerkraut and caraway seeds. Cook for 3–4 minutes, until hot, stir in sour cream and seasonings and heat through without boiling. Serve at once. Serves 2.

CHINESE PORK WITH WATERCRESS

Use noodles or Minute Rice with this dish. Double the quantities for 4.

Noodles or Minute Rice	½ pound pork, in thin slices
2 tablespoons peanut or vegetable	2 tablespoons soy sauce
oil	1 bunch watercress, washed and
1 clove garlic, chopped	dried
1 scallion, chopped	

Start the noodles or rice. Chop the pork into thin slices and heat the oil in a frying pan. Add the garlic and scallion and stir-fry for 2 minutes. Add the pork and soy sauce and cook for 3 minutes.

Check rice or noodles for doneness. Add the watercress to the frying pan and fry 2 minutes. Serves 2.

See also
SWEET AND SOUR PORK WITH CABBAGE, page 208

ESCALOPES OF VEAL
WITH CREAM AND MUSHROOMS

This won't be the cheapest meal you've cooked all week, but if you're serving just 1 or 2 it won't cost too much. Noodles are good with veal and they take only about 7 minutes to cook. Put them on before you prepare the veal.

4 escalopes of veal
2 tablespoons butter
¼ pound mushrooms, chopped
1 tablespoon lemon juice

½ cup heavy cream
Coarse salt and freshly ground
   black pepper

Pound the escalopes with the flat of a heavy knife blade. Heat the butter in a frying pan and brown the escalopes lightly on both sides. Add the mushrooms and cook for 3 minutes. Add the cream and seasonings and cook for another couple of minutes.

Drain the noodles, put the escalopes on top, and pour on the sauce. Serves 4.

ESCALOPES WITH TOMATOES

You can serve these with frozen peas and noodles.

4 escalopes of veal
2 tablespoons butter
2 tomatoes, chopped
1 scallion, chopped
1 clove garlic, chopped

½ cup white wine, cider, or chicken
   stock
Coarse salt and freshly ground
   black pepper

Pound the escalopes with the flat of a knife blade. Sauté in the butter lightly and remove. Add the remaining ingredients and simmer for 5 minutes; return the veal and cook 1 minute more. Serve on noodles if desired. Serves 4.

WIENER SCHNITZEL

This is made from escalopes of veal, thin slices of meat cut against the grain and flattened until thin with the flat edge of a knife. Allow 1–2 per person.

Serve the veal with noodles, which you should start first since they take 7–8 minutes to cook.

Slices of anchovy, hard-boiled egg, capers, and sliced pickles are good with Wiener Schnitzel. Place the slices on top of the meat.

Frozen peas, cooked at the same time as the noodles, would go well with the veal.

4 escalopes of veal
1 egg, slightly beaten
  Breadcrumbs
  Coarse salt and freshly ground
    black pepper

1 tablespoon oil
1 tablespoon butter
  Lemon slices
1 tablespoon chopped fresh parsley,
   to garnish

Pound the veal flat and roll it in the egg, then in the breadcrumbs. Fry in the butter and oil over high heat until brown. Season and serve garnished with the chopped parsley and lemon slices, with the noodles in a separate dish. Enough for 2–4.

KIDNEYS IN RED WINE

Frozen peas, cooking while you prepare the kidneys, would be good with this dish.

4 kidneys, cut in two	stock
4 slices bread	Coarse salt and freshly ground
3 tablespoons butter, or more as	black pepper
needed	1 tablespoon chopped parsley, to
½ teaspoon cornstarch	garnish
½ glass red wine, or beef or chicken	

Dry the kidneys with paper towels. In a frying pan, fry the bread in the butter. Remove, drain, and add the kidneys. Fry them for 3–4 minutes and remove. Put them on the bread. Add a tiny bit of the wine and the cornstarch to the frying pan, stirring until smooth, and scrape up the juices. Add the rest of the wine, bring to a boil, and pour over the kidneys. Season. Sprinkle with parsley, if desired. Serves 4.

KIDNEYS WITH MUSHROOMS

Serve these with Minute Rice or noodles, either of which should be started first. A frozen green vegetable would also be good with the kidneys.

½ pound mushrooms, sliced	Flour for dredging
4 tablespoons butter, or more as	4 kidneys, cut in two
needed	Cream (optional)

Dry the kidneys and slice the mushrooms. Heat the butter in a frying pan and cook the mushrooms over low heat. Remove to a warm plate. Add the kidneys rolled in flour and cook for 3–4 minutes, until done. If you like, scrape up the cooking juices with a little cream. Serves 4.

MUSHROOMS ON TOAST, AND SALAD

When you come in, put the eggs on to boil and start the toast. Wash and dry the salad greens. Make the dressing, then prepare the mushrooms.

Cheese and fresh fruit for dessert are all you need to make this a dinner.

4 hard-boiled eggs	and chopped
Buttered toast (don't forget that it is toasting while you cook)	Squeeze of lemon juice
	Salt
3 tablespoons butter	Freshly ground black pepper
1 tablespoon oil	¼ cup cream or sour cream
1 onion, chopped	1 tablespoon chopped fresh parsley
1 pound mushrooms, wiped clean	or chives

Melt the butter with the oil, and sauté the onion until soft. Add the mushrooms and lemon juice, and cook for 5 minutes. Season, and add the cream.

The toast and the eggs should be ready by now. Run the eggs under cold water, peel, and slice them in half. They should be slightly soft in the center. Spread the mushroom mixture on the buttered toast, put the eggs on top, and sprinkle with herbs. Serve immediately. Serves 4.

See also
MUSHROOMS PROVENÇALE, page 116
MUSHROOMS WITH SOUR CREAM ON TOAST, page 116

TOMATOES ON TOAST

Green peas or lettuce salad will turn this into a complete meal. Cook peas and make salad while the tomatoes are heating up and the toast is cooking. In about 7 minutes you should be sitting down to eat. This is a good meal for one.

1 can Italian tomatoes, drained	1 cup grated Cheddar cheese
Coarse salt and freshly ground black pepper	1 tablespoon chopped fresh parsley or chives (optional)
4 slices toast	

Put the tomatoes in a saucepan to heat up. Make the toast. Butter toast, season the tomatoes, and pour them on the toast. Sprinkle on lots of the cheese, and garnish with parsley if desired. Serves 2–4.

See also
FRIED GREEN TOMATOES, page 127
CHINESE METHOD OF COOKING VEGETABLES, page 85
BASIC STIR-FRIED GREENS, page 112
PEAS, page 120
CHEESE AND WATERCRESS SALAD, page 146
WELSH RAREBIT, page 161
CROQUE MONSIEUR, page 162

SAUSAGE AND CHICK PEAS

1 tablespoon oil	1 can pimientos, sliced
1 onion, chopped	Chopped fresh parsley to
3–4 hot sausages, sliced	garnish
2 cloves garlic, crushed	Hard-boiled eggs, sliced
Dash oregano	(optional)
1 can chick peas	

Heat oil in a heavy skillet and sauté onion. When onion is beginning to fry, slice sausages and add them to the pan. Add garlic and a dash of oregano.

When the sausages are cooked, in about 5 minutes, add the chick peas and the pimientos. Season, and heat through to very hot. Add sliced eggs if you wish. Sprinkle with fresh parsley before serving. Serves 2.

If you want eggs too, put them on to boil while you're preparing the main dish and remove after 7 minutes.

BUBBLE AND SQUEAK

Although it takes only ten minutes to cook this, it is not, strictly speaking, a ten-minute meal because you have to use leftovers.

This is a dish frequently served to British children the day after a dinner or lunch of cabbage and mashed potatoes. Although incredibly simple, it is delicious. You don't need anything else with it, unless you want a salad.

Leftover vegetables (cabbage,	1 onion, chopped
broccoli, cauliflower, etc.)	Extra butter, as needed
Leftover mashed potatoes	Coarse salt and freshly ground
2 slices bacon	black pepper

Chop the vegetables and mix them with the mashed potatoes. Cook the bacon, remove, and fry the onion in the fat. Get the fat really hot and add the potato mixture. Fry it like a pancake so that it gets brown and crispy on the outside. Add extra butter if you need it. Season and serve very hot with the bacon.

NOODLES WITH THREE-MINUTE TOMATO SAUCE

2 tablespoons olive oil	Basil
1–2 cloves garlic, chopped	Chopped parsley
½ pound noodles	Butter
4–6 tomatoes, chopped	Grated Parmesan cheese

Put a large pot of water on to boil. Add a teaspoon of salt.

Heat the oil in a skillet and add a chopped clove of garlic or two.

When the water is boiling rapidly in the pot, gradually add noodles. Stir and cook them for 8 minutes.

Meanwhile, add tomatoes to the skillet with some basil or chopped parsley. Don't cook for more than 3 minutes.

When the noodles are ready, drain them in a colander, melt a lump of butter in the pot and return noodles to pot, coating them well with the butter.

Put the noodles into a heated serving dish, sprinkle with lots of grated Parmesan cheese, and serve the sauce separately, also in a heated dish. Serves 4.

Note: To heat the dishes, either run them under the hot tap and dry them or put them in a warm oven while you're cooking. The latter method is less trouble.

NOODLES WITH MUSHROOMS

½ pound noodles	2 tablespoons chopped fresh
2 tablespoons butter	parsley
1 tablespoon olive oil	Butter
1–2 cloves garlic, chopped	Grated Parmesan cheese
¾ pound mushrooms, chopped	

Put on to boil a large pot of water with a teaspoon of salt.

Heat butter and oil in a skillet. Add garlic and sauté for 2 minutes.

When the water is boiling, gradually add noodles and boil rapidly for 8–10 minutes.

Sauté mushrooms in the skillet with the garlic until cooked. Add chopped parsley.

Drain the noodles in a colander, put a lump of butter in the pot, and turn the noodles in the butter until thoroughly coated. Put them in a heated dish, cover with the mushroom mixture, and serve grated Parmesan cheese on the side. Serves 4.

Foods for the Brain

That awful time of year comes around so suddenly. After a year of cutting classes, not taking notes, staying up too late, going to too many parties, making fun of the professors, and generally having a good time, you realize that final exams are upon you, time is running out—has run out—and there's nothing you can do about it.

Knowing that it won't do any good, you stay up late night after night trying to cram information and facts that you know will leave your head the next day. In your nervousness you can't concentrate anyway.

Finally, you go into the exam, exhausted and depressed after another sleepless night, hands shaking from too much coffee, no breakfast, and a week of living on snatched hot dogs and gulped hamburgers.

"If Balzac could write all those novels on nothing but black coffee, why can't I?" you think. But we're not all Balzacs, and they say that even he died of the effects of too much black coffee.

Obviously no one in the middle of studying for exams wants to do a great deal of cooking. Who has the time? But eating the right things really isn't a big deal, and it's not all that clever to eat garbage—and wonder later why you didn't do as well as you thought you might. You *can* be alert (and brilliant) all day long if you eat the right food.

First of all (what no one wants to hear), *you must have a good breakfast.* This is more important than any other meal of the day. If you don't have a decent breakfast, your blood sugar and your energy will drop, and by the middle of the day you will feel half dead.

A good breakfast ,doesn't mean corn flakes, toast, and six cups of black coffee. It means plenty of protein (eggs, bacon, ham, sausage, kidneys, even liver, if you can stand it first thing) and vitamins (juice). If you're going to have coffee (let's face it, you probably are), try to drink it with milk, or at least have milk on your cereal. The cereal, if you eat it, should be wholegrain, cracked wheat, buckwheat, Granola, Swiss Bircher Meusli, or some other *real* cereal from a health food store. See the cereal breakfasts on page 233.

Instead of sugar, use honey or molasses. If you can bear it in the morning, brown rice makes an excellent nutritional substitute for cereal.

Drink a glass of fresh juice if you have time to prepare it; otherwise, canned or frozen juice will do. If you eat toast, try to make it whole-wheat. The same applies to pancakes and muffins.

For lunch, eat some raw vegetables or a salad. You won't want a heavy meal anyway if you've got another exam coming up in the afternoon. See the section on salads for some good ideas. None of them takes long to prepare. Also try to eat a container of yoghurt (Homemade Yoghurt, page 237, is the best and the cheapest). If you don't like it plain, put some honey, molasses, or fruit on it.

Plenty of fruit or vegetable juices are important. Try to drink them instead of soft drinks.

If you feel hungry between meals, try not to eat those candy bars (ever read the label?), but chew some fresh, unsalted nuts instead. If you're passionate about candy, health food stores usually carry sesame candy and other seed candies that are good for you.

One of the hardest things to do during the exam period is to get to sleep at night. Calcium helps you to relax and sleep soundly, so a warm milk drink before you go to bed at night will help. If you still can't sleep, calcium tablets might help. They are much better to take than sleeping pills.

If it is possible, try to get unsprayed fruits and vegetables. This is almost impossible in most cities, unless you buy them through a health food store, but some college campuses are now running their own organic gardens. At the University of California in Santa Cruz the students got so fed up with the dreadful food in the cafeteria that they refused to eat it. They started their own gardens and now grow their own vegetables. Other universities across the country are doing the same thing. Organic gardening, once the normal way of growing things, is coming back again. However, for commercial purposes the Department of Agriculture still sanctions enough chemicals to fill a small telephone directory. And the use of these chemicals is by no means confined to our vegetables. It is almost impossible to buy food that does not contain one or another of them. Ralph Nader accuses the FDA of being soft on food chemicals and points out that most of the top people in the FDA are connected with the chemical industry in some way or other.

You can't work if you debilitate your body with junk. You only have to look at the skin of people who eat a lot of chemical foods—processed artificial food-substitutes that only take you another step away from the natural world—to see how harmful they are.

What to Eat

Raw vegetables
Raw fruit
Meat, fish, eggs, cheese, and milk for protein
Wheatgerm
Brewer's yeast
Yoghurt
Juice soybeans
Offal or organ meats (brains, kidneys, liver, etc.)

What Not to Eat

Corn flakes, puffed cereals, rice flakes
Imitation fruit drinks
French fried foods (hydrogenated fats)
Margarine
Processed cheese
Cola
Commercial ice cream
Sugar
Candy
Doughnuts
Packaged foods containing chemicals
Dyed and preserved meat (hot dogs)
White flour
White rice
Artificial sweeteners

I once heard a comedian describe a visit to a factory that made canned artificial whipped cream, the kind you spray on. He read the label on a can of whipped topping (as I think it was called), and after enumerating about twenty chemicals he came at last to "artificial color." "Artificial color!" he exclaimed. "Let me tell you why they put in artificial color. They got together all these scientists and they mixed up a whole bunch of chemicals in a big vat. Then the manager came down to look at it. It was *brown*. 'You can't put that stuff on strawberries!' he screamed. So that's why they put the artificial color in whipped topping."

None of the recipes in this chapter takes much time or requires a great deal of attention. They are here because they are especially healthy.

By taking enough time each day to prepare yourself a reasonable meal, you may help yourself during the gruesome period of exams.

MUESLI

This combination makes an excellent breakfast cereal.

2 bananas, sliced
2 apples, sliced
  Juice of half a lemon
3 tablespoons honey

½ cup ground or chopped nuts
½ cup yoghurt
½ cup rolled oats

Combine all the ingredients and mix together. If you like, add some fresh berries (blueberries are delicious with this when they are in season). The oats can be soaked overnight, but their crunchy texture will be lost. Serves 2.

WHEATGERM BREAKFAST

Some people don't like wheatgerm by itself. In this combination it is delicious.

1 cup wheatgerm
2 apples, chopped
2 bananas, chopped
1 cup yoghurt
  Juice of half a lemon

Mix together all the ingredients. Serves 2.

FRUIT AND VEGETABLE JUICES

Unless you have a juicer, it is impossible for you to make juices from fresh vegetables and fruits yourself. Assuming that a juicer is an unlikely feature of a college kitchen, we have included here a selection of drinks that you can easily make yourself, using canned juices and adding fresh fruits or herbs.

TOMATO JUICE WITH LEMONS

This is a very refreshing drink during the summer. It can be improved by fresh herbs such as basil or mint and a dash of ground mace.

Tomato juice
Lemons
Worcestershire sauce

Tabasco sauce
Coarse salt and freshly ground
   black pepper

For 1 glass of tomato juice, allow the juice of 1 lemon. Squeeze it into the tomato juice, add a dash of Worcestershire sauce and Tabasco, and season to taste.

TOMATO-CLAM JUICE WITH OREGANO

If fresh oregano and fresh clam juice are available, this drink will be even better.

1 glass tomato juice
1 glass clam juice
  Juice of 1 lemon
  Dash Worcestershire sauce

Coarse salt and freshly ground
   black pepper, to taste
1 teaspoon oregano

Mix the juices in a jug or pitcher with the lemon juice, Worcestershire sauce, and seasonings. Top each drink with a sprinkling of oregano. Serves 2.

VEGETABLE JUICE

If you are serious about vegetable juice, a juicer is essential. It can be bought at health food stores. The fresh vegetables are much better for you than the canned juice.

1 can V-8 juice, or other mixed
  vegetable juice
⅓ cup juice from canned beets
1 tablespoons brewer's yeast

Dash Worcestershire sauce
Squeeze of lemon, to taste
Salt
Freshly ground black pepper

Mix well and correct seasoning. Serves 1–2.

APPLE JUICE

1 cup organically grown apple juice
1 teaspoon brewer's yeast
  Dash of lemon juice
  Dash cinnamon

Mix together thoroughly and drink cold. Enough for 1 drink.

PRUNE JUICE

½ cup organically grown prune juice
½ cup organically grown apple juice
⅓ cup yoghurt
  Dash nutmeg

Mix well, with the yoghurt blended in well. Season. Enough for 1 drink.

LICUADO

This drink is popular all over Mexico. It would be great if more people would drink it instead of "refrescos," the terrible sticky soft drinks that the poor the world over have had thrust upon them and have accepted so gratefully.

A blender is really required for these drinks. The banana drink could be made with a lot of mashing, but the others would be difficult to make without a blender.

1 glass milk
  Chopped banana or
    Pitted peach
    Pitted apricot
    Raspberries
  Strawberries
  Blueberries
¼ cup honey
  Dash cinnamon
  Dash nutmeg

Combine milk with desired fruit, honey, cinnamon and nutmeg. Blend together or mix thoroughly by hand. Enough for 1 drink.

GRAPE AND APPLE JUICE

Try to get organically grown grape juice. Most health food stores carry the apple juice.

½ cup grape juice
½ cup apple juice
1 teaspoon brewer's yeast
⅓ cup yoghurt
   Dash cinnamon

   Mix well and serve. Enough for 1 person.

PAPAYA DRINK

   Papayas are very high in vitamin C. If fresh ones are available at a reasonable price, and you have access to a blender, use them instead of the canned juice.

½ cup papaya juice
1 teaspoon lemon or lime juice
½ cup pineapple juice
   Juice of 1 orange

   Mix thoroughly and serve. Enough for 1 person.

ADELLE DAVIS'S PEP-UP

   In her eye-opening and brilliant book, *Let's Eat Right to Keep Fit*,* Adelle Davis gives a recipe for a pep-up drink that will keep you bright-eyed and alert through any examination, even if you've made the fatal error of staying up all night for last-minute cramming.

   Keep this in the refrigerator and have it for breakfast, then continue drinking it throughout the day. She also suggests that you add ¼ cup soy flour, ¼ cup wheatgerm, bananas, crushed pineapple, and any frozen undiluted fruit juice. The ingredients for her recipe (below) can be obtained from health food stores.

   Combine and beat:

2 egg yolks or whole eggs
   (unless cooked preferred)
1 tablespoon granular lecithin
1 tablespoon vegetable oil or
   mixed vegetable oils
1½ teaspoons calcium lactate
   or 4 teaspoons calcium
   gluconate or 1 teaspoon
   bone meal

¼ cup yoghurt or 1
   tablespoon acidophilus
   culture
2 cups of whole or skim milk
¼ to ½ cup of yeast fortified with
   calcium and magnesium
¼ to ½ cup non-instant powdered
   milk or ½ to 1 cup
   instant powdered milk

   *Adelle Davis, *Let's Eat Right to Keep Fit*. Harcourt, Brace, Jovanovich, Inc., New York, N.Y. © 1954, 1970.

1 teaspoon pure vanilla or ½
   teaspoon cinnamon or
   nutmeg
½ cup frozen undiluted orange

juice
Magnesium carbonate,
   oxide or other magnesium
   salt

Put into a container and add the remainder of a quart of milk; cover and keep refrigerated. Stir before using.

HOMEMADE PEANUT BUTTER

A blender is essential for this. Perhaps you could make it at home over a weekend if you have no blender at school. It would keep for several weeks refrigerated, but you'll be lucky if you can keep Homemade Peanut Butter for 24 hours. It's *so* good and almost impossible to stop eating once you've started. It's a good base for sauces, particularly those served with tongue, as well as being excellent spread on black bread or in sandwiches.

1 pound raw, unshelled peanuts
  About ½–¾ cup peanut oil
Coarse salt and freshly ground
  black pepper

Shell the peanuts (a long and arduous task) and put them in the blender. Add a little oil and blend. Continue adding oil and blending until you have a smooth paste of the right consistency. Season and refrigerate.

HOMEMADE YOGHURT

Anyone who has tasted homemade yoghurt will never want to buy it ready made again. It is quite different and a hundred times better. Once it's made you can keep it going for at least six months, by reserving a little each week as a starter for the next batch. It is very easy to make, whether you have a yoghurt maker or not, and once it is made, you can add fruits and different flavors to it.

A yoghurt maker costs about $10 and the culture costs about $2. The culture is available at most health food stores, complete with simple directions.

1 package yoghurt culture
1 pint milk
1 package dried milk

Follow the directions on the package. You heat the milk near to boiling point, then let it cool to lukewarm. Add the milk powder (this will make it thicker) and stir in the culture. Put the mixture into clean pre-warmed jars, seal and incubate overnight in warm water. If you have a yoghurt maker, simply allow the mixture to stand in the jars overnight with the machine plugged in. Refrigerate, and your yoghurt is done.

Note: You may be able to start your own yoghurt by using a spoonful from commercial yoghurt. This often works and saves you the cost of the culture. You can also make yoghurt in a Thermos.

BUTTERMILK

This is as easy to make as Homemade Yoghurt (above). You simply keep the mixture at about 85 degrees for 10–12 hours, until it has turned to buttermilk. You can keep it warm in hot water sitting on the pilot light of a gas stove, or in a very low oven (keep turning it off).

3½ cups milk
½ cup commercial buttermilk

Add commercial buttermilk to milk in a large container. Mix well and incubate in capped glass jars, either on top of or inside the stove or on a yoghurt maker hot plate. Refrigerate when done.

LAMB PATTIES WITH WHEATGERM

This is an extremely good way to increase your day's intake of wheatgerm. Wheatgerm can often be substituted for breadcrumbs, and it is much more nourishing.

Serve the patties with brown rice and green vegetables. Remember to give rice ample cooking time; it requires a longer time than white rice.

1 pound freshly ground lean lamb
3 tablespoons wheatgerm
1 onion, chopped
1 tablespoon peanut, sesame, or soy oil
Dash allspice
Dash nutmeg
Dash Cayenne pepper
Freshly ground black pepper
1 tablespoon peanut, sesame, or soy oil, or enough to cover bottom of pan
Wholewheat flour
Coarse salt or soy sauce
1 tablespoon chopped fresh parsley

Put the lamb and the wheatgerm in a mixing bowl. Soften the onion in the oil over low heat, then add to the lamb along with the spices and seasonings.

Heat enough oil to cover bottom of pan. Dredge the patties lightly in the flour and cook for about 5 minutes on each side, until brown outside and pinkish inside. Season with salt or soy sauce, scatter parsley over the patties, and serve on a heated platter. Makes 4 patties.

CHICKEN LIVERS AND TOMATOES WITH RICE

This can be served on wholewheat toast or on rice. To reheat the next day, fold into rice and serve with grated Parmesan cheese.

2 strips bacon, chopped	1 can tomatoes, with juice
½ stick butter (2 ounces)	½ cup heavy cream
1 onion, chopped	Coarse salt and freshly ground
1 pound chicken livers	black pepper
¼ pound mushrooms, sliced	1 tablespoon chopped fresh parsley

Cook the bacon in the skillet and remove. Add the butter and cook the onion until soft. Add the livers and the mushrooms and cook for 3 minutes. Add the tomatoes with their juice and simmer for 3 minutes. When the chicken livers are almost done, add the cream and heat through without boiling. Season, and sprinkle with parsley. Serves 4.

See also
CREAMED CHICKEN LIVERS, page 206
CHICKEN LIVERS WITH MUSHROOMS, page 221
PINEAPPLE AND CHICKEN LIVERS, page 221

ORGAN MEATS

Liver, kidney, and heart are rich in iron and vitamins and help the body to resist colds and other illnesses. They must be eaten fresh. You can keep the meat overnight by wiping it and covering it with a little oil. Refrigerate.

Kidneys

Kidneys usually come enveloped in fat, which can be removed or not, depending on how the meat is to be cooked. They should have little or no smell and should be very fresh. Never overcook kidney or it will have a very hard texture. Remove it from heat when it is still pinkish inside.

Calf's kidney is the most delicate. Lamb kidneys are also delicate and tender and are cheaper than calf's. Sauté them or cook them in sauce.

Beef and pig's kidneys are coarser, stronger in flavor, and even cheaper than calf's or lamb's. They are best served in a strong-flavored sauce.

Liver

Liver is rich in vitamin A, iron, and copper and is also used in the preparation of medicines. It should be very fresh, smooth, and glossy, with no bluish tint. It should be sliced thinly and evenly. If it is not sliced properly, take it home and do it yourself with a sharp knife.

The nutritive value of different kinds of liver is the same, but the prices vary tremendously. Calf's liver is the best and is very expensive. It should be very pale. Lamb's liver is not so delicate as calf's but it is very good and can be cooked in the same way. Pig's liver is less delicate and beef liver is the cheapest and coarsest.

Prepare the liver by wiping it with a damp cloth and removing the veins and outer skin. It should be cooked very lightly, whether sautéed or braised, so that it is pinkish inside. Three to four minutes in the frying pan is enough; turn it when moisture gathers in beads on the surface.

Heart

It should be very fresh and have no smell. Calf's heart is the most tender. Lamb's heart comes next and is delicious stuffed and roasted. Beef heart is very big and tastes very much like beef. Sometimes it can be tough, but if it is marinated overnight it can be a delicious and very economical way to serve a large group of people.

Remove the outer covering and the tubes. Either chop it up or stuff it.

KIDNEYS WITH BROWN RICE

Make sure the kidneys are fresh. To serve, pour the kidneys with their juice over brown rice. A salad on the side would be a good accompaniment. Allow enough time for the brown rice to cook before starting the kidneys.

About 4 lamb or veal kidneys (depending on size)	1 teaspoon mustard Coarse salt and freshly ground
1 onion, chopped	black pepper
2 tablespoons peanut or vegetable oil	1 cup brown rice, cooked

Remove the membranes from the kidneys. Heat the oil and add the onion. Cook until clear. Add the kidneys and cook very quickly, turning the heat up a little so that their juices are sealed in and they don't toughen. Don't overcook them. Add the mustard, stir around, correct seasonings, and serve over the rice. Serves 4.

BAKED KIDNEYS

This is one of the simplest ways to cook kidneys. Serve them with mushrooms, tomatoes, and a green vegetable.

1 pound kidneys, with their fat on
  Coarse salt and freshly ground
    black pepper
1 tablespoon parsley

Preheat oven to 350 degrees. Put the kidneys in a baking dish and cook in the oven for 30 minutes. Remove, take off their fat, and cut them in half. Season and sprinkle with parsley. Return them to the oven for a few more minutes. Serves 3–4.

GRILLED KIDNEYS

Serve this dish with watercress and brown rice. You may grill halved tomatoes and mushrooms at the same time, if you like.

1 pound kidneys, split in half
8 strips bacon
  Coarse salt and freshly ground
    black pepper
  Parsley Butter (page 50)

Wrap pieces of bacon around the kidneys and grill them for about 5 minutes on each side. Season and serve them on brown rice, with the parsley butter on top. Serves 4.

BROILED LIVER WITH BREADCRUMBS

This is delicious with greens (see page 111), mushrooms, tomatoes, and brown rice, if you like.

4 slices liver
3 tablespoons mustard
1 tablespoon oil
1 scallion, finely chopped
2 cups fresh wholewheat

  breadcrumbs
  Melted butter
1 tablespoon chopped fresh parsley
  Coarse salt and freshly ground
    black pepper

Put the slices of liver in a mixture of the mustard, oil, and scallion. Then dredge with the breadcrumbs. Brush with melted butter and grill under the broiler (medium heat) for 5–7 minutes on each side, until the liver is done on the outside and pinkish in the middle. Season and serve. Serves 4.

STIR-FRIED CHINESE BEEF LIVER

This method of cooking beef liver seals in its juices and, provided it is not overcooked, prevents the liver from toughening. After the liver has been soaked for at least two hours in salted water, it should be sliced very thinly and any tough membranes removed.

Brown rice or wholewheat noodles are a good accompaniment.

1 pound beef liver, soaked in salted water for 2 hours

Marinade

¼ cup dry sherry
2 tablespoons soy sauce
1 teaspoon powdered ginger, or chopped fresh ginger, if available
1 teaspoon cornstarch mixed with

1 teaspoon water
Freshly ground black pepper
5 tablespoons peanut or vegetable oil
4 scallions, including tops, chopped

Slice the beef liver, remove membranes, dry it, and place in a bowl with the marinade. Marinade for at least 30 minutes. In a heavy skillet, heat the oil. Add the scallions and stir-fry for about 2 minutes. Add the liver and stir-fry for 1–2 minutes. Remove to a hot dish. Pour marinade into skillet and cook, stirring, until the sauce coats the spoon. Pour over the liver and serve. Serves 4.

BEEF LIVER IN RED WINE

Beef liver is delicious when marinated in a red wine mixture. The wine masks the rather strong taste.

Serve the liver with buttered potatoes, a green salad, and garlic bread.

1 pound beef liver, soaked for 2 hours in salted water
1 onion, chopped
1 clove garlic, chopped
1 tablespoon oil
1 tablespoon butter

Bay leaf
Dash thyme
Coarse salt and freshly ground black pepper
1 glass red wine
1 tablespoon red wine vinegar

Remove liver from salted water and cut into thin slices. Heat the oil and butter in a heavy skillet and cook the onion and garlic until clear but not browned. In a deep dish combine the remaining ingredients (except the parsley) and add the liver. Add the onion and garlic and marinate for 30 minutes. Remove liver and pour marinade into skillet. Bring marinade to a boil and return the liver to it. Reduce heat and simmer gently for about 5 minutes. Remove from heat, scatter parsley over the top, and serve. Serves 4.

See also
LIVER AND ONIONS, page 212

STUFFED HEART

This is good with peas, beans, zucchini, or broccoli. A beef heart, being quite large, may require twice the amount of stuffing given in the recipe below.

1 cup wholewheat breadcrumbs	Dash thyme
1 egg	1 tablespoon oil
2 scallions, chopped	Coarse salt and freshly ground
¼ pound sausage meat, chopped	black pepper
1 tablespoon chopped fresh parsley	1 heart

Preheat oven to 350 degrees. Combine the stuffing ingredients in a bowl. Trim the gristle and little pipes. Stuff mixture inside the heart and close the cavity with toothpicks. Put in a greased pan and bake for about 1½ hours.

STIR-FRIED HEART

Serve this with brown rice. Marinate the heart in the sauce for 1–2 hours, if you have time. Lamb or pig's heart is best for this dish.

1 heart	water, then diced
2 tablespoons soy sauce	1 package frozen peas, or 1 pound
2 scallions, chopped	fresh peas
2 tablespoons dry sherry (optional)	Coarse salt
2 tablespoons oil	Freshly ground black pepper
½ cup dried mushrooms, soaked in	

Trim the heart, remove the gristle, and chop heart into thin strips. Toss in a mixture of the soy sauce, scallions, mustard, and sherry. Marinate for a while, about 30 minutes, or longer if you can. In a frying pan, heat the oil. Add the scallion mixture and the beef and stir-fry for 3 minutes. Add the remaining ingredients and cook for 5 minutes. Serve immediately.

MARINATED BEEF HEART WITH BAKED ONIONS IN CHEESE SAUCE

These two dishes go very well together. If you buy a whole beef heart, you'll have enough to feed about 8 people. The recipe below is for 4, allowing about ½ pound per person.

It is hard to describe how delicious the beef heart is when it is cooked this way. If you could cook it over charcoal, it would taste extraordinarily good. However, it is excellent when done in the oven. You can broil the liver at the same time the onions are baking inside the oven.

2 pounds beef heart

Marinade

Juice of one orange   **¼ cup oil**
¼ cup red wine vinegar   **Dash cumin, if available**
2 cloves garlic, squeezed   **Freshly ground black pepper**

Wash the beef heart under running water. Cut away the tubes and gristle. Chop into 1-inch cubes. Combine the marinade ingredients in a bowl and soak the beef heart in it overnight.

Grill the cubes (on skewers, if available) when the onions are almost cooked. Heat up the sauce and spoon it over the hearts. Serves 4.

Baked Onions with Cheese Sauce

4 large onions, peeled and chopped   **Coarse salt and freshly ground**
¼ cup butter   **black pepper**
4 hard-boiled eggs   **Sauce Mornay (page 115)**
Dash thyme   **¼ cup wheatgerm**
Dash nutmeg   **1 tablespoon chopped fresh parsley**

Preheat oven to 350 degrees. Soften the onions in the butter without browning. Put in a mixing bowl. Mash the eggs and add to the bowl with the spices and seasonings. Make the sauce. In a baking dish put the onion mixture, cover with the sauce, sprinkle on the wheatgerm, and bake for about 25 minutes. Sprinkle with parsley. Serves 4.

Brains and Sweetbreads

Brains and sweetbreads are similar in flavor and texture. Some people are put off by the idea of eating brains. However, eating animal brains is no worse than eating part of an animal's stomach or one of its legs.

Brains are a rich source of vitamin B and lecithin and, together with sweetbreads and other organ meats, are the parts of the animal best for you. They are also cheap since there is little waste and there are no bones.

Organ meats should be washed thoroughly in cold water. The filament surrounding the brains and the opaque white stuff at the bottom should be removed. Sweetbreads are connected by a tube which should also be removed and can be saved for stock.

Brains and sweetbreads are often soaked for a few hours in cold water with a tablespoon of vinegar. Do this if you like, but you will lose many of the vitamins and minerals. Sometimes they are parboiled before being cooked, to firm them up, but this method not only removes much of the nutritional value, it also removes much of the flavor.

BRAINS IN BLACK BUTTER

Thes are delicious with potatoes and green vegetables.

1 pound brains, washed and trimmed	1 tablespoon capers
1 tablespoon oil	1 tablespoon chopped parsley
2 tablespoons butter	Coarse salt and freshly ground
1 tablespoon vinegar, or a mixture	black pepper
of vinegar and lemon	

Dry brains, slice, and fry them in the oil. Meanwhile, heat the butter in a saucepan and, when it starts to turn brown, add the remaining ingredients. Pour over the brains. Serves 4.

SAUTÉED SWEETBREADS OR BRAINS

Chop the brains or sweetbreads coarsely and fry them in a mixture of hot oil and butter. Garnish with lemon slices and chopped fresh parsley. You can dredge them with flour before frying, if you like.

Serve them with potatoes or brown rice, plenty of green vegetables, and a salad.

SCRAMBLED BRAINS OR SWEETBREADS

This dish is delicious on toast with spinach.

**1 pound brains or sweetbreads,
    washed and trimmed
4 eggs
    Butter**

Beat the eggs and add the brains or sweetbreads, finely chopped. Melt plenty of butter in a skillet, add egg mixture, and cook as you would scrambled eggs, until just firm.

CREAMED BRAINS OR SWEETBREADS

This is delicious on toast. Serve with tomatoes and green vegetables.

1 tablespoon butter	**1 pound sliced brains or sweetbreads**
1 tablespoon flour, preferably	**Coarse salt**
wholewheat	**Freshly ground black pepper**
1 cup hot milk	**Paprika**
1 teaspoon Worcestershire sauce	**1 tablespoon chopped fresh parsley**

Heat the butter in a saucepan. Add the flour and cook together for a couple of minutes without browning. Add the milk gradually and cook until slightly thickened. Add the Worcestershire sauce and reduce heat to a simmer. Add the brains and simmer gently for about 10–15 minutes. Season, and sprinkle with paprika and parsley. Serves 4.

BREADCRUMBED PIG'S FEET

Pig's feet are extremely cheap, and it is said that one helping of them can provide you with as much calcium as three cups of milk. Although they have to be simmered for a long time, the resulting broth is simply delicious. They are great as hors d'oeuvres.

4 pig's feet

Ingredients for Stock

1½ quarts water	**A few cloves**
1 carrot, sliced	**1 onion, chopped**

1 stalk celery, chopped   Coarse salt
Lemon peel   Freshly ground black pepper
Herbs (thyme, bay leaf, parsley)

Melted butter
Breadcrumbs
Sauce Tartare (page 23)

Bring ingredients for stock to a boil. Tie the pig's feet together with
string to keep them from falling apart. Simmer for 3½ hours, or until
the meat starts to fall away from the bone. Remove pig's feet and drain.
Reserve the broth for soup.

Preheat oven to 400 degrees. Roll the feet in melted butter and
breadcrumbs. Put in a baking dish and bake for 15 minutes. Serve with
Sauce Tartare. Enough for 2–4.

SALAD APHRODITE

This recipe is from *The Alice B. Toklas Cook Book* and was sent to her
by Princess D. Rohan, London. I quote it here in full.

"Apples, quickly peeled and finely chopped, celery chopped fine,
yoghurt, black pepper, salt.

"The beauty of this salad depends entirely on how quickly the apples and celery are stirred *into* the bowl of yoghurt. This prevents their
becoming brown. To be served on the crispest lettuce leaves.

"This is inspired by the famous Bicht's Moussle of the Bicht Sana-
torium at Zurich. Ideal for poets with delicate digestions." *

And ideal for delicate, hungry, undernourished students short of
time when studying for exams.

CABBAGE IN WHITE SAUCE

For people who don't like milk, this is a good way to get your daily
dosage. The vitamins that seep out of the cabbage during cooking are also
preserved, because the cabbage milk is used in making the white sauce.

Serve with pork chops, chicken, or fish. A little cooked bacon sprinkled
on top adds extra flavor.

*Toklas, Alice B., *The Alice B. Toklas Cook Book*, Harper & Row, New York,
N.Y. © 1954.

1 head cabbage, shredded
1 cup milk
1 onion, stuck with cloves
  Nutmeg
  Celery salt

3 tablespoons butter
1 tablespoon wholewheat flour
  Coarse salt and freshly ground
    black pepper
  Cooked, chopped bacon (optional)

In a large saucepan bring the milk to a boil with the onion. Add the cabbage and seasonings and simmer until the cabbage is tender. In another saucepan, heat the butter. Add the flour and cook on low heat, stirring constantly, for about 5 minutes. Do not let the flour brown. Drain cabbage milk through a sieve directly into the roux. Stir constantly and bring to a boil. Boil, stirring, for about 10 minutes, until the sauce thickens enough to coat the spoon. Pour over the cabbage. Serves 4–6.

RAW CARROTS WITH LEMON JUICE

Everyone knows what a healthy food carrots are (and they're supposed to help you see in the dark, which is an asset for late-night students). Carrots are very good raw, and retain the vitamins often lost in the cooking process.

2 cups raw carrots, grated
2 tablespoons lemon juice
¼ cup olive oil

1 teaspoon finely chopped parsley
  Coarse salt and freshly ground
    black pepper

Place the grated carrots in a bowl. Mix the remaining ingredients in another small bowl and season. Pour over the carrots. Serves 4.

CARROT AND ONION CASSEROLE

If you are staying up late at night studying, this is what you need to keep your eyes good until 4 A.M. It has eggs and milk in it and if you serve it with brown rice you'll feel so healthy you won't ever want to go to sleep.

4 tablespoons sesame, soy, or
    vegetable oil
1 pound carrots, sliced
2 onions, sliced
1 clove garlic, crushed
1 tablespoon wholewheat flour
1 cup boiling milk
½ cup boiling stock or bouillon

  Dash rosemary
  Dash nutmeg
1 tablespoon raw or brown sugar
  Coarse salt and freshly ground
    black pepper
2 egg yolks
1 tablespoon chopped fresh parsley

In a heavy ovenproof casserole or skillet, heat the oil. Add the carrots and the onions and cook over very low heat for about 30 minutes.

Add the garlic and the flour, tossing the vegetables so that they are well coated. Bring the milk and bouillon to a boil. Add all at once to the vegetables and stir well. Add the herbs and sugar and cook, simmering, for about 20 minutes. Season, and remove from heat. Carefully stir a small amount of the hot mixture into the egg yolks in a small bowl. Then very gradually add egg yolk mixture to pan, stirring constantly. Cook over very low heat, always stirring, until the sauce thickens. Garnish with parsley. Serves 4.

GLAZED CARROTS

Carrots cooked this way are good with most meat dishes, particularly roasts; or for a vegetarian meal with brown rice and a green vegetable.

1 pound carrots, chopped	Coarse salt and freshly ground
1 cup stock or bouillon	black pepper
1 tablespoon brown sugar or	1 tablespoon chopped fresh parsley,
molasses	to garnish
¾ stick butter	

Combine the carrots with the stock, sugar or molasses, and butter in a heavy pan. Cover and simmer gently for 30–40 minutes. By the time the carrots are tender, the liquid will have reduced to glaze the carrots with a thick syrup. Season, garnish with parsley, and serve. Serves 4.

CREAMED CARROTS

None of the vitamins will be lost when the carrots are cooked in milk used to make a thick white sauce. This dish is good with ham or pork and all roasts.

1 pound carrots, chopped	1 tablespoon flour
1 cup milk, or more as needed	Coarse salt and freshly ground
½ cup water	black pepper
Dash nutmeg	1 tablespoon chopped fresh parsley
3 tablespoons butter	

Simmer the carrots in the milk, water, and nutmeg until almost tender. In a small saucepan, melt the butter. Add the flour and cook for 5 minutes, stirring constantly, without browning. Add the boiling milk-water from the carrots. Stir until smooth and return to the carrots. Season and simmer for about 10 minutes, or until the sauce coats the spoon. Add the parsley and serve. Serves 4.

See also carrot recipes in
VEGETABLE chapter, page 98

EXTRA-HEALTHY CAULIFLOWER CHEESE

This dish is high in protein. If served with steak or chops and a green salad, you will have a really nourishing meal. Don't put the cauliflower mixture on high heat after you have added the eggs: you will have rather nasty half-scrambled curdled eggs and not the smooth yellow sauce you are supposed to produce.

1 cauliflower, broken into flowerets
1 cup milk
2 eggs, beaten
Coarse salt
Freshly ground black pepper

½ cup grated Parmesan or Cheddar cheese
Nutmeg (freshly grated, if possible)

Cook the cauliflower in milk for 10–15 minutes. Remove from heat. Remove cauliflower, drain, and reserve. Add a little of the hot milk to the eggs in another container, stirring constantly. Gradually add egg mixture to hot cauliflower milk, always stirring. Season, add the cheese, and cook over very *low* heat until sauce is slightly thickened. Do not overcook. Return the cauliflower to the sauce, sprinkle with nutmeg, and serve. Serves 4.

Soybeans

One of the most economical ways to add protein to your diet is to eat soybeans. They have twice as much protein as meat or fish, and three times as much as eggs. They contain little starch and half the carbohydrates of other beans. They contain vitamins A, B, and some D, as well as lecithin, calcium, phosphorus, and iron.

You can get the beans dried, canned, or in the form of bean sprouts which are sold at health food or Chinese stores. Bean sprouts are also now available in many supermarkets. To cook them, see Chinese Method of Cooking Vegetables (page 85).

A cup of dried soybeans equals about 3 cups after being soaked overnight. They should be cooked as for Basic Beans (page 180), and are extremely good when chopped celery and tomato juice are added to the water.

Canned soybeans can be enhanced by fresh tomatoes, celery, and onion. While they are not as good for you as dried ones, they have plenty of vitamins and make an excellent, healthy last-minute meal.

Wine

Wine is a luxury that can be enjoyed alike by the poor college student and the rich international banker. Perhaps the banker is swilling down his pâté de foie gras with a Château Lafite Rothschild, while the student is eating his fried chicken with a glass of Gallo Chianti, but both are probably enjoying their meal with equal satisfaction.

It may be the fault of Prohibition, but in many parts of the country wine is regarded with suspicion as something un-American and unmanly. To drink it with meals is weird and "foreign," and to cook with it is outrageous extravagance.

The same people who knock back three or four martinis before dinner may look shocked if someone suggests having wine with the meal. A few egg-cup-size glasses are brought down from a high shelf and carefully dusted, filled with wine to the brim—and in one gulp it's gone. You spend the rest of the meal wondering if they will ever offer you more, but that's it; they manage to toy with their one egg-cup for the whole meal. More often than not it isn't, as you might think, some rare and ancient wine that's lain in the cellar for fifty years, but good old California red that is best served in ordinary glasses.

At the same time, there is an awful lot of pretentious nonsense spoken and written about wine. To quote Thurber, "It's a naïve domestic burgundy, without any breeding, but I think you'll be amused by its presumption."

Andre Launay, in *Posh Food*, says, "There is more rubbish talked about wine and wine tasting than anything else. It is the perfect subject for the snob, the one-up man and the bore because the true experts are patient, polite people who prefer drinking wine to talking about it; only the views of the amateur are expressed and they become more and more banal as time goes on."

The so-called rules about wine often make people so nervous that they are afraid to serve it for fear they will make a mistake. If you like a certain wine with a certain food, by all means drink it. The line should be drawn, however, in serving a sweet wine with a savory dish, spoiling both the wine and the food. Strong wines overpower delicate dishes, light wines are overwhelmed by spicy foods, dry wines taste sour with desserts. In general, dry wines should be served with the main course, and sweet wines used with desserts.

Light wines are generally served before heavy ones, white before red, when you are serving more than one wine for dinner. Sauces can also help guide you to the right wine; a delicate cream sauce is best with white wine, and a strong tomato sauce would be better with red.

In general, this is how it goes:

Light Dry White Wine   Seafood, eggs, salads, cold meat

Robust Dry White Wine   Fish, poultry, brains, sweetbreads, veal in cream sauces.

Rosé Wine   Salads, aspics, cold food, eggs, ham, pork, and curries

Light Dry Red Wine   Roasts, chicken, veal, lamb, stews, cheese and vegetable casseroles

Robust Red Wine   Italian food and pasta, beef, marinated meats, cheese, tomatoes

Sweet and Sparkling Wine   Desserts

Wine is drunk with food because it complements the food. If you care about what you eat, it follows that you care about what you drink with it. You would rather spend a few extra cents, perhaps, to drink a rough and ready wine with your stew than to have a bottle of soda pop, which ruins not only the food but your stomach and teeth as well.

If it is a special occasion and you are opening a really good wine, remember that cocktails and cigarettes will ruin it. Sherry and vermouth are the best aperitifs to have before dinner.

While you may not be able to afford vintage French wine, 1-gallon bottles of California, Spanish, Portuguese, or Italian wine are economical and quite pleasant. A good French red wine, such as a Côtes du Rhône, can often cost as little as $1.19 a bottle. There are many very good French and German wines in this price category. You might also split the cost of a case with someone else and thus get a discount. If the liquor store man is amiable and knows that you're interested, he might advise you when the cheaper wines are available.

Serving Wine

Red wines should be served at room temperature unless they are very rough or you want to serve a cheap wine chilled in the summertime. If it is a good wine, open it and let it sit for a couple of hours.

White and rosé wines should be chilled for about three hours in the refrigerator. If they are too cold, they lose much of their taste. Sparkling wines and most sweet wines are better served cold.

A bottle of wine can stretch for four people, but it is usually better to count on half a bottle per person. Half bottles are meager for two people, and they cost proportionately more than half of a whole bottle. But a half bottle is better than none.

If you have wine glasses, fill them only half full so that the bouquet of the wine has room to develop. The basic tulip wine glasses are the best kind—just the right size and not embarrassingly dainty. Rough, peasanty wine is perfectly acceptable served in ordinary drinking glasses. In France, Spain, and Italy they often serve a *vin ordinaire* in straight glasses.

Wine and Cheese

Wine and cheese are natural partners. Red wine is best with most cheese, although white can be drunk with cream cheese. Although some wines taste unpleasant when drunk after certain cheeses, as a rule strong cheese goes with strong wine.

Cooking with Wine

"The only difference between cooking with wine and not cooking with wine is that you put some wine in."—Paul Gallico.

Cooking with wine seems a great extravagance to some people, but suppose you figure paying a little over a dollar for a bottle of wine. Then 1 glass costs less than a quarter. That makes it absurd not to try it. And the addition of wine can transform a dish.

Do not try to use up old, stale vinegary wine in cooking. You can ruin a dish if the wine is bad. Once the alcohol has evaporated, you are left with the concentrated taste of the wine. If the wine is no good, the dish won't be either.

Since the wine must almost always be boiled, it should be added to casseroles and stews at the beginning in order to mingle with the other ingredients and produce a delicious rich sauce. When added to a sauce, it is cooked much faster. The heat is turned up and the cooking juices are scraped up with the wine, producing a thick, syrupy sauce in just a few minutes.

Use too little wine rather than too much. The wine should accentuate the other flavors and complement them, not drown them out.

In the recipes where red wine is suggested, a good, young, dry red wine is meant. Claret, burgundy, chianti, or Spanish or Portuguese dry red wine will do, but *never* use a sweet wine.

White wine called for in the recipes means a dry white wine or even a dry white vermouth. Never use a sauterne or a sweet dessert wine.

Soup is improved with the addition of a little dry sherry or madeira. Improve fish dishes and potato salads with dry white wine; add a little red wine to meat dishes; and use either red or white with chicken. Port, sweet sherry, madeira, liqueurs, rum, and brandy are good in desserts.

In the sections on meat, you will find several marinades containing wine. Left for 24 hours in a wine marinade, the tough fibers of the meat are broken down, and the meat becomes tender and acquires a delicious flavor. Wine marinades are much more satisfactory than artificial meat tenderizers.

Index